CW00517023

Children of God

Towards a Theology of Childhood

Edited by
Angela Shier-Jones

EPWORTH

British Library Cataloguing in Publication data

A catalogue record for this book is available from the British Library

978 0 7162 0619 4

First published in 2007
by Epworth
4 John Wesley Road
Werrington
Peterborough PE4 6ZP

Typeset by Regent Typesetting, London
Printed and bound in Great Britain by
William Clowes Ltd, Beccles, Suffolk

Contents

Contributors ix

Introduction xi

1 Expecting or On Being Open to Children 1
Natalie K. Watson

2 Birth: Pain and Potential 21
Esther Shreeve

3 Babes in Arms: Speechlessness and Selfhood 41
Jeremy Worthen

4 Moulding and Shaping: Education 63
David Deeks and Angela Shier-Jones

5 Re-Imagining, Re-Thinking and Re-Doing: Deconstucting our Biblical and Theological Perspectives on the Christian Nurture of Children 84
Anthony Reddie

6 Maturity, Delinquency and Rebellion 111
Sheryl Anderson

7 Being and Becoming: Adolescence 135
Jocelyn Bryan

8 Collecting Memories: Identity, Nostalgia and the Objects of Childhood 159
Terry J. Wright

9 The Never-Land of Religion and the Lost Childhood of the Children of God 181
Angela Shier-Jones

O Lord, my heart is not lifted up, my eyes are not raised too high; I do not occupy myself with things too great and too marvellous for me. But I have calmed and quieted my soul, like a weaned child with its mother; my soul is like the weaned child that is with me.

Psalm 131.1–2

Contributors

Natalie K. Watson is a theologian, writer and editor based in Peterborough, UK. She is Head of Publishing at *mph* and prior to that was Tutor in Church History and Ecclesiology at Ripon College Cuddesdon. Natalie is a member of the Meissen Commission English Committee and of the Church of England's Faith and Order Advisory Group as well as a local tutor for the Eastern Region Ministry Course. She is the author of several books and articles on feminist theology and related areas, including *Introducing Feminist Ecclesiology* (Continuum, 2002) and *Feminist Theology* (Eerdmans, 2004).

Esther Shreeve is Director of the BA in Christian Theology in the Cambridge Theological Federation, and a Church Historian. She is a Methodist Local Preacher. Publications include *The Gingerbread House, a Journey of Faith through Bereavement* (Inspire, 2004) and, with Philip Luscombe (eds), *What is a Minister?* (Epworth, 2002).

Jeremy Worthen is Principal of the South East Institute for Theological Education and Honorary Lecturer at the University of Kent. He is an Anglican priest who completed his doctoral studies at the University of Toronto's Centre for Medieval Studies and has since published articles on a variety of topics relating to theology and cultural history.

David G. Deeks is a Methodist minister who, since 2003, has been General Secretary of the British Methodist Church.

Anthony G. Reddie is a Black theologian and Christian educator working for the British Methodist Church and the Queens Foundation for Ecumenical Theological Education in Birmingham. He is the author of a number of books, including *Nobodies to*

Somebodies (Epworth, 2003) *Acting in Solidarity* (Darton, Longman & Todd, 2005) *Dramatizing Theologies* (Equinox, 2006) and *Black Theology in Transatlantic Dialogue* (Palgrave Macmillan, 2006). He is also the editor of *Black Theology: An International Journal.*

Sheryl Anderson is a Methodist minister, currently stationed in the London Mission (South) Circuit, and Director of the South London Mission, a Methodist social outreach project in South East London. Her background is in youth justice, working in both the statutory and voluntary sector. Immediately prior to entering the ministry she was senior manager for young offender services in South East Kent.

Jocelyn Bryan is a member of the core staff at the Wesley Study Centre, Durham with responsibility for Foundation Training. She is married to Steve, and they have three children. Her PhD is in Psychology and she teaches Psychology and Christian Ministry at Masters Level as well as teaching on courses in ministry, formation, pastoral theology and practical theology. Her research interest is in the interface between psychology, theology and Christian ministry. She is a Local Preacher and member of the Faith and Order Committee of the Methodist Church.

Terry J. Wright, although an Anglican, is employed by the Connexional Team of the Methodist Church and is studying at a Baptist college for a PhD on the concept of causality in the doctrine of providence. He is the inaugural winner of the Society for the Study of Theology/International Journal of Systematic Theology Colin Gunton Memorial Essay Prize (2004).

Angela Shier-Jones is the Director of Academic Studies and Research at Wesley College Bristol. She is a Methodist minister who completed her doctoral studies in the development of Methodist Doctrine. She was a co-editor of *Unmasking Methodist Theology/Methodist Theology Today* (Continuum, 2004). Her most recent publication is *A Work In Progress: Methodists Doing Theology* (Epworth, 2005) Her specialist research interest is the doctrine of Christian perfection. She is also the editor of the *Epworth Review*.

Introduction

Things are better than ever for children now – children have rights, infant mortality has plummeted in almost all western societies and campaigns are underway to ensure that this trend continues over the whole world. Governments insist on 'education, education, education' as the cornerstone of policy and even school dinners have been reviewed and revamped, with suet puddings, chips and crisps giving way to healthier, balanced nutritional meals.

Yet we are also living at a time when paediatricians will fight for the life of a premature baby born at the same age as another foetus that has just been legally aborted and child trafficking and child pornography is on the increase. In the western world, child obesity is a serious drain on medical resources. Bullying and acts of child vandalism and violence have reached unprecedented proportions. At the same time, children are clearly becoming the latest fashion accessory: designer made or custom ordered, test-tube fertilized, carried or surrogated they are a 'must have'.

The very fact that children can be perceived in this way hints at just how far we have objectified, separated out – alienated – children as people while at the same time, managing to convince ourselves we have, of course, been doing exactly the opposite.

At the heart of this dichotomy is the very real separation between childhood and adulthood. Adults are not children, though most remember what it was to be a child, and at times almost all forms of what society will term 'childish' behaviour are possible. All that adults can know of the state of childhood today, however, is second hand.

They have passed through that state – they are children no longer – as the apostle Paul writes:

> When I was a child, I spoke like a child, I thought like a child, I reasoned like a child; when I became an adult, I put an end to childish ways. (1 Corinthians 13.11)

Attempts to rationalize the state of childhood often begin by superimposing a remembered childhood onto that of the current age – something doomed to end in the exasperated retort – 'it was never like this in my day!' The more deliberately anthropological approach to understanding children compounds the problem of separation through the need for 'objective' – and hence non-interactive – analysis. Sociological studies tend to be similarly remote and statistically based. Yet children are dependent upon adults for their survival and for their safe progress through this state of childhood.

How then can this separation and its negative effects and/or consequences be minimized? What role, if any, does the Church or faith have to play in bridging this gap? More importantly, what is God saying to us in the existence of childhood, in the necessity of our life beginning with this peculiar time of separation and dependence? Childhood is not merely a phase or a stage in life, it is a part of our being before God. We were created to be children before we were adults – not just for a day – but for long enough for it to make a substantial difference to how we perceive ourselves and form our relationships with others and the world. It would be natural to assume therefore that Scripture and the Church have something substantial to say about childhood, that theologians and pastors have reflected upon the state of the child before God and have something to contribute to how childhood is perceived today.

As this volume makes clear, childhood *qua* childhood has not been the subject of a great deal of theological enquiry, although the abstracted moral and spiritual status of the child has. The subject is immense and warrants a more detailed systematic treatment than this volume could ever hope to provide. What this volume attempts to do, therefore, is to offer a primer – a way into the subject at various levels that it is hoped will encourage and enable further work to be undertaken.

The volume takes into account the ambiguity of childhood and so begins with expectancy and ends with teleology, intending to cover each major stage of childhood in-between in chronological order. Thus from expectancy we move to birth, from birth to babe in arms, and from thence to that most mysterious stage of being educated and more obviously 'related to'. Delinquency and adolescence are not synonymous, although they do share some characteristics; they are therefore dealt with as a twinned pair before we move to consider the effect of all of this on the child in adulthood. The volume thus concludes with an exploration of the interdependence of biological and spiritual childhood and asks whether or not the children of God can ever grow up, and what they would become if they did.

It should not be surprising that a volume on childhood contains many surprise discoveries. Although the original intention was that each chapter participate in an orderly, disciplined theological dialogue through the various phases of childhood – engaging biblically with the interdisciplinary and doctrinal issues that arise naturally from the chronology – the reality was that the volume took on a life of its own. In some places the dialogue stretched presumed boundaries, in other places, it ignored them completely. In doing so it made explicit the fact that there is no real scriptural warrant for the idealized romanticized image of childhood as a protected time of innocence and purity and the so-called stages or phases of childhood are as much culturally as biologically determined and thus should never be presumed to be definitive.

Nonetheless, there remains a clear order to the volume which mirrors the fact that even when children are less well behaved than expected, and even if they insist that they are five and a half going on sixteen, their lives are still, in the main, subject to the discipline and natural order imposed by time. Thus the children described in the volume – whether conceptual or actual – age.

Children begin their existence in the mind of God, who, in an act of prevenient grace, plants the longing for them in the hearts of those predestined to bear them, whose existence is thereby justified and whose future is therefore assured and saved. This account of the purpose of procreation is, of course, a parody of the *ordo salutis*. The first chapter demonstrates that the terms 'justification', 'assurance' and 'salvation', when used with regard to procreation, need to be understood differently according to the context and framework in which they are used. When set in a human individualistic framework, the 'assurance' and 'salvation' offered by God is limited to those who are able, biologically, to bear children. This seems contrary to the Christian experience of God as the one who offers salvation to all of creation through the birth of a child – not just to Mary and Joseph. Clearly, therefore, when it is set within the context of the redemption of creation, from within the framework of the whole community of the people of God, the justification, assurance and salvation carried by the gift of children is somehow different. Natalie K. Watson explores this difference by examining the concept of child-bearing and child-caring as a community vocation rather than as a private occupation, which opens up the possibility of reconciling and healing some of the pain inflicted by societal (and ecclesial) attitudes to childlessness.

Pain continues to act as the counter-balance to the joy of childhood in Esther Shreeve's essay. The inescapable, intricate, intimate weave of pain and pleasure, hope and despair that are the woman's experience of childbearing and birth are explored in dialogue with traditional, feminist and womanist readings of Scripture. The challenge to the historical, traditional understanding of the source of a woman's pain in childbirth comes from an examination of the assumptions, expectations and even manipulations of the relationships that develop between mother, Church, society and infant: relationships that are as embryonic as the life that they are created by – but which therefore have the same potential for joy or pain.

But the mother is not the only parent of a child. When the embryo becomes an infant the network of relationships that has the child at its centre becomes more tangible and inclusive. The babe in arms can be seen and held separately from the mother who carried it. It can be held by a father, perceived and recognized as a person in its own right. Now the question of dependency is wedded to that of identity. In his essay, Jeremy Worthen draws heavily on both the Jewish and Christian traditions to explore what it means to regard an infant as a person. Does this automatically mean that they should be seen as sinful? How does the infancy of Jesus illuminate the state of human childhood – and of the relationship of the child to its father? Worthen's contention that only by juxtaposing Christology and anthropology can we begin to give a proper account of either, sets the framework for his dialogue with Scripture and the role of the infant in salvation. His theological explorations lead implicitly to the question of whether it is in this time of infancy, of radical dependency, when potential and providence converge, that personhood is truly formed?

Formation is, of course, the central issue in education. The acquisition of facts and figures takes second place – always, to the formation of lives and the moulding of minds. But who should be responsible for this – the state, the Church or the family? The implicit question, 'to whom do children belong and who should determine how and what they are taught?' is explored in two chapters on education. The use, abuse and exploitation of children in the name of education and formation is perpetrated (deliberately or otherwise) by state, Church, and family. Children are all too often victims as well as beneficiaries of their parents' behaviours, emotions, beliefs and anxieties.

The relationships between Church, democracy and education are critiqued in the co-authored essay by David Deeks and Angela Shier-Jones. The state's need to control and, where possible, limit the consequential damage to social structure often forms the real basis for a policy-driven vision for the education of children. But what can be said of the role of the Church in the implementation of such visions? Does the Church have a better or alternative vision for children's education and formation, and if so what? The way in which Scripture is read and engaged with the Church's teachings can, as Anthony Reddie details in his chapter, prove just as abusive and manipulative of a child's formation as any deliberately, determinedly secular approach can be. Both papers therefore argue for a revisiting of the underlying theology of divine–human relationships as well as a re-reading of Scriptures on the basis that these things still inform the overarching values for how we treat and engage with children. This alone, it is believed, will end the current widespread practice of assaulting children (emotionally, or physically) and then justifying it on the grounds of Christian, biblical or even democratic formation and the 'salvation' of the community.

But children do need control and discipline, particularly in the latter stages of childhood. Adolescent rebellion is a real problem, which is writ as large in Scripture as it is in any current juvenile court record. What then can we learn of the nature of childhood from the Bible's delinquents? Sheryl Anderson's essay brings the social worker's perspective to bear on the rogues of the Bible, and explores the theological consequences of God's apparent favouritism of the rebel, the miscreant and delinquent. When is 'bad' behaviour 'good' and what determined the acceptability of mischief? The chapter explores the way in which a slavish devotion to obedience as a great Christian virtue may in fact be repressive and unproductive as well as decidedly un-scriptural. The relationship between obedience and maturity as recorded in Scripture is much more complex than certain orthodox hymnody or teachings would have us believe. It is, however, precisely this complexity that offers real potential for human growth and development.

Jocelyn Bryan's perspective as a psychologist on this most puzzling time – when the movement to maturity disturbs the child's identity – leads to the same conclusion: identity is not a passive but a dynamic component of the nature of childhood. Obedience and subservience to those who hold the identity of a child in trust is eventually challenged to allow for a fuller expression and discovery of self. That this is all a part of God's intended design for humanity is the wonder that provides the theological framework for the chapter. The dialogue between Scripture and psychology that she opens up invites a discussion of the theology of 'being and becoming', which seeks to inform our understanding of the potential for growth in all human relationships.

The final section of the volume is more explicitly concerned with the child within than with the biological child. Terry Wright's contribution explores the theological justification and motivation for the all too human attachment to childhood and even childish behaviour. In so doing he touches on the importance of memory and nostalgia in maintaining our identity, spiritually as well as practically. Is there something in the injunction and desire of adults to remember events from their past, and to want to re-animate memories, that is more than just a longing for gentler times? Is all nostalgia nothing more than escapism from the demands of the design imperative to grow to be more than we once were? The links that are made between memory, nostalgia and identity offer a valuable insight into how Christian identity might be supported and nurtured through sacramental practices and regular religious observance.

The task of the final essay is to engage with the parallel questions that arise through the Church's proclamation of God as father and human beings as God's children. What can we learn from the dialogue between Scripture and the social sciences concerning the nature of biological childhood that will facilitate our understanding of what it means to be a child of God? Is childhood in this context a metaphor which cannot – dare not – be taken though to its logical conclusion – or are the children of God destined to 'grow up'? By drawing on the doctrine of recapitulation, the chapter argues for a growth and maturity that will do justice to the image of God in humanity and the cost of its redemption. The goal of humankind should be nothing less than to grow into its full perfection or state of *theosis*. The chapter concludes by offering a taster of some of the liberating and transforming consequences for humanity, and in particular for the way in which children are raised, if society ever came to believe that humanity is called to be like Christ, rather than imitators of Christ's best behaviour.

The volume is offered as a primer with the deliberate intention of opening up theological questions rather than closing them down. The contributions were therefore selected in order to make explicit the complex interplay of religion, biology, sociology and culture, which inform our current understanding and engagement with the theology of childhood, with the inescapable conclusion that even as adults (?) we really can only see through a glass dimly. There are, inevitably, all too many areas where further work is warranted but which lay outside of the initial remit of this project: childhood sexuality, gender identity, imagination, play, sibling community, to name but a few. It is hoped, however, that by beginning with a more limited and – to some extent – predictable chronological approach, the necessary theological tools will have been uncovered to encourage and enable the subject to be more systematically investigated by others. Any in-depth investigation of childhood will, of course, depend on all the major doctrines of the Church: the conclusion of this volume is that childhood – whether biological or spiritual – contains its own narratives of creation and fall, of justification, assurance, redemption and even perfection. The way in which certain concepts, ideas and insights can be found repeated throughout this volume, however, offers a tantalizing glimpse of which doctrines might provide the best theological light in which to explore further. Questions of identity and belonging, of learning and growing, for example, appear from this admittedly limited appraisal to be more pressing than those of sin and innocence. Regardless of which doctrines or traditions are explored, however, the scriptural dialogue alone suggests that God in Christ may be more directly involved in the nurturing and caring, shaping and forming of young lives – with or without parental consent – than we may have hitherto been prepared to admit.

Sing, O barren one who did not bear; burst into song and shout, you who have not been in labour! For the children of the desolate woman will be more than the children of her that is married, says the LORD. Enlarge the site of your tent, and let the curtains of your habitations be stretched out; do not hold back; lengthen your cords and strengthen your stakes. For you will spread out to the right and to the left, and your descendants will possess the nations and will settle the desolate towns. Do not fear, for you will not be ashamed; do not be discouraged, for you will not suffer disgrace; for you will forget the shame of your youth, and the disgrace of your widowhood you will remember no more. For your Maker is your husband, the LORD of hosts is his name; the Holy One of Israel is your Redeemer, the God of the whole earth he is called.

Isaiah 54.1–5

1. Expecting or On Being Open to Children[1]

NATALIE K. WATSON

Conflicting messages

'When you have got your own children, you'll understand.'
'When I have got my own children, I'll do it differently.'

These were sentences often heard and even more frequently thought during my own childhood. Of course, I would get married and have my own children when I was old enough to do so. That was what all adults I knew did and there was no reason why I should be different.

When I was about six years old I encountered the celibate female members of a religious community to which my mother was chaplain. I asked how these women managed not to have children. For me this question was not about the 'facts of life', the mechanics of human reproduction, but something far more obvious: grown-up women have children. These women don't. How come?

Later the picture changed, at least as far as I was concerned: I began to hint that I was planning not to be a parent myself. Now I began to encounter a different set of reactions, ranging from a patronizing 'You'll grow out of it' to the accusation of selfishness 'Who will pay for your pension?' 'Isn't it about time you produced a grandchild for your father?' In other words, it must be 'unnatural' for human beings, and for women in particular, not to want to have children. And furthermore, those who choose not to reproduce opt out of the society that has enabled them to grow and develop.

The attitudes reflected in these anecdotes from my own experience reflect the confusion, the conflicting messages, found in society at large. While on a global scale many countries struggle to feed the increasing populations of sub-Saharan Africa, South East Asia and Latin America, modern industrialized societies in North America and Western Europe react to fears of an ageing society and plead with their citizens to have children, offering incentives to those who are willing to do so. While governments and NGOs in the Two-Thirds World are desperately trying to educate their populations in the use of methods of birth control, citizens of western industrialized nations find themselves struggling with increasing rates of infertility and desperate attempts to have children by artificial means, sometimes going to extremes such as the attempt to use a deceased ex-partner's sperm or a 62-year-old woman travelling to another country to have an ovum implanted after she was 'denied' the same by the National Health Service in the UK.

More conflicting messages: in dialogue with Scripture and tradition

While the other essays in this book will look at different stages of childhood and attempt to offer contributions towards a theology of being children of God and children of men and women, I want to go back a step and to reflect in dialogue with Scripture and tradition on the fact that thinking about children begins long before physical contact between potential parents and conception, and takes place in a context much wider than the relationship between birth parents or between parents and children. What we are reflecting on is essentially the fact that human beings find it within themselves to be open to reproduction and procreativity and to create communities in which children are received, at times even welcomed. Yet, as we will see, Scripture and the traditions of the communities that regard these ancient texts as sacred offer a conflicting array of messages with regard to what such openness to reproduction and procreativity might mean. The task of the Christian theologian is to develop a framework in which critical theological and ethical reflection is possible in dialogue with these texts and with the history of the communities that have sought to interpret them in order to develop patterns of responsible living as part of the global and the Christian community, but most essentially in response to the love of the Triune God.

The Hebrew Scriptures

The Hebrew Scriptures, received as sacred texts by Jewish and Christian communities, begin with the search for an answer to the universal question for the beginning and the origin of all things, found in the creation narratives. The opening chapters of Genesis assert the fact that it is JHWH who created heaven and earth and thus also humanity, and thereby firmly establishes a qualitative distinction between the creator and the created. These texts assert the place of human beings within creation, and resulting from that, the responsibility human beings have as stewards of creation. God then charges human beings to 'be fruitful and multiply'. It is interesting to note that this charge appears twice in the first chapters of Genesis – once in the context of the creation of humankind (Genesis 1.28) and then again after the flood (Genesis 9.1). In the first instance, the text is read as a blessing on humankind, repeating the blessing on all living creatures in Genesis 1.22. The abundant fertility of the earth that will enable creation to continue and to flourish is framed within God's creative activity and only exists as a consequence of it, not separate from it. After the flood the same words occur again. However, in Genesis 9, the charge to 'increase and multiply' has become a commandment,[2] one of the roots of the centrality of procreation in Judaism. In the context of Judaism, procreation is seen as an obligation. In fact, one of the objections raised against same-sex relationships is that they are by nature not procreative.

The idea of children as a blessing and as divine favour is particularly strongly expressed in the Abraham narrative, but also in the stories of barren women such as Hannah (1 Samuel 1 and 2). The importance of human co-operation in this can be found again in the Abraham narrative where Abram's wife Sarai presents Abram with a slave woman whose duty it is to bear his son. It can also be found in the responsibility of a man who is to marry his brother's widow, not merely to ensure social protection for the woman, but to ensure offspring and the continuation of the family.

Throughout the Hebrew Scriptures children are regarded as both essential to survival and as a blessing from God. It is the responsibility of human beings, and this is addressed to men in particular, to co-operate with God in this act of continuing creation. In fact, not to do so, to waste one's seed, is seen as sinful, as the story of Onan in Genesis 38, source of many detrimental attitudes to masturbation in Jewish and Christian contexts, indicates. Broadly speaking we can say that in the context of the Hebrew Scriptures and the first communities that received them as sacred texts procreation and reproduction are an essential aspect of participating in God's covenant with humanity. It is therefore unthinkable for members of God's chosen people to opt out of this by choice or as an act of religious activity.

The Christian Scriptures

The picture presented in the New Testament and in the earliest Christian communities, however, is a very different one. I find little encouragement let alone obligation for procreation and parenthood in the Gospels. On the contrary, Jesus rejects the emphasis of family ties in favour of faithful discipleship (Mark 3.31–35 and Luke 11.27f.). While Jesus himself is born of a woman and spent the early years of his life in the context of a human family (though very little is said about this and the only story about his childhood told in the Gospels speaks of him breaking out of the context of his human family to be in the temple (Luke 2.41–51)), Jesus himself was not a parent. When the Gospel writers speak of children, children are presented not so much in terms of biology and in the context of parent/child relationships, but as models for a particular understanding of what it means to be human and to be a disciple. This is a move from children as property, as objects essential to the covenant relationship, to being subjects who can be disciples in their own right. The interest here is not in whether or not children are being born and whether or not adults can be parents, but in the idea that there will be children in the communities in which models of discipleship emerge and develop and that these children will have something to contribute to the community and its understandings of discipleship. We do, however, have to bear in mind that these texts were written before 'childhood' was developed as a separate social concept. The emphasis here is not on childhood or parenthood but on what Herbert Anderson and Susan Johnson call 'childness'.[3]

The focus in the Gospels is not on the domestic unit (though other New Testament writings do speak about the ordering of domestic relationships/families) but on the Christian community as a whole: Jesus speaks of receiving children in his name as a mark of true discipleship (Mark 9.33–37). 'What appeared to be an undistinguished activity – care for children, belonging to the domain of women, similarly marginalized people – becomes a prime way for all disciples to demonstrate the greatness that corresponds to the reign of God.'[4]

Yet, our understanding of the earliest Christian communities would be incomplete if it was restricted to the Gospels alone. These communities and their patterns of living emerged and developed in the context of societies where children were born and therefore domestic life needed to be ordered. While the Gospels themselves contain no encouragement to procreate, other texts such as the pseudo-Pauline Pastoral Epistles do. The author of 1 Timothy states that women will be 'saved through childbearing, provided they continue in faith and love and holiness with modesty' (1 Timothy 2.15).[5] Linda Maloney reads this as a shocking statement that excludes women from the saving activity of Christ and argues that they must save themselves. Elsa Tamez sees the verse as an assertion of the traditional roles of women in the context of the patriarchal family and essentially as an argument against extreme (Gnostic?) groupings within the Church, who sought to forbid marriage (4.1–5).[6] What we see here is evidence of different interpretations of Genesis and of gender roles within the earliest Christian communities rather than necessarily an argument for procreation as normative. Tamez warns against an ahistorical reading of the text and, from her own context of the poor barrios of Costa Rica, proposes to re-read these texts in the light of the praxis of Jesus.

In the letters of the apostle Paul we find next to no mention of the possibility of reproduction and parenthood: '. . . marriage, for Paul, was not for the proper ordering of sex in the interest of procreation, but in the interest of propriety. For Paul, the last thing one should want to do is to produce little Christians. Marriage is not for the having of children, but a prophylactic against passion, a curb on concupiscence.'[7]

While the earliest Christian texts remain at best ambivalent about parenthood and children, we discover a third strand within the later Christian tradition. This is most clearly expressed by the fourth- and fifth-century Church father Augustine of Hippo and has penetrated Christian thinking about marriage and human sexuality much more profoundly than the other two hitherto identified. His treatise 'On the Good of Marriage' describes children as one of the 'goods of marriage'. In fact for him children appear to be the only good that can come from the sexual union of man and woman in marriage:

> Marriages have this good also, that carnal or youthful incontinence, although it be faulty, is brought unto an honest use in the begetting of children, in order that out of the evil of lust the marriage union may bring to pass some good. Next, in that the lust of the flesh is repressed, and rages in a way more modestly, being tempered by parental affection. For there is interposed a certain gravity of glowing pleasure, when in that wherein husband and wife cleave to one another, they have in mind that they be father and mother.[8]

This is, for example, reiterated in the list of 'causes for which Matrimony was ordained' in the Book of Common Prayer:

> It was ordained for the procreation of children, to be brought up in the fear and nurture of the Lord and to the praise of his holy Name.

In the context of Roman Catholic moral theology this is used as an argument against artificial birth control: every act of sexual intercourse has to be open to the procreation of children. The Second Vatican Council asserts that:

> God Himself is the author of matrimony, endowed as it is with various benefits and purposes. All of these have a very decisive bearing on the continuation of the human race, on the personal development and eternal destiny of the individual members of a family, and on the dignity, stability, peace and prosperity of the family itself and of human society as a whole. By their very nature, the institution of matrimony itself and conjugal love are ordained for the procreation and education of children, and find in them their ultimate crown.[9]

The post-conciliar encyclical *Humanae Vitae* asserts:

> The transmission of human life is a most serious role in which married people collaborate freely and responsibly with God the Creator.[10]

Later in the text it adds:

> The Church, nevertheless in urging men [sic] to the observance of the precepts of the natural law . . . teaches that each and every marital act must of necessity retain its intrinsic relationship to the procreation of human life.[11]

We can conclude that in searching the Scriptures and the Christian tradition of reading, re-reading and acting on them as part of the process of discerning appropriate and responsible action we are faced with another set of conflicting messages. Our task here is to develop a critical, creative and constructive theology of the expectation that children will be born in the context of the human community and that, as part of being the Church in the world, the Christian community needs to engage with this reality and the realities in which human beings become parents and children are born. This is part of the calling to stewardship and discipleship, which applies to all Christians.

Receiving children: gift – responsibility – vocation

In contrast to the Jewish tradition, the Christian tradition has always had within itself the possibility of voluntary childlessness as a vocation for individuals, yet in the majority of cases such an affirmed calling to foregoing the possibility of parenthood also entailed the absence of a commitment to a partnership such as heterosexual marriage, for example, in the context of (clerical) celibacy, consecrated virginity or the religious life.[12] The narrow focus on the 'family', meaning the hetero-patriarchal nuclear family in which much writing on the subject of children is framed, is in contrast to ample precedent of children being raised by adults other than their biological parents.

Writing, as I do, from the point of view of a celibate feminist theologian in an affluent western industrial society, it is important to recognize that in a global context, the number of those for whom parenthood or childlessness is an absolute choice is relatively small. Unfortunately, the debate about whether or not there will be children has been dominated by issues such as the at times violent abortion vs. pro-life debate, the debate about the use of artificial methods of birth control and contraception and issues of reproductive choice such as in vitro fertilization and pre-natal diagnostics. All of these are issues to be discussed in the context of Christian ethics and the use of natural and moral law. Yet, from my point of view as a feminist theologian, they require a theological debate that needs to take place prior to discussing any of these specific ethical questions, a debate about what it means to be a community of human beings in the image of God and in response to God's creative love.

The Church as the community of disciples is a space where having children and being a child is no longer the task of individuals. The community of disciples is a space that in its own way can embody openness and hospitality to children and thereby to God's creative commitment to the future of his creation. Stanley Hauerwas argues that the Christian Church should seek to become and be a community where children are actually welcome.[13] Such a welcome, however, cannot be to children in general or in principle but must be to actual children and their parents, regardless of who they are and who their parents are.

The basic premise for this chapter is that children are a gift from God. Yet, this gift is given to a community not to individuals. The living in God's covenant as well as the life of Christian discipleship is a shared and communal calling. It is a calling to stewardship and discipleship, responsibility and vocation.

One of the achievements of the Protestant Reformation of the sixteenth century is an understanding of all human activity as potentially vocational. Vocations to the priesthood or the religious life are no longer perceived as superior paths to perfection. All baptized Christians are called to glorify God in what they do and it is the Christian community which is to support them in doing so. This means that the rejection of parenthood (as advocated by St Paul) is no longer seen as superior to parenthood. This does not mean, however, that the reverse is now true. The unjustified elevation of so-called family values, which see the creation of hetero-patriarchal nuclear families as superior to all other forms of human relationships and their creative potential, must be avoided. The responsibility for making choices, for realizing and growing into what might be our vocation, be it parenthood or not, lies in the community of the baptized as a whole and begins long before children are begotten and conceived. It lies in the responsible construction and re-construction of the desire to participate in the creative, redemptive and sanctifying activity of God, of which biological parenthood is but one realization. Celibacy as a vocation to be free from the ties of marriage and family life, for the sake of the gospel, is a gift and vocation for some. Yet, we might have to re-think what celibacy might mean in a context where more and more people are single, and living in life-long committed relationships is an option for some but definitely not for all. This could also mean that the Christian community could reinvent itself as a space where children are welcomed and received and where parenthood is rethought as a vocation that needs to be held and supported by the community as a whole. Stanley Hauerwas sees having children as a form of prophetic practice, proclaiming hope in a future that is God's, and not something we can secure through our own activities (as in some societies children are a form of 'insurance' for old age).

'Receiving children' as the calling and the responsibility of the Christian community as a whole is to be distinguished from expecting that individuals will have children and from the 'right to have a child' voiced by individuals. While the number of childless households in industrialized western societies increases, we also find a growing number of individuals who are prepared to go to great lengths to conceive and have a child and regard this as part of their personal self-fulfilment or to fulfil the expectations of others. The idea that one has the 'right' to have a child implies that children are property, possessions, rather than gifts entrusted to us from God with the responsibility to care for them to the best of our abilities. Stanley Hauerwas argues this point rather strongly by saying that Christian parents are called to serve their children, to bring them up in the Christian faith, precisely because they are not the property of their parents but God's gift to be received by the community as a whole.[14]

It is the responsibility of the Christian community to work towards and create an environment in which human beings can receive God's gift responsibly and to consider how abilities of individuals to make choices are shaped and shared. A woman's right to choose can be both an empowerment and an abdication of responsibility on the part of the wider social context.

The Christian vocation to 'receive children as a gift from God' is a response to a creative and loving God who desires all human life to flourish and who entrusts human beings with the gifts of free will and autonomy. These gifts of free will and autonomy, to live responsibly before God, are given to all human beings and it is the task of the Church as a moral community to create spaces where human beings are empowered to live with these gifts in a way that we can indeed see the glory of God in human beings fully alive. I noted earlier that the commandment to procreate is essentially given to men, yet barrenness is often seen as a sign of the absence of God's favour for women and is indeed regarded as a valid reason for a man to divorce his wife in many patriarchal societies. On the other hand, we hear of the destruction of the physical and mental capacities of women through more pregnancies than their bodies are able to sustain. A Christian community that takes its vocation to receive children in its midst seriously can therefore not subscribe to a patriarchal ordering of reproductivity but to has to take into account the interests of all involved. This begins with women who give birth to children. Ann Loades and others call for a 'woman-centred ethic of procreativity'.[15] What does it mean for women to give birth to children? Are women's experiences of the pressure to reproduce, pregnancy and childbirth taken into account in our thinking about human reproduction and procreativity? Beverly Wildung Harrison remarks that the 'elevation of procreation as the central image for divine blessing is intimately connected to the rise of patriarchy'. In patriarchal societies it is the male's power that is enhanced by the gift of new life. Throughout history, women's power of procreation has stood in definite tension with this male social control.[16] Our creative and constructive thinking in this area must seek to disconnect from this connection with (hetero-)patriarchy. Elina Vuola questions the coherence and credibility of liberation theological discourses on praxis and the poor if it fails to reflect as a matter of urgency on sexual ethics and women's reproductive rights.[17] Regina Ammicht-Quinn and Hille Haker challenge the Roman Catholic Church to take seriously the dimension of experience with regard to pregnancy and childlessness as experiences in their full extent and formative power as it develops its thinking on sexual ethics and reproductive medicine.[18]

Speaking about children as models of Christian discipleship is ultimately meaningless unless it happens in a Christian community where actual children are welcome and are seen as fellow disciples in Christ. Any Christology that speaks of Christ being born of a woman remains abstract and empty if it does not result in an understanding of human particularity, which sees the parenting of children as a social process in which the voices of biological mothers must be heard. The Christian community's openness to children as the embodiment of God's creative love for all humanity is ultimately measured by its openness to 'unwanted' children and their mothers. Christ himself was technically conceived 'out of wedlock'; in other words: the incarnation transcends boundaries of legitimacy and illegitimacy. It is a fundamental affirmation of all human life, which has to be realized in creating conditions where such human life can indeed be received as God's gracious gift and where the rejection of such a gift of life is regarded as a rejection of Godself. The Christian tradition contains both experiences of rejecting such children and their mothers and of welcoming them. Examples of the former are the notorious wash houses of the Magdalen Sisters and the rejection of all 'illegitimate' children as 'bastards'. Examples of the latter include the welcoming of abandoned children by the communities of the earliest Christian communities, child oblates in monastic communities and family communities that are wider than the nuclear. Ann Loades remarks in an essay on sexual abuse:

> Little attention has been given to the value and significance of the lives of those who may or may not flourish in the period between birth and social maturity, and to the abuse which may be present in their lives. Insofar as we do not have children as the focus of our attention, except to the extent that we spend time and energy trying to prevent their conception and birth or to ensure our own procreativity in having them, we are not likely to find ourselves well-equipped for evaluating their abuse, sexual or other.[19]

There is a fundamental difference between the commandment to procreate as given to God's chosen people and the calling to 'welcome children' given to the earliest Christian communities. For a small desert tribe, which saw itself as God's chosen people, reproduction was essential in order to survive. To bear children, and indeed many children, meant that God was committed to the survival of his chosen people and its future. The charge to receive children, on the other hand, is not tied to human reproduction, but is rather a response to the fact that in the world in which Christ's disciples live, there will be children and to receive them is part of the universal call to hospitality and the welcoming of strangers, others, as the people they are.

For the Christian community in its earliest days, and throughout its history, the challenge to 'receive children' is not merely about whether or not particular individuals will be parents, but it is about receiving all children, especially those who may not be welcomed into existence by their biological parents. The Christian community is to be a place where those who are abandoned, the 'bastards of society' are welcomed and received and where the development of a flourishing life is possible on the premise that all children are welcomed and loved into being by God.

Rethinking procreativity

Human procreative activity, embodied in the begetting, conceiving, bearing, giving birth to and raising of children, is essentially participation in the creative and sustaining activity of God. Yet, does this really mean that human reproduction is the only way in which human beings can participate and embody this aspect of the life of God? The challenge for Christian communities is to develop a sexual ethic that is able to distinguish between openness to reproduction and procreativity. It means that sexual intercourse is best placed and experienced as an experience of 'the body's grace' if it takes place in the context of relationships that are open to being hospitable to another, a third, and that can thus participate in the welcoming of new human life. This is by no means restricted to heterosexual couples alone. Same-sex couples modelling permanent, faithful and stable relationships are a vital part of the Christian community's practice of hospitality as participation in God's mission. They embody the fact that participation in divine creativity is not restricted to human reproduction but is a shared activity in the life of the body of Christ where the body of the other and one's own body are received as God's gift.

To parent children, to give birth, to foster and enable the growth and development of children does offer insights into the nature of God; it offers the possibility to participate in the creativity of God, in the life of God the creator in a particular and profound way. And yet, our understanding of what this means is so frequently tied up within the social construct of the modern hetero-patriarchal nuclear family unit. It is almost exclusively focused on biological parenthood and even more frequently on biological motherhood. We have to bear in mind that the activity of God the creator is communicated to human beings with the charge to be responsible stewards of creation. Procreativity therefore cannot mean mindless and unlimited reproduction of individuals; it is a responsibility that is realized in the communities in which human beings find themselves. One could, for example, argue that the fact that homosexuality could have disappeared in the evolutionary process but has not indicates that it would not be sustainable for all human beings to reproduce and that communities and families need those who are responsible adults but not necessarily themselves birth parents.[20]

David Matzko McCarthy writes of the 'neighbourhood' (in contrast to the consumptive economies of isolated domestic units), in which 'all adults have children'.[21] For him, reproduction, a fundamental activity of the household, implies more than biological parenthood. It is set within a 'grammar of hospitality' in which surplus resources are shared. One could think about this from the point of view of children: the first and most essential human relationship, the bond between parents and child, gradually develops in the context of a web of other human relationships. Where the relationship between parents and children remains exclusive of other adult–child relationships, children grow up to be unable to perceive their parents and essentially themselves as fallible human beings who are part of the community of shared humanity.

What does it therefore mean that all sexual intercourse should be open to conception? Perhaps our thinking on this point needs to move beyond thinking purely in terms of human reproduction to the meaning of human sexuality as such. Perhaps it could mean that human sexuality is most appropriately celebrated and shared in relationships of human beings who accept their role as responsible members of a human/ecclesial community that is open to new life. Openness to biological parenthood is one expression this can take, but it is one among many others.

Much of our thinking around the fact that somehow children will happen is centred on the expectation that adults will be parents, women will be mothers and that men will be fathers. Yet a Trinitarian understanding of God does not restrict the divine to God the Father, the creator. God's creative activity is also the activity of the Son, of God incarnate, and it is the activity of the Spirit, God as present in his creation and in his Church. If God the creator and giver of new life is present in the womb, in the conception and growth of new life, then this cannot be isolated from the community of love, support, role models and anti-models that a child needs to encounter. In the body of Christ, the Church, we are all at once those who are parents and those who need to be parented. The revolutionary character of the gospel allows both for existing kinship ties to be sanctified, to be the holy ground where God is encountered, and for new and different relationships to develop and to be recognized as sacred social spaces where we find ourselves in the image of God. It is to the detriment of the Church and essentially a weakening of the gospel if it restricts itself to becoming an instrument of perpetuating the hetero-patriarchal nuclear domestic unit and to reducing women (and men) to being agents of biological reproduction.

Retrieving diversity

What is fascinating to see is that even in the Early Church, the Christian tradition does not present a single line of argument with regard to the expectation of whether or not there will be children. Throughout the New Testament we can watch the earliest Christian communities wrestle with the search for appropriate responses to the creation and the ordering of inter-generational life in a community that sought to forge patterns of discipleship between imminent eschatological expectation and developing culturally appropriate ways of living in existing structures. We therefore have to recognize that any Christian sources on the subject are shaped by the norms and expectations of the cultural context. If they are, they can and need to be shaped and re-shaped in the light of the reading and re-reading of the call of the Christian community as a whole to stewardship and discipleship.

Yet, we can go further than this. Gerard Loughlin argues:

> The Church receives children, not in the hope of reproducing herself, so as to achieve some spurious immortality, but simply and only as the new life that burgeons from the life of Christ, who is yet to come, but even now arriving, not least in the new-born child. As already hinted, this way of thinking of the matter understands children as born to the Church, and not merely to their parents. For the latter are not isolated couples, but part of the one body. This is why everyone has a responsibility for the children of the Church, symbolized in the practice of godparenting and of adoption. And it is also why not everyone in the Church has to look for the gift of children, why not every particular relationship or

sexual act has to be open to the gift of children, in short, why there can be infertile straight couples and gay couples; why there can be celibates, consecrated virgins and single people. For in the imagination of the Church, children are first and foremost gifts that arrive through the nuptial union of the Church with her beloved, Jesus Christ.[22]

Transcending expectations

What does it then mean to chose to have children, or, as the case may be, not to have children? While for the majority of the world population choices with regard to reproduction are rather limited, be it through lack of access to methods of birth control or through social and cultural expectations, knowledge and access to contraception do open up spaces in which (responsible) choices can and have to be made. It is part of the calling of the Christian community to enable human beings to make responsible choices before God and in the wider community in which they live. While in earlier times the idea of vocation frequently meant to respond to God's calling and as part of it to forsake parenthood and the protection that came with having children, perhaps Christians in modern western societies need to support and encourage those who regard it as their vocation to provide healthy and welcoming environments in which children can grow and develop. Frequently this happens at considerable cost to them and is not well respected by the society in which they live.

Yet, we have to bear in mind that the hetero-patriarchal nuclear family is by no means the only environment/structure in which children can and will flourish. Vocation means the calling of the whole body of Christ to respond to the God who sends God's Church into the world. This calling is embodied in the manifold callings of different members of the body of Christ to share in the life of God in the world. We must therefore challenge any thinking about a calling to parenthood or away from it that is in any way individualistic or selfish. Yet, the calling of an individual has to be carried and upheld by the whole body of Christ and regarded as part of its corporate calling. David McCarthy speaks of the family being grounded in 'a vocation that cannot be pursued alone'.[23] It is essentially a response to the self-giving of God in the incarnation and in creation. In responding to it we receive the gift of being able to participate in the activity of God in the world. This response is framed in the dual calling of all human beings to stewardship and discipleship, to worship and mission, to living in a world that is both God's creation and fallen. It is God we worship with our bodies and whose love we potentially (and by no means exclusively) experience in sexual intercourse, which is open to procreation and the conception of children. This is not a rejection of a general openness of all human life as a gift from God, but part of a life of stewardship and discipleship in the interest of the whole body of Christ and for the life of the world.

What about those, however, who do not have a choice? While, on the one hand, the choice of a life of celibacy has been part of the Christian tradition, Christian theology has had very little to say about the experience of barrenness and the pain of involuntary childlessness. A community that is open to receiving children as God's gift of new life also has to acknowledge that some will experience childlessness, for a variety of reasons, as a painful experience wherein they believe they are not only being judged and being abandoned by human beings, but also by God. The focus on 'family-friendly' churches is not always helpful, if such churches are not at the same time open to all human beings and willing to engage with the pain of barrenness and infertility. Involuntary childlessness can be experienced as a source of pain and feeling rejected and abandoned by God. To say anything else, or to take verses such as Isaiah 66.9 out of context, would be advocating a form of Christian fatalism, which is nothing other than cruel. As God incarnate and crucified suffers with God's creation, God also shares the pain of frustrated creativity on the part of humans. As the Christian community in the image of God we are called to do nothing less.

In this chapter I have noted that there is indeed a variety of different attitudes and expectations with regard to children to be found within the Christian tradition. What we can say is that the Church and individual Christians will find themselves in a world where children are born and where choices about the well-being of these children will have to be made. For some this may mean a calling to parenthood, for others a calling to care for children who are not biologically their own, to forsake the gift of fertility for the sake of another vocation. In any case, children – all children – are to be received as a gift from God that has to be received and treasured with responsibility and care. This may mean challenging assumptions made by the societies in which we live about reproductive choices, about the expectation that particular individuals will be parents and about what it means if, by choice or for other reasons, they do not become biological parents. The theological task before us is to transform our thinking about the expectation that children will be born in particular circumstances towards welcoming children, all children, as fellow citizens of the kingdom of God. This may mean recognizing that our attitudes to children themselves, as well as childhood, are socially and culturally constructed and therefore to some extent historically contingent. It is therefore possible and necessary to think anew in every generation what it means to receive children in the image of God. In reconsidering this and finding within it a range of different expressions of the one vocation, to participate in the creative activity of God in patterns of responsible stewardship and discipleship, the Christian Church as a moral community could provide an interesting and important counter-cultural challenge to a number of potentially destructive attitudes in society and thus fulfil its calling as leaven in the lump of society. But perhaps this challenge needs to begin in the Christian community itself in recovering the wealth of different models of parenthood and childhood, biological, social, ecclesial and theological, that exist within the Christian tradition, to find behind them the gospel principles that have shaped them and their constant need to be challenged and re-shaped in their light.

This is not the place to discuss in any detail the rightness or wrongness of abortion or fertility treatment. This I must leave to ethicists. What is at stake is rather the calling to an openness of life, the embodied encounter with the creativity of God in human procreativity and the fact that in the communities in which we live we find children and their parents. These children are an expression of 'God with us'. Our challenge as Christian (feminist) theologians is to develop patterns of responsible Christian living that focus on the lives of the actual human beings we meet.

Notes

1 I dedicate this chapter to the children who have not taken no for an answer and who have taught me much about life and about God: my step-daughter Hannah-Rose Davies, Frances and John Rolfe, Eleanor Thomas, Jack McLean and Hugh Wells.

2 I am indebted to Timothy Potts for bringing this to my attention.

3 Herbert Anderson and Susan Johnson, *Regarding Children: A New*

Respect for Children and the Family, Louisville, Westminster John Knox, 1994, passim.

4 Judith M. Gundry-Volf, 'The Least and the Greatest: Children in the New Testament' in Marcia Bunge (ed.), *The Child in Christian Thought*, Grand Rapids, Eerdmans, 2001, p. 44.

5 For a feminist reading of these texts see Linda M. Maloney, 'The Pastoral Epistles' in *Searching the Scriptures vol. 2 A Feminist Commentary*, ed. Elisabeth Schüssler Fiorenza, London, SCM Press, 1995, pp. 361–80.

6 Elsa Tamez, '1 Timothy' in Daniel Patte et al. (eds), *The Global Bible Commentary*, Nashville, Abingdon, 2004, pp. 509f.

7 Gerard Loughlin, 'Sex after Natural Law' in Lisa Isherwood and Marcella Althaus Reid (eds), *The Sexual Theologian. Essays on Sex, God and Politics*, London, T&T Clark, 2004, p. 96.

8 Augustine, 'On the Good of Marriage', 3; http://www.newadvent.org/fathers/1309.htm

9 *Gaudium et Spes* 48: http://www.vatican.va/archive/hist_councils/ii_vatican_council/documents/vat-ii_cons_19651207_gaudium-et-spes_en.html.

10 *Humanae Vitae I*: http://www.vatican.va/holy_father/paul_vi/encyclicals/documents/hf_p-vi_enc_25071968_humanae-vitae_en.html.

11 *Humanae Vitae*, English translation by Alan Clark and Geoffrey Crawfurd in John Horgan (ed.), *Humanae Vitae and the Bishops: The Encyclical and the Statements of the National Hierarchies*, Shannon, Irish University Press, 1972. The original Latin is even stronger here: 'ut *quilibet matrimonii usus* ad vitam humanam procreandam per se destinatus permaneat.'

12 But see, for example, Helen Stanton, 'Obligation or Option? Marriage, Voluntary Childlessness and the Church' in Adrian Thatcher (ed.), *Celebrating Christian Marriage*, London, T&T Clark, 2001.

13 Ann Loades, *Feminist Theology: Voices from the Past*, Cambridge, Polity Press, 2001, p. 64. See also Samuel Wells, *Transforming Fate into Destiny: The Theological Ethics of Stanley Hauerwas*, Carlisle, Paternoster, 1998, pp. 172–9.

14 Stanley Hauerwas, 'The Radical Hope in the Annunciation: Why both Single and Married Christians Welcome Children' in John Berkman and Michael Cartwright (eds), *The Hauerwas Reader*, Durham and London, Duke University Press, 2001, pp. 512 and 515.

15 Ann Loades, *Feminist Theology: Voices from the Past*, Cambridge, Polity Press, 2001.

16 Beverly Wildung Harrison with Shirley Cloyes, 'Theology and Morality of Procreative Choice' in Carol S. Robb (ed.), *Making the Connections: Essays in Feminist Social Ethics*, Boston, Beacon Press, 1985, p.117.

17 Elina Vuola, *Limits of Liberation: Feminist Theology and the Ethics of Poverty and Reproduction*, London, Continuum, 2002.

18 Regina Ammicht-Quinn, Hille Haker et al., 'Women in the Practice of Reproductive Medicine and in Bioethical Discourse – an Intervention', *Concilium* 2006:2, pp. 119–36.

19 Ann Loades, 'Dympna Revisited: Thinking About the Sexual Abuse of Children' in Stephen C. Barton (ed.), *The Family in Theological Perspective*, Edinburgh, T&T Clark, 1996, p. 258.

20 I am indebted to Rabbi Mark Solomon for drawing this point to my attention. Personal conversation with the author 23 July 2006.

21 David Matzko McCarthy, *Sex and Love in the Home*, London: SCM Press, 2004.

22 Loughlin, 'Sex after Natural Law', pp. 96f.

23 McCarthy, *Sex and Love in the Home*, p. 7.

So Jacob called the place where God had spoken with him Bethel. Then they journeyed from Bethel; and when they were still some distance from Ephrath, Rachel was in childbirth, and she had a difficult labour. When she was in her difficult labour, the midwife said to her, 'Do not be afraid; for now you will have another son.'

As her soul was departing (for she died), she named him Ben-oni; but his father called him Benjamin. So Rachel died, and she was buried on the way to Ephrath (that is, Bethlehem), and Jacob set up a pillar at her grave; it is the pillar of Rachel's tomb, which is there to this day.

Genesis 35.15–20

2. Birth: Pain and Potential

ESTHER SHREEVE

Excitement and joy are inextricably bound together with pain when it comes to the miracle of new life. We see it on the occasion of the delivery of a healthy child to parents who are eager to welcome her into the world; the tears from the pain of labour quickly become tears of happiness, relief and thanksgiving. The words of the hymn writer, George Matheson, seem apposite: 'O joy that seekest me through pain'. The tension between the two is profound, and is located at the heart of the human condition; the fact that we are human means that we feel, and express, conflicting emotions. But how they came to be so intimately entwined is not immediately apparent. Is this how it always was, and was meant to be – or did something untoward, unplanned for and unlooked for, happen along the way? If so, why? And what might we learn about God from exploring the questions? It seems that many of the core Christian doctrines are related to the discussion – creation, original sin, the incarnation, the problem of suffering, and the importance of relationship and community.

Creation

In the Christian tradition (Genesis 2—3) we start with the narrative of the creation of the Garden of Eden, paradise on earth, inhabited by Adam and Eve, who were created by God, not born. The creation story is told, starting with Genesis 1.27: 'So God created humankind in his image, in the image of God he created them.' This concept of being made in the image of God, bearing his divine imprint (in much the same way that a computer's silicone chip determines what it can do) reflects the nature of God and involves our God-given ability to make choices and live in relationship with God and with each other. Humanity has been given the freedom and responsibility to know God, to learn of his will, and to choose whether to work with him towards that future which he has prepared for the whole of his creation (Romans 8.12–21). It is vital to the well-being of the whole of creation that we recognize that humans are stewards, not owners, of creation. We have our limitations.

Teresa of Avila is attributed with extending this notion of stewardship with the words familiar to most of us:

> Christ has no body now on earth but yours,
> no hands, no feet on earth but yours.

Is this why we enter this world in the first place? Are we simply about our master's business? Or is there a more transcendent dimension to life? We could do worse than look at what the Christian tradition has taught, and about which Catholics and Protestants agree. The Catechism of the Roman Catholic Church asserts:

> God, infinitely perfect and blessed in himself, in a plan of sheer goodness, freely created man [sic] to make him share in his own blessed life. For this reason, at every time and in every place, God draws close to man. He calls man to seek him, to know him, to love him with all his strength.[1]

Calvin's sixteenth-century catechism for the church in Geneva is even more direct and affirms:

> Master: What is the chief end of human life?
> Scholar: To know God by whom we were created.
> Master: What reason have you for saying so?
> Scholar: Because he created us and placed us in this world to be glorified in us. And it is indeed right that our life, of which himself is the beginning, should be devoted to his glory.[2]

Creation then is good – it is God given, and carries divine responsibilities.

Small wonder that we feel overwhelmed when we witness the miracle of birth. Margaret Hebblethwaite wrote of the awe-inspiring effect of giving birth:

> Every woman thinks she has done the cleverest thing in the world when she has produced a baby. . . (she) knows reverence at the creation of her new-born baby, who is so obviously a person from the first moment she sees him. More reverence still would a mother feel if she could already see with the eyes of God all that her little child would grow to – the talent and beauty and strength and love that are already written into his make-up.[3]

Although this passage does need to be read critically, given that not every birth happens in the joyful circumstances she envisages (see below), it reflects a generally accepted attitude to the birth of a child.

The fact is, however, that not everyone is able to play a part in the miracle of procreation. One in six couples is infertile, that is around 17 per cent of the population. The many stories of infertility in the Bible, with their miraculously happy endings, work together to paint a picture of one of the pinnacles of creation being in the act of procreation, and that somehow we are less than fulfilled if we are not able to play our part in this. The life of the woman, in particular, is stunted, and shame is attached to her condition. On occasion God intervenes directly. Genesis chapter 18 tells of the visitation of the three angels (depicted by Rublev in his famous icon of the Trinity) to Abraham, and the promise of a son to Sarah, who was old and barren. There are the stories of the gift of a son to Hannah (1 Samuel 2.1–10), Samson to Manoah (Judges 13.3–4) and the twins, Jacob and Esau, to Rebecca (Genesis 25). Mary's cousin, Elizabeth, spoke in a familiar vein to the words used by Hannah when she conceived John the Baptist after what must have seemed like a life-time of infertility: 'This is what the Lord has done for me when he looked favourably on me and took away the disgrace I have endured among my people' (Luke 1.25). The same theme is picked up in the Magnificat. Fertility was – and often still is – seen as a mark of being a true woman. Only in bearing healthy children to term could one really be fulfilled and valued. Never mind the pain of childbirth – a more enduring and inescapable pain may well be the inability to conceive and the emotional trauma that accompanies it. Small wonder then that Mary herself came to be linked with the ability to overcome infertility; she was, and is, asked to intercede with regard to fertility, or fears of the pains of childbirth.[4]

Pain

Jesus, in John 16.21, clearly knew what the physical pains of childbirth could mean: 'When a woman is in labour, she has pain, because her hour has come.' There is an inevitability about it, and an overwhelming sense of knowing there is no way out of it, but of having to go through it. Margaret Hebblethwaite compared it with the Passion of Christ in Gethsemane, as she went through the transition stage: 'Anything, but anything, only take this pain away.'[5] We can only surmise that Rebekah must have had a difficult time of it when she was delivering the twins, Jacob and Esau, as Jacob emerged holding Esau's heel (Genesis 25.26).

The pain of labour may be seen as a physical manifestation of the emotional and spiritual pain that inevitably follows as the parenting role develops. Parenting is a challenging and often painful business, taxing those involved to the absolute limit. It may be because of rivalry between siblings – Rebekah favoured Jacob, and Isaac loved Esau (Genesis 25.28). Jesus went off without telling his parents where he was and they endured three days of anxiety as they searched (Luke 2.43–50) – was this a precursor of the three days between Jesus' burial and resurrection? And he told the story of the wayward, prodigal son (Luke 15.11–32), with its subtexts of rebellion, jealousy, woven into a compelling narrative to illustrate the enduring power of love, forgiveness and reconciliation.

Jairus had to watch his daughter sicken and die (Luke 8.49–56). This must be the worst pain of all, and God knows exactly how we feel in this situation. Jesus begged for the cup to be removed from him (Mark 14.36), but that was not to be. In this case God was actually allowing her Son to suffer when it would have been possible to allow a reprieve:

> There is no threshold of grief that she cannot have known in seeing her innocent and dearly loved child nailed up to die with no means of escape or anaesthesia. How could she have allowed these unthinkable experiences if it did not have to be this way? Must she not grieve again with us when she sees those terrible hours reflected in any way in our own experience? Must she not long to take our hand and weep with us for the burden of memories that cannot be borne and cannot be forgotten? If anyone knows what it feels like to suffer, it must be God, who saw her son die in agony, and had to let it be.[6]

Of course the pain of loving one's children is not restricted to biological parents. In this country, the process of adoption is as fraught as any pregnancy, with pitfalls, highs and lows. Would-be parents have to negotiate the social services vetting procedures and the legal system. Right up to the moment of adoption things can go wrong, and prospective parents feel they are walking on a tight-rope until the papers are finally signed and sealed. So the joy of the new arrival is tinged with pain and uncertainty in a way that the majority of biological parents simply never experience. How does this relate to God's adoption of us into his family? I suspect he goes through the same heart-breaking uncertainties and yearnings that all parents experience.

It is important to acknowledge also that giving birth in many cases is not the joyful experience that is implied by Hebblethwaite's words quoted near the start of this chapter. Not every child is planned, or welcome. Some are born as a consequence of rape. They may have inherited a drug-dependency from a mother who is addicted; they may be born with AIDS. There may be too many children in the family already, and too many mouths to feed in a context of economic and social deprivation. Post-natal depression may well come into play. For some women, the rapid change in hormone levels following childbirth can wreak havoc with their sense of identity and well-being, and they find themselves unable to cope with their new baby, perhaps even to the point of rejecting them, and spiralling into a pit of despair and guilt. 'Why did you bring me forth from the womb? Would that I had died before any eye had seen me, and were as though I had not been, carried from the womb to the grave' (Job 10.18–19).

Original sin

The process of bearing a child is, as we have seen, usually a painful business. The Bible explains the pain of childbirth by the story of the Fall, and Eve's part in it. Before Adam and Eve became parents, Eve had her encounter with the serpent (Satan), disobeyed God and ate the fruit from the Tree of Knowledge. As a punishment, they were cast out of the garden, and God said to Eve: 'I will greatly increase your pangs in childbearing; in pain you shall bring forth children, yet your desire shall be for your husband, and he shall rule over you'

(Genesis 4.16). God was even-handed; the serpent and Adam were also cursed – the serpent to creep on his belly, Adam to toil over the land and to face his own mortality: 'You are dust and to dust you will return' (Genesis 4.19).

Thus, the joy of Eden was turned to pain, and the seeds of patriarchal theology surrounding procreation and birth were sown, drawing on Aristotelian philosophy, which saw woman as inferior to man:

> A woman, having no positive sexual reality of her own, is only a failure to become a man. Aristotelian embryology claimed that, because all form, like the soul, is in the semen, and only formless matter is contributed by the mother, it is the true nature of all pregnancies to result in boys only. If girl babies are born, it is because of some failure in the gestation process.[7]

Looking at it from the standpoint of an educated western Protestant woman in the twenty-first century, it feels as if a sort of theological or philosophical shorthand came into play, which conveniently made the connection between prevailing philosophical trends and the need to explain the problem of evil, neatly demeaning the role of woman in God's creation.

Origen, writing in the third century AD believed:

> Everyone who enters the world may be said to be affected by a kind of contamination . . . by the very fact that humanity is placed in it's mother's womb, and that it takes the material out of its body from the source of the father's seed, it may be said to be contaminated in respect of both the father and the mother . . . Thus everyone is polluted in father and mother.[8]

So, having begun with humankind being created in God's own image (Genesis 1.26), we have moved to being lumps of perdition. In the Christian tradition, woman fares particularly badly.

> In the faeces and the urine – Augustine's phrase – of childbirth, the closeness of woman to all that is vile, lowly, corruptible, and material was epitomized; in the curse of menstruation, she lay closer to the beasts; the lure of her beauty was nothing but an aspect of the death brought about by her seduction of Adam in the garden.[9]

This was simply an extension of the ancient view which despised matter; the woman's role in reproduction was basic and inferior to that of the man's spiritual, noble and infinitely superior function of imparting life.

The medieval tradition saw woman as womb, and womb as evil.[10] Jerome wrote: 'As long as a woman is for birth and children, she is different from man as body is from soul. But when she wishes to serve Christ more than the world, then she will cease to be a woman, and will be called man.'[11]

A false dualism had emerged, which identified women as weak and inferior, controlled by bodily passions and functions, as compared to men, who might identify with Adam, sinning through self-will and pride, but who also identified themselves with Christ, the saviour. This could be taken to pernicious extremes, in the denial of pain relief to women in childbirth, because the pain was seen as women's natural punishment.[12] Is it any wonder that women have struggled to be treated as equals in the Church, as we have seen in their deliberate barring from positions of leadership, in both lay and ordained ministry? Even the clarion call of Paul in Galatians 3.28, 'There is no longer Jew or Greek, there is no longer slave or free, there is no longer male and female; for all of you are one in Christ Jesus', implies that there is an intrinsic inferiority, which is only removed by baptism. A feminist interpretation of original sin challenges this mindset, and sees sin as 'violence done by human beings to each other, as exemplified by Cain's murder of Abel. Such violence constitutes a break in relationships which cannot be remedied. This fits the notion of *sin* much better than the concept of experimentation, sharing and learning, which is the true meaning of Genesis 1—3'.[13] If we are made in the image of God, we must therefore have in us the potential to reflect something of the harmony and co-operation intrinsic in the Trinity. How we relate to God, and to one another, is crucial, and men and women share equal responsibility for this – as indeed they did in the story of that first act of disobedience.

Taking the lens of birth to look at how sin manifests itself in the world, it is worth looking further on in the book of Genesis. Jealousy was a major factor in the story of Abraham, Sarah and Hagar (Genesis 16.1–6). When Abraham and Sarah had given up all hope of having a child, Sarah's servant, Hagar, slept with Abraham, with Sarah's blessing, and became the mother of Ishmael. It could only end in tears. A few years later, after Sarah (miraculously) gave birth to

Isaac, trouble broke out again and Hagar was banished to wander in the desert with Ishmael (Genesis 21.9–14). What was Hagar's role and significance? Picking up the theme of the exploitation of women, this passage has become a very significant one for womanist theologians:

> The themes of the meaning of motherhood, poverty and homelessness, the expendability of black women and children, the ongoing use of black women's bodies for assorted forms of surrogacy correlate the story of Hagar with African American women's experiences.[14]

A womanist interpretation of sin makes it *external* to the human being – Delores Williams talks of any abuse or defilement of the human body being sin, if we are made in God's image.[15]

This, surely, goes to the core of what the doctrine of original sin is about. It has nothing to do with the process of procreation, but everything to do with our humanity, and the ways in which we give way to the temptation to act as controllers, rather than stewards, of God's creation. By the very fact that we are made in the image of God, we are prone to forget our dependence on our creator and try to behave like gods – and power struggles ensue. This is our human nature.

The incarnation

The Christian faith is based on the belief that at a particular and specific stage in human history God did, in fact, become a human being – in the words of Charles Wesley: 'Our God contracted to a span, incomprehensibly made man.'[16] Where does the most famous biblical birth narrative fit in to this complexity of thought about the purpose of our creation? Given the weight that the Christian tradition gave to the role of Eve in the Fall, we can understand how the doctrine of the virgin birth came to be so important. Mary was 'Theotokos' – God-bearer – but Jesus was as little contaminated by the physical process of conception as he could have been. The doctrine of the immaculate conception concerning how the Virgin Mary herself was conceived, promulgated as official doctrine of the Roman Catholic Church by Pope Pius IX in 1854, made Mary unique in the history of the world – she herself was conceived (having two human parents) without being contaminated by original sin.[17] The idea of the virgin birth takes it one step further. Augustine wrote:

> Only Jesus my Lord was born without stain. He was not polluted in this respect by his mother, for he entered a body which was not contaminated . . . For Joseph played no part in his birth other than his devotion and affection, and it is on account of his faithful devotion that Scripture allows him the name 'father'.[18]

Mary has a key role to play in the unfolding of the salvation narrative. In marked contrast to Eve, she was obedient to the point of apparent foolhardiness,[19] responding to the angel Gabriel's Annunciation of Jesus' birth with the historic words: 'Here am I, the servant of the Lord; let it be with me according to thy word' (Luke 1.38). It is interesting to note that it is only in the Gospel of Matthew that we find an unequivocal and clear statement of the virgin birth.[20] Hence the link with Adam – she has been called the mother of the second Adam, or a second Eve.[21] Humanity is given another chance. It is worth noting that this role fits in with a long tradition in classical mythology and ancient religion, 'where the Goddess as mother, sister, or spouse functions to rescue and establish male kingly power, rather than to uplift the power of women'.[22] Nevertheless, the part that she was asked to play was crucial, laden with potential, as Hauerwas comments, comparing Mary's sacrifice with the possible offering up of Isaac:

> God restrained Abraham's blow that would have sacrificed Isaac, but the Father does not hold back from the sacrifice of Mary's son. Jesus's command that Mary should 'behold your son' is to ask Mary to see that the one born of her body was born to be sacrificed that we might live. As Gregory of Nyssa put it: 'If one examines this mystery, one will prefer to say not that his death was a consequence of his birth, but that the birth was undertaken so that he could die.'[23]

What is often perceived as the submissive tone of the Magnificat poses problems for many women today and it has certainly been taken as a key text for generations of Christian men in a patriarchal society to assert their dominance over women. Feminist theologians have worked hard to counterbalance this, working with a hermeneutic of suspicion and insisting 'that *the* litmus test for invoking Scripture as the word of God must be whether or not biblical texts and traditions seek to end relations of domination and exploitation'.[24] Mary's position must be viewed in a more positive light, moving her a long way from apparently supine, submissive obedience, if we recognize that 'Jesus becoming human should be regarded as a continuum of the manifestation of divine spirit beginning with Mary, becoming an abundance in Jesus and later overflowing into the life of the church'.[25] In her encounter with Gabriel, she may not have been given a choice, but it is important to recognize that this was in the context of her relationship with God, who does not force anyone to do what they really do not want. Far from a prospect of exploitation and suppression, what was on offer was liberation and salvation for the world. In terms reminiscent of the catechisms, which we looked at earlier, Mary was told she 'had found favour with God' (Luke 1.30) and hence this great honour was to be given to her. By assenting to play the part assigned to her, she was displaying immense courage and determination – attributes which the Church would do well to rediscover! Thus 'the role of women in birthing new realities through openness to the Spirit is informed by Jesus' incarnation, which becomes a possibility for each generation'.[26]

Mary's role in giving birth to the Christ child epitomized this 'birthing of new reality' in a physical sense. In marked contrast to Augustine, Luther waxed eloquent about the process. Far from being squeamish, he revelled in the very ordinariness and messiness of the occasion:

> They must have marveled that this Child was the Son of God. He was also a real human being. Those who say that Mary was not a real mother lose all the joy. He was a true Baby, with flesh, blood, hands and legs. He slept, cried and did everything else that a baby does, only without sin . . .
>
> Think, women, there was no one there to bathe the Baby. No warm water, nor even cold. No fire, no light. The mother was herself the midwife and the maid. The cold manger was the bed and the bathtub. Who showed the poor girl what to do? She had never had a baby before. I am amazed that the little one did not freeze. Do not make of Mary a stone. It must have gone straight to her heart that she was so abandoned. She as flesh and blood and must

have felt miserable – and Joseph too – that she was left in this way, all alone, with no one to help, in a strange land in the middle of winter. Her eyes were moist even though she was happy and aware that the Baby was God's Son and the Saviour of the world.[27]

This passage is rather fun to read in view of Luther's clarion Reformation cry of 'Sola Scriptura!' – here is a highly embroidered account of the Nativity, based on a collective inheritance of western fantasy.[28] Not much of the biblical narrative is evident at all. But this is not to dismiss it. It speaks to our modern context of displaced peoples, refugees, and life on the margins. Christ was born at the heart of human need at its most acute, and Luther's interpretation of events is eloquent and challenging.

Disability?

Christ was born perfect in every way. This means not only was he born without sin, but that his physical being was (as far as we know – and it surely would have been reported if there had been any problem!) in perfect working condition. He had ten fingers and ten toes, all his vital organs worked as they were designed to do. But what about disability? Psalm 139 has posed problems for those who read it as a hymn of thanksgiving and praise for perfection in creation, although I would argue that it does not have to be interpreted in this way:

For it was you who formed my inward parts;
you knit me together in my mother's womb.
14 I praise you, for I am fearfully and wonderfully made.
Wonderful are your works;
that I know very well.
15 My frame was not hidden from you,
when I was being made in secret,
intricately woven in the depths of the earth.
16 Your eyes beheld my unformed substance.
In your book were written
all the days that were formed for me,
when none of them as yet existed.

We are all 'fearfully and wonderfully made', but we are not all perfect – or maybe not perfect in the eyes of the world. God, of course, looks at us differently. In John's Gospel we read the story of Jesus and the blind man.

> As he walked along, he saw a man blind from birth. His disciples asked him, 'Rabbi, who sinned, this man or his parents, that he was born blind?' Jesus answered, 'Neither this man nor his parents sinned; he was born blind so that God's works might be revealed in him'. (John 9.1–3)

Here we have the assumption that disability was the result of the parents' sins. Luther is notorious for suggesting on more than one occasion that a 'changeling' child be suffocated, or thrown in the river, the assumption being that the devil had somehow taken over the human being – but we must be careful to see this in the context of many, many more of his writings which affirm the importance and potential of the grace of God operating in human beings. The work of Jean Vanier and the l'Arche movement affirms the concept touched on above – that God is to be found in each and every one of us, and therefore everyone, regardless of their physical/mental/emotional state is worthy of the utmost respect, honour and love.

> In our l'Arche community in the Ivory Coast, we welcomed Innocente. She has a severe mental handicap. She will never be able to speak or walk or grow very much. She remains in many ways like a child only a few months old. But her eyes and whole body quiver with love whenever she is held in love; a beautiful smile unfolds in her face and her whole being radiates peace and joy. Innocente is not helped by ideas, no matter how deep or beautiful they may be; she does not need money or power or a job; she does not want to prove herself; all she wants is loving touch and communion. When she receives the gift of love, she quivers in ecstasy; if she feels abandoned, she closes herself up in inner pain – the poorer a person is, old or sick or with a severe mental handicap or close to death, the more the cry is solely for communion and for friendship. The more then the heart of the person who hears the cry, and responds to it, is awoken.[29]

This is not where much of our society is today. Television regularly offers programmes that are basically the modern equivalent of freak shows, featuring tragic (and yes, fascinating) case studies of unusually affected individuals. Thus, I heard for the first time of 'Mermaid Syndrome' or Sirenomelia, a congenital abnormality which affected a baby girl born in South America with her legs fused together.[30] She had no external genitalia and one of her kidneys was affected. Without surgical intervention, she would surely die. Her father was asking what he had done wrong to deserve this, and her mother's response reflected the devastation she felt: 'Oh God, why did you allow her to live? If she lives, we will both suffer.' The village perceived the birth to be the result of a curse, perhaps because the mother had been seen at the lake, which was believed to be cursed. This is not so very far removed from the biblical concept of handicap being the result of parental sin. The way the story unfolded demonstrated, and played its own part in, a media circus – as the result of which the girl got the very expensive help she needed. The Mayor of Lima ended up as her godfather, because the doctor who treated her wanted a career in politics.

The reason for recounting this particular story is because it reflects the way society generally deals with disability, and it does us no credit. Dominic Lawson wrote about the birth of his daughter who has Down's Syndrome in a very moving article, which describes the pain and frustration his family have experienced since her birth in respect of the way health professionals and others have reacted. 'You didn't need to have this child, you know' is a comment heavy with implicit assumptions. He concludes: 'Down's is not a disease or an illness or, as some members of the public still appear to believe, an infection. There is nothing to be cured – save the fear and hostility of the medical profession and the misery that causes to countless women who are cruelly confronted with a life or death choice.'[31] This is another aspect of the cultural norms surrounding birth, which dictate the way we deal with our children, both those already born, and the unborn, and it feeds in to the debates which wage about abortion. Has Christianity got a distinctive perspective on this – a way of seeing potential through the mists of pain?

A Church that saw reality through Jesus Christ would witness to the world through a way of life that would express those truths about human existence, its origin and its destiny, which are known in him. This way of life, in what is done as much as in what is said, would be welcoming of children, female as well as male, disabled as well as able-bodied, planned as well as unplanned. Such a way of life would find expression in countless practical endeavours, just as Christian witness always has, to support and assist those who are seeking to live the life of discipleship to which the gospel calls us, aware as Dietrich Bonhoeffer put it, that 'guilt in these matters may often lie within the community than with the individual'. In that life of discipleship there would be nothing of the despising of human existence, the despair in its course, and the estrangement of one from another, which presently characterize our dealings with the unborn, but not only the unborn. Instead, where there is faith, hope and love, there would be a life of joy in which abortion would not first of all be thought wrong, but would be quite simply, as Bonhoeffer says, unthinkable.[32] It is interesting to see how key the notion of relationship is in this context, just as it was when we looked at understandings of original sin. But Elizabeth Templeton sounds a note of caution:

> It is an act of heroic and Christlike faith to trust that God will transform situations of immense pain and stress into creative possibilities. It cannot be taken for granted that people are capable of that, and certainly it cannot be prescribed as a response by a Church which lives as much by prudent self-conservation as by heroic faith . . . If the Church is to be witness to that post-ethical community of a new earth, it misinterprets that vocation by trying to impose the conditions of eschatology on to a pre-eschatological world.
>
> It would be great if the church were to take full responsibility for looking after the children who would otherwise be aborted – but there is no evidence that either the Churches or the community are able and willing to meet the additional strain on resources . . . we are invited to 'sin boldly', not in pride or complacency at our decisions, but in confidence that God himself suffers with us in all the ambiguity of our imperfect choices.[33]

Death – and eternal life

Rachel's travail and subsequent death is one of the few biblical accounts we have of a hard labour (Genesis 35.18). A new report from the charity Save the Children, *State of the World's Mothers*,[34] indicates that every minute a woman meets her death during pregnancy and childbirth – nearly all of them in the developing world where 60 million women per year give birth at home without a skilled person to help. The scandal is that something could so easily be done to prevent this: cheap, low-tech solutions could prevent the shameful mortality rates among mothers and new-born babies. But change will only come about when we begin to take community seriously, on a global scale.

But wherever the birth may happen, whether it be in a western hospital with all the clinical paraphernalia regarded as the norm, or in a rural, remote setting, when giving birth we find ourselves in a very 'thin' place, where the barrier between earth and heaven seems almost non-existent. Women die in childbirth, babies die just before being born, in the process of coming into the world, and shortly after birth. When our second baby died after living for only an hour, we had a profound sense that we held a child who had come very recently from God, and who was now on his way home. On a rational and theological level, we could appreciate that the time we have on earth is but a blinking of an eye in God's economy:

> You have made my days a few handbreadths,
> And my lifetime is as nothing in your sight.
> Surely everyone stands as a mere breath.
>
> Psalm 39.5

We were grateful that our son had lived for a short time. Yet how important is it, that a new-born baby should actually draw breath? If they are still-born, does that imply that they have not lived? Surely not – the debate about abortion posits several points at which life may be considered to have begun: conception, implantation at 6–10 days, transition from embryo to fetus at 8 weeks, quickening at around 20 weeks, birth, a year or so after birth – these are all points at which, it has been argued, life begins.[35] Jeremiah makes an even more challenging statement: 'Before I formed you in the womb I knew you, and before you were born I consecrated you' (Jeremiah 1.5). Recent scientific experiments have shown that a baby in the womb has a memory, recognizing, after birth, nursery rhymes that her mother sang to her *in utero*. The biblical tradition makes a strong link between life in the womb and what follows, so that if life in the world is not to be, it can be viewed as an 'early' death, rather than a life that did not happen. A joyful example of this is in the story of the unborn John the Baptist leaping in the womb when Mary visited Elizabeth (Luke 1.44).

Potential

We are made to be in relationship with God – and with each other. Jesus' commandment, that we love one another as he loves us, makes this abundantly plain (John 13.34). The individualism of Descartes' 'I think, therefore I am', is destined for aridity; John Mbiti's African perspective: 'I am because we are' places enormous significance in the communities that form us.[36] It is in our relationships with one another that much of the pain surrounding birth (apart from the pangs of childbirth itself) are rooted. Were it not, for example, for the norms of the ways in which we order society, the experience of childlessness could be very different. We can begin to see this in the way China has imposed the 'one child' policy on the country; social norms there have changed, in marked contrast to the context in many other countries and cultures, where large families are deemed to provide security for the future. But they are in the process of changing back again, as the realization dawns that through this policy the new generation may end up supporting not only two parents but potentially four ageing grandparents. Hence some bending of the rule, so that if both parents are only children, they may be given permission to have two children. The 'circle of life' is dependent on relationships.

Implicit in the creation of life are contradictions of life and death. 'As for mortals, their days are like grass; they flourish like a flower of the field; for the wind passes over it, and it is gone' (Psalm 103.15–16). But grass has seed, and the seeds propagate:

> All living beings give life. Thus from generation to generation we have birds, fish, animals, trees, flowers and fruit – the incredible fecundity of creation as life flows from one being to another. Man and woman together give life, conceiving and giving birth to a child. And that is just the physical and biological aspect of procreation. Once the baby is born, and even before birth, the parents give life to the child, and reveal to him/her its beauty by the way they welcome and love it. Or they may bring inner death to the

child, making it feel ugly and worthless through the way they reject or over-protect it. Through love and tenderness, through welcome and listening, we can give life to people.[37]

Community and relationship, as we have seen, are of the essence of what is life-giving. Sin, and the capacity to abuse power and bring hurt, arise from relational failure. We may be made in the image of God but perhaps the beauty of the dance of the Trinity, perfect relationship within itself, eludes us. The process of giving birth is an utterly overwhelming experience in physical, emotional and spiritual terms. The mother is totally absorbed in the business of bringing new life into the world. She risks her life to do it – just as God risked everything in the incarnation of Jesus. It is not just the new-born baby who is naked, the mother too is in a place where all pretence, any denial of what is actual and true, is impossible. This is a moment of intense vulnerability – both before God, and in the world. Such occasions are rare.

What happens in the hours, days and weeks following the birth is crucial to the well-being of mother and child. If all has gone well, there will be a natural inclination to give thanks and rejoice. But there is also a great need for support and encouragement. How much more is this the case when the outcome is not one of unmitigated joy – for whatever reason. This is the point at which the love of God needs to be seen in action, in the body language, words and deeds of those around the mother and child, as Teresa of Avila envisaged.

Paul writes of us being 'clay jars' (2 Corinthians 4.7), with our 'outer nature wasting away' (verse 16). These clay jars are capable of doing tremendous good for God's kingdom on earth. This is the potential with which we are all born. But fulfilling that temporal relational potential must not become an end in itself; we should not lose sight of the ultimate goal 'that I may gain Christ and be found in him' (Philippians 3.8–9). This is what we mean when pray in the baptism service:

Pour out your Holy Spirit
That those baptized in this water
May die to sin,
Be raised with Christ
And be born to new life in the family of your Church.[38]

So we can sing of the new birth in the words of Charles Wesley:

Changed from glory into glory,
Till in heaven we take our place
Till we cast our crowns before thee
Lost in wonder, love and praise.[39]

Notes

1 <http://www.christusrex.org/www1/CDHN/prologue.html#life> 12.04.06.

2 <http://www.reformed.org/documents/calvin/geneva_catechism> 12.04.06.

3 M. Hebblethwaite, *Motherhood and God*, London, Geoffrey Chapman, 1984, p. 94.

4 M. Warner, *Alone of All Her Sex*, Picador, London 1976, p. 281.

5 Hebblethwaite, *Motherhood and God*, p. 79.

6 Hebblethwaite, *Motherhood and God*, p. 76.

7 S. Gunew, *A Reader in Feminist Knowledge*, London, Routledge, 1991, p. 97.

8 A. McGrath, *The Christian Theology Reader*, Oxford, Blackwell, 1995, p. 215

9 Warner, *Alone of All Her Sex*, p. 58.

10 Warner, *Alone of All Her Sex*, pp. 41 and 57.

11 Warner, *Alone of All Her Sex*, p. 73.

12 L. Isherwood and D. McEwan, *An A to Z of Feminist Theology*, Sheffield, Sheffield Academic Press, 1996, p. 166.

13 Isherwood and McEwan, *An A to Z of Feminist Theology*, p. 167.

14 Stephanie Y. Mitchem, *Introducing Womanist Theology*, Maryknoll NY, Orbis, 2002, pp. 82–3.

15 Mitchem, *Introducing Womanist Theology*, p. 110.

16 *Hymns & Psalms*, Peterbrough, Methodist Publishing House, 1983, No.109.

17 Warner, *Alone of All Her Sex*, p. 236.

18 McGrath, *The Christian Theology Reader*, p. 215.

19 Gunew, *A Reader in Feminist Knowledge*, p. 299.

20 Warner, *Alone of All Her Sex*, p. 19.

21 Warner, *Alone of All Her Sex*, p. 59.

22 Gunew, *A Reader in Feminist Knowledge*, p. 278.

23 Stanley Hauerwas, *Cross-shattered Christ*, London, Darton, Longman & Todd, 2005, p. 52.

24 Gunew, *A Reader in Feminist Knowledge*, p. 266.

25 D. S. Williams, *Sisters in the Wilderness: The Challenge of Womanist God-Talk*, Maryknoll NY, Orbis, 1993, p. 168.

26 Mitchem, *Introducing Womanist Theology*, p. 116.

27 Roland H. Bainton, *The Martin Luther Christmas Book*, Philadelphia, Fortress, 1983, p. 39.

28 Warner, *Alone of All Her Sex*, p. 14.

29 Jean Vanier, *Community and Growth*, London, Darton, Longman & Todd, 1979, pp. 97–8.

30 Channel 4, *Body Shock*, 30.1.06

31 The *Independent*, 23.6.06

32 M. Banner, *The Practice of Abortion*, London, Darton, Longman & Todd, 1999, pp. 56–7.

33 Church of Scotland Board of Social Responsibility, *Abortion in Debate*, Edinburgh, St Andrew Press, 1987, pp. 26–7.

34 Save the Children <http://www.savethechildren.org>

35 D. Gareth Jones, *Brave New People*, Leicester, IVP, 1984, p. 161.

36 Mitchem, *Introducing Womanist Theology*, p. 35.

37 Vanier, *Community and Growth*, p. 87.

38 *Methodist Worship Book*, Peterborough, Methodist Publishing House, 1999, p. 79.

39 *Hymns & Psalms*, No. 267.

Guided by the Spirit, Simeon came into the temple; and when the parents brought in the child Jesus, to do for him what was customary under the law, Simeon took him in his arms and praised God, saying, 'Master, now you are dismissing your servant in peace, according to your word; for my eyes have seen your salvation, which you have prepared in the presence of all peoples, a light for revelation to the Gentiles and for glory to your people Israel.' And the child's father and mother were amazed at what was being said about him. Then Simeon blessed them and said to his mother Mary, 'This child is destined for the falling and the rising of many in Israel, and to be a sign that will be opposed so that the inner thoughts of many will be revealed – and a sword will pierce your own soul too.'

Luke 2.27–35

3. Babes in Arms: Speechlessness and Selfhood

JEREMY WORTHEN

The great and mighty God whom no eye has seen, who has neither form nor image, who said, 'For man may not see Me and live' (Exodus 33.20) – how shall I believe that this great and inaccessible *Deus absconditus* needlessly entered the womb of a woman, the filthy, foul bowels of a female, compelling the living God to be born of a woman, a child without knowledge or understanding, senseless, unable to distinguish between his right hand and his left, defecating and urinating, sucking his mother's breasts from hunger and thirst, crying when he is thirsty so that his mother will have compassion on him. Indeed, if she had not suckled him, he would have died of hunger like other people.[1]

Baptism lets us recognize completely what we first recognized in Christmas: for Christianity the beginning replaces redemption, the beaten path replaces consummated life. Every baptism renews the adoration of the divine infant. Christianity is wholly young. For in every individual, in every soul, it begins anew.[2]

Introduction

Outsiders can sometimes perceive things with more sharpness than those close up. Both of the quotations given at the start of this chapter are from Jewish authors trying to identify critical issues for their own people's intellectual engagement with Christianity. They are from very different periods and contexts. Joseph Kimhi wrote his dialogue in twelfth-century France in what might be called the genre of comparative polemic that was the normal mode for such formal theological exchange as there was between representatives of different faiths until relatively recently. Franz Rosenzweig's *Star of Redemption*, first drafted on postcards scribbled out while he was serving with the German army in World War I, represents one of the first and most enduring attempts to write about two religions together, Judaism and Christianity, in a quite different way, without the colouring of either polemic against the other or indeed apologetic for one's own. Yet both Kimhi and Rosenzweig perceive that the willingness to identify God with an infant is somehow near the heart of what makes Christian belief so astonishing and so alien for Jews, but also so powerful for those who accept it, although Rosenzweig is much more ready than Kimhi to concede and explore the positive. Rosenzweig also makes the link between Christology and liturgical spirituality, between Christian beliefs about God and the lived culture of Christian traditions, rightly stressing the profound and complex interchange between practices and ideas. Just as Christianity makes distinctive and difficult claims about one infant being 'the great and mighty God', in Kimhi's words, so it also generates a particular set of attitudes and expectations, according to Rosenzweig, about the infants it continues to welcome into its midst, most visibly through baptism.

The perspectives of these outsiders, then, suggest that Christian theology ought to have a substantial – though not uncontroversial – contribution to make towards the understanding of infancy. In order to outline some of the potential features of such a contribution in the contemporary context, the chapter will begin by reviewing some general questions about what it means to regard an infant as a human person. It will then consider two texts from the Gospel of Mark where Jesus is reported to have taken children – conceivably infants – into his arms as symbolic actions, and ask how these texts might speak to us today. The question of whether infants should be seen as sinful will then be briefly reviewed in the light of the discussion's emerging themes. Finally, the chapter will conclude with some reflections on the account in Luke 2 of Jesus himself being taken as a 'babe in arms' by the aged Simeon, who saw salvation in the figure he held. These investigations of the theology of infancy are premised on the assumption that only by juxtaposing Christology and anthropology can we begin to give a proper account of either. The statement from *Gaudium et spes*, 'The truth is that only in the mystery of the incarnate Word does the mystery of man [*sic*] take on light', needs to be set alongside Thomas Merton's summary expression of a major theme of the Christian spiritual tradition: '. . . we know him in so far as we become aware of ourselves as known through and through by him.'[3]

The infant as human person

The normative position of Christian orthodoxy, that both human and divine natures are fully present in Jesus Christ from the moment of conception, was firmly established at the Council of Chalcedon in AD 451. This sets a certain limit for speculative theology within the Christian tradition, or, to change the metaphor, indicates that the tendency to deny or diminish the fullness of either nature in Christ can only lead down a blind alley for thought. It does not, however, determine for all time the understanding either of the divine nature or indeed the human nature of the Word made flesh. The layers of our comprehension of human existence at the beginning of the twenty-first century include strata that would have been unimaginable to the bishops at Chalcedon, while the foundations of their own understanding have hardly survived intact. The subject of changing conceptions of the soul and the self through the western Middle Ages and into modernity is too vast to be addressed here.[4] One undeniable factor, however, is the influence of dynamic psychology at the level of both popular culture and intellectual discourse. Just as Darwin taught modern people to see the physical world as the latest stage of an incomplete process driven by competing powers, rather than an ordered cosmos whose pattern was established 'in the beginning', so Freud introduced the vision of the internal landscape of the self as the outcome of a conflictual and for the most part irretrievable history, a fragile balance of forces achieved at great cost and always susceptible to dissolution. As with Darwin, so with Freud, it is not the particular components of the theory that are of determinative significance or the debates and qualifications of his successors and opponents, so much as the 'way of seeing' that he opened up – a way of seeing that was simply not available to those who lived in earlier generations but that we cannot now blank out from our horizons. The working assumption of this chapter is that the thesis of the dynamic self in modern psychology is a perspective with which Christian theology should seek to engage both critically and creatively.

Changing conceptions of the self have inevitably been bound up with changing evaluations of childhood generally and infancy specifically. The first quotation at the start of this chapter characterizes infancy as dependency. To be an infant – literally in Latin 'without speech' – is to be without knowledge and without power, to lack those things that constitute the dignity and the glory of human beings from this point of view. The infant needs another to do anything, indeed to survive; and surely we can read in Kimhi's words not just the misogyny that has been common currency in all forms of discourse for so much of human history, but also a contempt for the child in its helplessness and vulnerability. Now, clearly just as the prevalence of misogyny does not mean that husbands never loved their wives, so the contempt for children as such does not mean that fathers did not cherish their infant sons and daughters. Nevertheless, the linkage in this text between ambivalence towards women and ambivalence towards children remains striking. By contrast, if we were to seek a word to describe the perspective on childhood in Rosenzweig's text, it might be not so much dependency as dynamism – the potential of the child as new beginning, its inherent dynamic for growth and development, its capacity to be a catalyst for change in the wider world. In this respect, Rosenzweig, like Kimhi, is not untypical of the long-term mentality regarding children in his context. For all the deep hostility shown towards Rousseau among the great majority of thinkers from his contemporaries onwards, his 'way of seeing' infants as free and open potential, rather than as direly lacking the goods of adulthood, exercised an enormous influence on the cultural imagination from the early nineteenth century onwards.[5]

To set up these contrasting emphases as an either/or for the understanding of infancy would, however, be dangerously simplistic. The insights of both psychology and theology would indicate that the dependency and the dynamism of the human being as infant are in fact profoundly interwoven. At one level, there are obvious truths here. To be a living thing is, as Aristotle expressed it, to have one's principle of movement within oneself – it is to have an inherent dynamic for growth towards the 'end' of maturity for the species to which one belongs. Living things only survive by developing towards their distinctive ends, and therefore to say the infant needs adult others to survive is also to say that it needs them to fulfil its own dynamic potential. Yet it is also true that the human infant 'needs' adult others in a still more radical sense than other animals. The relative weakness of instinctual behaviours in their young and a correspondingly greater need for a protected environment in which they can learn appropriate modes of interaction seems to be a general feature of animals who have moved further along the evolutionary process.[6] The need of the human infant for parents is not simply a need for warmth, food and shelter. In order to function as an adult in a human society, the infant – the one without speech – must become a talking animal, and this too is something it cannot achieve in isolation, but only out of the constant interchange of affectionate relationships. As the child learns speech, so with the words it forms it begins to inhabit a particular human culture with its indescribably complex patterns, and is then on the way to being able to live within a human society, where communication and action are premised on shared language and shared cultural codes, not only on bodily power and gesture.

The human infant is both profoundly dependent and vulnerable, yet also possesses the dynamism to move through stages of development that are without parallel in other species, including the capacity for articulated self-reflection. The changes within the first 18 months of a person's life are arguably the most far-reaching that will ever befall that person; still limited mobility and speech at the end of it should not blind us to that fact, nor the awareness that these changes lead to the construction of a kind of platform for obviously dramatic developmental progress in the next few years. And somehow it would seem that the depth of infant dependence is necessary to 'clear the space' for this dynamism to be nurtured into actuality, while on the other hand the dynamism itself – towards appropriate autonomy, towards the perceived goods of the adult others – drives the infant to move beyond its original dependence towards the eventual interdependence of human maturity.

One important theological question that arises from these initial observations about our understanding of the infant as characterized by a dialectic of dependency and dynamism is in what sense an infant is human. Put in this way, the question may sound rather brutal, but the operative notions of humanity in many theological approaches can at best regard the humanity of infants as somewhat anomalous. Nor is this simply a matter of the emphasis of post-Enlightenment culture, now challenged and indeed castigated by the standard-bearers of post-modernity, on rationality as the differentiating feature of human beings. Augustine himself, having identified the image of God with the mind's capacity for remembering, knowing and loving to be turned within itself and thereby towards God, has to acknowledge in the *De trinitate* that he is simply unable to explain how infants carry this indelible image which defines the human person before God in his theology.[7] Crucially, for Augustine it is language that enables us to be encouraged to turn away from the images of the external world to self-knowledge via self-reflection, while infants by definition are wholly unresponsive to such a strategy. Yet modern thought would suggest that the problems are in fact more profound than Augustine may have imagined; is not the very idea of that 'inwardness' in which Augustine locates the image of God a cultural – and linguistic – construction? Wittgenstein criticized Augustine's account of learning to speak in the *Confessions* on the grounds that Augustine imagines learning language as such to be functionally equivalent to learning a second language, as though we are born with a conceptual grid that maps onto the external world and then simply have to learn the particular terms by which we can communicate that 'mapping' to those around us.[8]

Wittgenstein may well have oversimplified Augustine's position, and certainly in the passage from the *De trinitate* just referred to Augustine shows a healthy sense of the limits of our capacity to understand the infant's mind.[9] Wittgenstein himself, however, is one of the founding fathers of the notion of the constructed self that has now become a virtual commonplace in much academic discourse. Philosophy of language, cultural studies and psychological investigation of infancy would seem to converge on the view that the self that Augustine wanted his readers to 'know' is itself formed by the early (and continuing) history of interpersonal exchange, not given or innate.[10] At one level, the earliest self is fashioned by a complex process of language acquisition and induction into a specific culture; at another, the very sense of continuous identity is – when it emerges – the outcome of a fraught and painful history involving the negotiation of growing separation from the parent-figure and the difficult exploration of power and its limits.[11]

If this broad consensus in the humanities and the human sciences is right about the (culturally) 'formed' self rather than the universal soul, then 'self' is an achievement that comes only at the end of infancy, and exists at best in fragmentary form within it. Can it then make sense to speak of the infant as a human person when there is such a large question mark against the meaningful presence of a 'self'? Chalcedonian Christology would at least discourage us from seeing human nature as something that only comes to exist at a specific point in human development, given that Christ is proclaimed to be 'in two natures' from the moment of conception. It could also be the case, however, that the outline characterization of human infancy as a dialectic of dependency and dynamism gives us a way of affirming the distinctive reality of human personhood prior to language – an important matter not just for the understanding and treatment of infants but also of other human beings who, for whatever reason, find themselves in various degrees unspeaking, without language. Dependency and dynamism find their interface in desire: desire that needs the other, and desire that seeks the horizon of 'more', 'further'. Such desire is both trust and thirst, and is the root of the selves constructed from infancy on and of our conscious relatedness to the divine through these variously constructed selves. From the perspective of Christian theology, all human desire – including the desire of the unspeaking, 'unselved' infant – strives towards the horizon of the God who created us for Godself, beginning and ending in trust in that God and in God's self-gift. Just as the connection of the desire for the good – for beatitude, in Augustine's argument – to the desire for the eternal and thereby for God does not depend on the link being consciously accepted in the case of adults, so it does not depend on the capacity for its being consciously articulated in the case of children. Of them too, Augustine was right to say: 'You have made us for yourself, and our hearts are restless until they find their rest in you.'[12]

Receiving (as) the child in arms: Mark 9.33–37 and 10.13–16

It is not easy to establish unambiguous references to infants in the Gospel narratives, aside from the birth narratives relating to Jesus himself in Matthew and Luke. On two occasions, however, in passages which have clear parallels in Matthew and Luke, Mark in contrast to the other two Synoptic accounts uses the word *enankalisamenos*, 'taking in [his] arms' (Mark 9.36 and 10.16).[13] Mark therefore seems at least to hint at the possibility that the children referred to in these narratives could be – or include – infants, who might most readily require or accept being held by adults in a public context. The stories come close together in Mark, and serve as part of the journey that leads from Peter's declaration that Jesus is the Christ at 8.29 to arrival at the outskirts of Jerusalem in 11.1; a journey during which Jesus seeks to explain repeatedly to the disciples what conformity to God's will means for him, and what following him means for them – without success, as Mark reports it. Indeed, the pairing of these two stories about children is one of the many ways in which the writer of Mark underlines the disciples' stubborn resistance to Jesus' teaching about the way of the cross. They recount symbolic actions by Jesus the interpretation of which is somehow lost on his first followers. What is it, however, that these narratives about Jesus receiving children in his arms might have to say to us today about the understanding of infancy in the light of God's revelation?

The first passage seems the more straightforward. Jesus has been trying to explain to the disciples on their journey that he will be handed over and killed. Not only have they not understood, however, they have actually been having a secret argument among themselves instead about their own comparative status. At this point,

> He sat down, called the twelve, and said to them, 'Whoever wants to be first must be last of all and servant of all.' Then he took a little child and put it among them; and taking it in his arms, he said to them, 'Whoever welcomes one such child in my name welcomes me, and whoever welcomes me welcomes not me but the one who sent me.'
>
> Mark 9.35–37

This passage mirrors the one that recounts the specific request of James and John for a special place in the kingdom at Mark 10.35–45, which is the last exchange between Jesus and the disciples on this journey. The central message is more or less identical, but on this occasion Jesus uses fewer words and instead deploys the 'acted parable' of receiving the child. In this context, it would seem that the child is chosen primarily because it is in human terms 'last of all' in the pecking order of the band of disciples: it has the least power, the least recognition. It will not be consulted when there are decisions to be made; it will not be listened to for advice or wisdom. Yet Jesus suggests that if the disciples want to welcome him and the one who sends him they should welcome such a child 'in his name'. By so doing, it would seem, they enter the upside-down order of things in the kingdom of God. By looking out for the first and the greatest, on the other hand, and giving honour and attention accordingly, they will miss the Jesus whom Peter has rightly identified as God's chosen – God's chosen who will be rejected, mocked and put to death.

The second, more famous story needs to be read in the light of this.[14] Jesus has told the disciples that welcoming and embracing a helpless child in his name is a way to welcome him and welcome the God who sends him, yet when at a halting place people bring children to him for him to touch, the disciples shoo them away. They still live in the logic of a world where only important people get to see really important people, and as Jesus is obviously the most important person around he quite clearly cannot be bothered with those who are 'last of all' – children, and perhaps especially infants. At this point, Mark says, Jesus becomes angry (*eganaktesen*, a word Mark uses sparingly) and tells the disciples,

> 'Let the children come to me; do not stop them; for it is to such as these that the kingdom of God belongs. Truly I tell you, whoever does not receive the kingdom of God as a little child will never enter it.' And he took them up in his arms, laid his hands on them, and blessed them.
>
> Mark 10.14b–16

Jesus has to reprise the message and the acted parable in the face of the disciples' stubborn inability to grasp his meaning, yet this time there is also an important change. In this case, it is not the way that Jesus receives the child that is the parable, but the way that the child receives Jesus' embrace, Jesus' acceptance. What might this mean? It could point to the teaching that it is through relation to Jesus as God's chosen that people enter the kingdom. Just as Jesus welcomes sinners into the kingdom by feasting with them, so he welcomes children – marginalized for different reasons in most visions of God's redemption – simply by embracing them and blessing them. In this way Jesus' symbolic actions with children also recall the prophetic discourse about God taking up and carrying the helpless child Israel (Isaiah 63.9 and Hosea 11.3–4). All we have to do is to receive the reception, accept the acceptance, from the hands of Jesus, to enter the kingdom – to begin the new life that starts the other side of such entry, for there is no suggestion here that such acceptance of itself constitutes the beginning *and end* of the kingdom of God. In this matter too dependence and dynamism remain in dialectical tension.

Still, the problem for Jesus' first followers (and perhaps for Mark's own readers), it would seem, is the tendency to think that it is the acting out of our own dynamic capacities in ways that gain us palpable power and status in the Christian fellowship that gives us right of entry into the kingdom or indeed some kind of priority once established within it. In fact, while simple acceptance of Jesus' acceptance of us brings us into the kingdom, the dynamic of growth within its life – towards conformity to Christ crucified and risen – points towards an ever deepening self-giving embrace of the last and the least, not the achievement of visible degrees of progress and achievement.

Of course, it is easy to sentimentalize the 'simple' acceptance of the child by the parent and of the parent by the child, which the acted parables of Jesus in relation to children clearly recall. Welcoming the infant is in fact in ordinary human experience an intensely demanding task, both practically and emotionally, precisely because of the acuteness of the dialectic of dependence and dynamism at this stage of development. Such welcome requires self-giving – we might say self-emptying – to a far higher degree than perhaps most people are likely to experience at any other point in their lives. The sheer physical dependence of the infant means that those in a position of parental responsibility can never simply stop thinking altogether about the needs of this fellow human person, while the dynamism of human development always already in train means that needs requiring speedy satisfaction are constantly shifting and, most of all while language is unknown, only communicated in the most rudimentary ways – although when unmet, the crying that declares their frustration is specifically designed to be beyond our adult capacity to tolerate. As we who are adult have achieved the maturity of interdependence only after a painful struggle to move beyond original dependence, it should not be surprising that the reprise of physical dependence in becoming parents of infants ourselves should be so often unsettling as well as exhilarating; indeed, feelings of frustration, resentment and aggression are likely to be compounded with guilt that I 'ought' to be feeling nothing but loving affection for this helpless creature. This may be one dimension of the difficulties experienced by many individuals and couples in the early years of child-rearing, indicated for instance in the cluster of statistical instances of separation around precisely this point.

In order to enable the intrinsic dynamism of the human person to move forward, the parent figure needs to sacrifice a large measure of her own autonomy. In order to help the baby to learn mobility, the parent needs to spend long hours restricted to a few rudimentary motions and movements in holding and accompanying it. In order to bring the child to the point of being able to eat, drink, urinate and defecate without constant assistance, the parent must spend many hours dealing with sick and slobber, piss and shit. In order to enable the infant to speak, the adult has to re-learn how to communicate solely through touch, tone of voice and gesture, how to inhabit the space of repetitive play where the child enjoys being endlessly surprised by exactly the same thing, how to greet with patient affirmation the first obscure stammerings of verbal communication without frustration on one side becoming ignited by frustration on the other. Surely there are few more demanding tasks in human life than welcoming the new-born child into the home and nurturing it towards selfhood, enduring the demands of dependence and fostering each glimmering of the dynamic potential that leads towards the capacity to give and receive love in the conscious freedom of human maturity.

In these ordinary – yet extraordinary – human experiences as in Mark's Gospel, there is a close relationship between receiving the child and receiving as a child, becoming (like) a child. It has already been suggested that rearing an infant requires from parents a willingness to tolerate a partial loss of independence that may well recall the dependence of childhood and also to practise a certain empathy with the horizons of the infant's pre-linguistic world, so restricted at one level and yet at another so overwhelmingly rich with wonder and terror, trust and rage, pleasure and pain. Moreover, perhaps it is true that, in order to sustain the unconditional positive regard with which they first greeted the new-born child, parents are likely to need to draw – unconsciously for the most part – on their own experiences of parental love, love that did not crumple at disappointments, defiance or outraged aggression. For all the bonding that takes place between parents and children, it is no easy thing to keep caring for one from whom one cannot expect any reciprocity, any responsiveness to one's own changing needs and moods. Their deepest memories of acceptance from a human other are part of what enables the parents to sustain the offering of acceptance to this new human other through all the frustrations that must accompany the welcoming of the littlest and least of the human race. It is the image of one giving love and giving self without limit that appears at the horizon here; a gesture towards the divine? To receive the infant we have to renew, it would seem, in a range of intersecting ways, the roots of our own selves in now distant infancy.

The shadow of sin

At this point, we might usefully confront what has been an intensely disputed question in the history of western Christian theology: are infants born sinful? The positions sketched out in this chapter so far would perhaps suggest a negative answer to this question. Children are born into a world which 'lies under the power of the evil one' (1 John 5.19b), and are therefore exposed from and even before birth to the distortions and disfigurements wrought by evil's reality. As they learn by imitation and participation, so they cannot help but be drawn into the life-undoing dynamics of fallen human existence. Yet, to call a person sinful is to say more than this; it is to say that they contribute in their freedom to the sin of the world, that they have sometimes chosen evil over the good, and that they stand in need of forgiveness. Sinfulness in this sense requires the exercise of conscious intentionality, and we have already suggested there are good grounds for regarding the foundations of such conscious intentionality, a distinguishing feature of human selves, as an outcome of the period of infancy, and not as subsisting throughout it. I noted earlier Wittgenstein's criticism of Augustine for attributing a wholly implausible level of conceptual organization to the pre-linguistic child; Augustine's analysis of the sinful tendency of infants, repeated and rendered more extreme by later voices in the western tradition, relies precisely on this same assumption which it has been suggested is no longer tenable.[15] To abandon it, however, is not necessarily to keep company with Rousseau and argue for the 'original goodness' of human beings. Everything in creation, by virtue of being a creature, shares in the transcending goodness of the creator; and everything in creation is nonetheless radically open to the mystery of evil. The myth of Genesis 2—3, read without the controlling lenses of the dominant exegetical tradition in western Christianity, presents evil as a reality that both arises from within the freedom of the human person yet is also (in the figure of the snake) encountered by human beings as always already present outside themselves in the world that God made good.[16] Adam, the 'earth creature', first names what is around him, and is then divided so that male and female enter the world; only then does the question of obedience or disobedience arise. Analogously, after entering into the realms of language (and therefore culture), consciously differentiated identity (beyond the 'oceanic fusion' of our earliest days and months) and thence constructed selfhood, we face the first glimmerings of the reality of moral choice, the freedom for good and the freedom for evil – and somehow, like Adam and Eve, we slip towards evil even with our very first hesitating steps in exercising this freedom.

The idea of a certain homology between the narrative of the first chapters of Genesis and the narrative of individual human development is an old one; it was Irenaeus of Lyons in the later second century who argued forcefully (against Gnostic speculation) that Adam was created as a child needing time to grow towards divine perfection, although the explicit denial of that position later became axiomatic in the dominant doctrinal traditions of East and West alike.[17] Such a homology remains, however, suggestive and in itself indicates a way of escaping the sterile debate in the western Christian tradition about whether young children are morally good or morally evil. Infants live the dialectic of dependence and dynamism, which drives them forward – in most cases – towards the formation of a self with some moral freedom, at which point they discover the capacity for good and evil and, in a world fractured by sin, find their choices for the good are inextricable from overt and covert collusion with the bad.

For Irenaeus, the salvation of the world comes about when God in Christ 'recapitulates' the original narrative of the fall in which the dynamic potential of the 'child' Adam for growth into the image and likeness of God and thereby participation in the divine life was blocked and broken, so that the route towards the fulfilment of that potential may be repaired and opened anew for all humanity. Does the participation of human adults in this redemption require an analogous return to their own origins in sheer desire, prior to the construction of selfhood and the shadowed history of our subsequent moral failures? Here we are close to the theological language of being born again/from above that appears most prominently in John 3, which puns repeatedly on the dual meaning of *anothen*. Nicodemus' revulsion at Jesus' suggestion recalls the contempt for the weakness and dependency of earliest childhood that was noted in relation to the quotation from Joseph Kimhi. Some scholars have indeed suggested that John's Gospel is at this point providing a commentary on the *logion* that appears at Mark 10.15, as cited above.[18] In John 3 as in Mark 9 and 10, those who would be followers of Jesus flinch away from the implication of the erasure of status and dignity that becoming a new-born child immediately carries for them. Yet in John 3 it is perhaps clearer that this resistance is also about our unwillingness to contemplate the possibility of as it were starting again, becoming beginners again – and this does seem to be part of what John's Jesus means to convey.

Being born again is an expression that cannot be held in isolation from the Pauline language of death and resurrection in union with Christ – language that is explicitly linked to the rite of baptism in Romans 6.1–11, whereas the allusions to baptism in John 3 remain more enigmatic. Indeed, the convergence of the discourses of death/resurrection and of new birth in the liturgy of Christian baptism underlines the need for the theologian to hold these two in creative tension. Both seek to express the radical otherness of the gift that comes through faith in Christ, while acknowledging that it is still *us* to whom the gift is given – and that *us* must include our past, our history, our childhood, however profoundly transfigured by redemption. To ask the question of whether birth from above by water and the Spirit in John 3 relates at any level to a return to the sources of our human personhood in the experiences of infancy is perhaps to engage in a certain level of anachronism, in that this is not a question that can have any kind of answer in terms of historical exegesis, but this does not necessarily mean it should simply be closed down. After all, birth again/from above cannot mean the erasure of all our history prior to that point, any more than the resurrection of the body can do away with *this* body; somehow, it has to gather up the fragments of our life prior to that point and set them into a new pattern, a new context. The gift that was there in infancy, for the dynamic of human desire to unfold in conformity to the image and likeness of God in Christ – can it be retrieved or, to use Irenaeus' term again, recapitulated? At the very least, we cannot leave our origins as human persons behind as we enter the kingdom of God; Jesus' saying about receiving it as a child might suggest that acceptance of our own infancy – dialectic of dependence and dynamism, trust and thirst – as an enduring dimension of our continuing selves might be one part of opening our eyes to the gospel of self-giving love and the inversion of cherished perspectives that it requires.[19]

So far, questions of gender have been generally bracketed in this chapter, but it is clear that further development would have to explore this area carefully. To what extent is the conversion to which Jesus seems to be calling his disciples by his symbolic actions of receiving children in Mark's Gospel one that hinges on the cultural construction of gender roles and thereby remains itself shadowed with the sinfulness of patriarchy? A man 'taking up' a child in his arms means something different – above all in rigidly patriarchal cultures – from the same gesture by a woman. There is certainly some evidence that in the Roman world, for instance, a new born child would be presented to the *paterfamilias* for his decision: if he took it up into his arms, it was accepted as a new member of the household, and if not, it might be abandoned and exposed.[20] Men have the power to signify acceptance into a community or society by receiving a child with an embrace; Jesus may be using a symbol embedded in patriarchal culture for a liberating end, the acceptance of the least in the kingdom of God, but there is no simple way to extricate any symbol from the cultural context within which it functions. Perhaps still more importantly, the fear of loss of power/autonomy through receiving (as) an infant is perhaps most characteristically a male concern in patriarchal contexts – that 'position' carefully gained through competitive interaction in public space will be lost through association with those who are wholly incapable of gaining any purchase within that frame. We are back with the immediate juxtaposition of contempt for women with contempt for infants in the initial quotation from Joseph Kimhi. For all Augustine's perhaps unique awareness of and interest in the world of infancy among pre-modern Christian writers, it is telling that he only names and describes his one child, Adeodatus, in the *Confessions* when he reaches the age of being able to discuss philosophy and theology with his father; prior to such capacity, it would seem, Augustine can see no value in interacting with him, or at the very least in recounting such interaction.[21] If Jesus had wanted to act a parable of the kingdom for the sake of his female followers, would he have chosen the embrace of a little child? Would he have needed to?

Perhaps not. In my own, limited experience of hearing stories about people's vocations, it is interesting that men as well as women sometimes describe the advent of parenthood, the welcoming of a baby, as bringing with it a profound renewal of spiritual awareness. Yet it may be more common for such experiences to have particular power in the case of mothers.[22] One of the most striking examples of a person being 'born again of water and the spirit' while passing through the human experience of receiving and nurturing the new life of an infant is that of Dorothy Day, whose 'Christmas Story' about the birth of her daughter was written in 1928 as she was emerging from atheism to faith and, with its theological 'frame' only indicated in the title, widely reprinted in the radical press at the time.[23] In *The Long Loneliness*, an autobiographical text written much later, Day makes clear that, for her, receiving the gift of a child, first in her womb and then into her hands and her home, was the catalyst for seeking the kingdom of God, and gave her the strength to break with the past – most immediately with her much-loved partner, who made it clear he would leave her if she sought baptism for her child let alone for herself. Day therefore began a fresh stage in her life simultaneously as a single mother and as a Roman Catholic convert.[24] In her case, it was the encounter with this new human life that enabled her, as Rosenzweig puts it, to 'begin anew' through accompanying her infant daughter to the font in baptism. Day's case would also confirm Rosenzweig's instinct, as an outsider, that infant baptism is not simply compatible with Christian doctrine but expresses in a concrete way the profound affinities between the journey of discipleship to which the gospel summons us and the journey towards selfhood that we all must make in our earliest days. The baptism of infants proclaims that the way of Christ draws together the whole of our being, the whole of our time into God's gracious purpose, including the time before we knew time, the person that loved and longed before the self was formed that freely knows and chooses. It also proclaims that in order to receive God's gift in Christ, even the most mature among us must be born again, begin again, become as a little child – so that our deepest desire and most marvellous potential, to grow to maturity in Christ and share in the divine life, might find fulfilment.

Seeing salvation in the child in arms: Luke 2.25–35

In the previous section, I reviewed two passages from Mark's Gospel where Jesus takes children – perhaps infants – into his arms as symbolic actions of the kingdom. In Luke's Gospel, Jesus as an infant himself receives the embrace of the aged prophet Simeon:

> Simeon took him in his arms and praised God, saying, 'Master, now you are dismissing your servant in peace, according to your word; for my eyes have seen your salvation, which you have prepared in the presence of all peoples, a light for revelation to the Gentiles and for glory to your people Israel.'
>
> Luke 2.28–32

Simeon is a prophet who discerns in the present the horizon of God's coming future. Having praised God for the blessing that is coming for Israel and the nations through the child he cradles, he turns to Mary and tells her that the path towards this blessing will not be a straightforward one – that her child will be 'a sign that will be opposed . . . and a sword will pierce your own soul too' (Luke 2.34–35). Yet while Simeon perceives what is coming, he also sees the glory that will be revealed here and now on the face of the child he holds: 'my eyes have seen your salvation.' This infant, unable to speak, unable even to crawl, is God's salvation, God's Word become flesh.

A Christian theologian is unlikely to agree entirely with Franz Rosenzweig that 'for Christianity the beginning replaces redemption, the beaten path replaces consummated life'. Yet there is a sense that the gospel Christianity exists to proclaim concerns the beginning of redemption, and it is this that the Church constantly strives to reiterate, to keep beginning at the (right) beginning, rather than holding some special and fixed knowledge about the end of all things. There is as yet no finality, nor will there be in human history, but there is still a 'beaten path', and Christian faith is finding a way to start walking along it. In the western daily office, Simeon's song is the canticle before sleep at Compline. Just as he could face his own end because he had glimpsed God's beginning, so we can enter the death-like darkness of sleep because we have seen salvation, not achieved, but unfolding, not moving smoothly forward in triumphal procession, but taking the hard and fractured path through human limitation and sinfulness. And it is the infant Jesus who remains in the liturgy the sign of this. As we sing the song of Simeon, we take the child into our own arms, our own embrace. Trusting ourselves to God at the end of the day, recalling the night of the cross, rehearsing for our own death, we also accept anew God's gift to us, the fragile life of the infant Jesus, the sign of divine and eternal life; '. . . what was from the beginning, what we have heard, what we have seen with our eyes, what we have looked at and touched with our hands . . .' (1 John 1.1).

Simeon turns to Mary and addresses her. The infant is radically dependent; the mother cannot be far away. In infancy, the weakness of the one who will be handed over to the power of others is anticipated without violence, in the ordinary order of human love. Yet still the Christian imagination may be haunted by the failures of thought that the Council of Chalcedon sought to teach us to lay to one side. In so much traditional iconography, the infant Jesus sits peaceful, composed, self-contained, even upright. It remains somehow faintly shocking to see an image such as the statue by Willi Soukop in the Pilgrim Chapel at St Mary's Abbey, West Malling, where Mary cradles Jesus on her ample lap and gently supports his lolling head. What it shocks, however, is the residue of heresy within orthodoxy, the resistance to the truth of the full humanity of the incarnate Lord. We know that an infant is not a miniature adult; we know that infants are not self-contained and self-controlled, that their needs are frequently overwhelming for themselves and for those who care for them, that in incomprehension of frustration they can only cry until satisfaction or sleep relieves them. Yet still thousands sing the line from the nineteenth-century carol, 'But little Lord Jesus no crying he makes', without flinching at its unwitting docetism. The corollary of the view that a sinless Jesus would not have cried to make his needs known might well be that sinful infants that do insist on crying should be beaten until they learn to cry less, a practice defended by John Wesley's mother, who wrote that 'Crying is a fault that should not be tolerated in children . . .'[25]

If we are truly to affirm the reality of Jesus' humanity, then we must face some hard questions about what it would mean for a real human child to grow up without sin – following the position outlined earlier on in this chapter, what it would mean for a person to form a self which is not immediately enmeshed in sinful choices as it emerges into stable, language-informed consciousness. Dependency would suggest that his mother must indeed have had some part in making this possible, and that therefore there is a need for careful reflection on the traditional teaching about Mary's unique relationship to human sinfulness, without necessarily simply affirming the modern Roman Catholic dogma of the immaculate conception.[26] It would also mean that we have to ask what the dialectic of dependency and desire means for a human person whose *hypostasis* – in the terms of traditional doctrine – is the eternal Son of God: for human dependency and incompletion to be always open to utter trust in the self-giving Father, even in the fears and frustrations that are part and parcel of human infancy, and for the dynamism of human development to be always unfolding in desire for the divine source. Finally, we must also ponder the question that lies within Joseph Kimhi's painful polemic: do we dare to affirm that Jesus, truly human, was exposed to the changes and chances of this life, as with any human being most intensely in his early years? Is it possible that Jesus could have died in infancy from disease, or some accident, or was he the object of some kind of special protection – and in that case again somehow exempt from the full reality of the human condition? What does the doctrine of providence mean in the face of the tragic character of our existence, if it is something other than the claim that some people are specially shielded from its effects, while billions of others are not?

At the beginning of his book on Dante, Auerbach wrote, 'In entering into the consciousness of the European peoples, the story of Christ fundamentally changed their conceptions of man's fate and how to describe it. The change occurred very slowly, far more slowly than the spread of Christian dogma.'[27] For Auerbach, Dante's work represented the culmination of that process, but it is perhaps better to regard it as still going on, indeed continuing indefinitely. It is possible that we may have in our time the opportunity to engage in new depth with the full implications of an orthodox, Chalcedonian faith in the incarnation: one that looks the human infant Jesus full in the face, and sees there salvation, in the flesh, not in some projection of our ideas and imagination, some proto-adult in full control of all its needs and desires. As we seek to sustain that gaze more truthfully and reverently, listening to the stories of fathers and mothers and attending to the partial insights of academic psychology as well as inhabiting the tradition of scriptural orthodoxy, we may find fresh contributions to what Christian theology might say about all infants in the light of this one infant, chosen of God, Word become flesh.

Notes

1 Joseph Kimhi, *The Book of the Covenant*, trans. Frank Talmage, Toronto, Pontifical Institute for Mediaeval Studies, 1972, pp. 36–7.

2 Franz Rosenzweig, *The Star of Redemption*, trans. William W. Hallo, Notre Dame / London, University of Notre Dame, 1985, p. 374.

3 Second Vatican Council, 'Pastoral Constitution on the Church in the Modern World', section 22, in Walter M. Abbott and Joseph Gallagher (eds),

Documents of Vatican II, London, Geoffrey Chapman, 1966, p. 220; Thomas Merton, *Contemplative Prayer*, London, Darton, Longman & Todd, 1969, p. 103.

4 Cf. Charles Taylor, *Sources of the Self: The Making of The Modern Identity*, Cambridge, Harvard, 1989.

5 Dawn DeVries summarizes some of the background here in her article '"Be Converted and Become as Little Children": Friedrich Schleiermacher on the Religious Significance of Childhood', in Marcia J. Bunge (ed.), *The Child in Christian Thought*, Grand Rapids / Cambridge, Eerdmans, 2001, pp. 331–5.

6 Cf. Clifford Geertz, 'The Growth of Culture and the Evolution of Mind', in *The Interpretation of Cultures: Selected Essays*, New York: Basic Books, 1973, pp. 55–83.

7 Augustine, *De trinitate* XIV.5.7–8.

8 Ludwig Wittgenstein, *Philosophical Investigations*, trans. G. E. M. Anscombe, Oxford, Blackwell, 1968, I.1–32, pp. 2–16; cf. Augustine, *Confessions* I.VIII, quoted by Wittgenstein at I.1.

9 'What, then, is to be said of the mind of an infant, which is still so small, and buried in such profound ignorance of things, that the mind of a man which knows anything shrinks from the darkness of it?', Augustine asks at the beginning of *De trinitate* XIV.5 (NPNF III: 186). At the end of the section, he offers the following as a justification for not exploring the question further: 'But let us pass by the infantine age, since we cannot question it as to what goes on within itself, while we have ourselves pretty well forgotten it.'

10 Cf. Alistair I. McFadyen, *The Call to Personhood: A Christian Theory of the Individual in Social Relationships*, Cambridge, Cambridge University Press, 1990, especially chapter 3, 'The Social Formation of Persons'.

11 For a summary of some of the psychological literature on the 'formation of the self', see Franco Imoda, *Human Development: Psychology and Mystery*, trans. Eugene Dryer, Leuven, Peeters, 1998, pp. 293–303.

12 Augustine, *Confessions* I.1. Henri de Lubac defended humanity's natural desire for the supernatural as an intrinsic and determinative feature of pre-modern Christian anthropology; for a recent discussion of his significance, see John Milbank, *The Suspended Middle: Henri de Lubac and The Debate concerning The Supernatural*, London, SCM Press, 2005.

13 The rather different arrangement of the parallel material relating to these two passages in the Synoptic Gospels raises some interesting exegetical questions about Mark's reasons for shaping it in the particular way he does; cf. Morna D. Hooker, *The Gospel according to Mark*, Black's New Testament Commentaries, London, A&C Black, 1991, pp. 226–8.

14 As emphasized by John T. Carroll, 'Children in the Bible', *Interpretation* 55:2 (2001), pp. 121–34; see in particular pp. 128–9.

15 Augustine, *Confessions* I.VII; cf. the careful discussion of the sinfulness of infants in subsequent Calvinist theology in Catherine A. Brekus, 'Children of Wrath, Children of Grace: Jonathan Edwards an the Puritan Culture of Child Rearing' in Bunge (ed.), *Child in Christian Thought*, pp. 300–28.

16 Paul Ricoeur, *The Symbolism of Evil*, trans. Emerson Buchanan, Boston, Beacon, 1969, pp. 257–8.

17 See for example Irenaeus, *Against Heresies* IV.38.

18 E.g. Barnabas Lindars, *The Gospel of John*, New Century Bible, London, Oliphants, 1972, p. 150; compare C. E. B. Cranfield, *The Gospel according to Saint Mark*, Cambridge, Cambridge University Press, 1959, p. 324.

19 Karl Rahner makes a powerful case for our lived childhood and its deepening appropriation as integral to our growth towards God in 'Ideas for a Theology of Childhood', *Theological Investigations* VIII, trans. David Bourke, London, Darton, Longman & Todd, 1971, pp. 33–50.

20 The complex issues regarding the practice of exposing babies in the ancient world are helpfully reviewed in Konstantinos Kapparis, *Abortion in the Ancient World*, London, Duckworth, 2002, pp. 154–62.

21 Augustine, *Confessions* IX.VI (compare also the mention of Adeodatus at the description of Monica's funeral rites, IX.XII); otherwise, there is just a fleeting reference to the son whom his (nameless) concubine leaves with him when she is sent back to Africa (VI.XV).

22 Cf. the brief survey of theological literature relating to the experience of motherhood in Bonnie J Miller-McLemore, '"Let the Children Come" Revisited: Contemporary Feminist Theologians on Children', in Bunge (ed.), *The Child in Christian Thought*, pp. 452–6.

23 Dorothy Day, 'Having a Baby – A Christmas Story,' reprinted in *The Catholic Worker*, December 1977, 8, 7; text available via Dorothy Day Library on the Web: at <http://www.catholicworker.org/dorothyday/>.

24 Dorothy Day, *The Long Loneliness*, New York, HarperSanFrancisco, 1997, pp. 132–51.

25 Quoted by Richard P. Heitzenrater, 'John Wesley and Children', in Bunge (ed.), *Child in Christian Thought*, p. 284.

26 For a recent example of ecumenical exploration of this teaching, see the report of the Anglican-Roman Catholic International Commission (ARCIC), *Mary: Grace and Hope in Christ*, New York, Continuum, 2005.

27 Erich Auerbach, *Dante: Poet of the Secular World*, trans. R. Mannheim, Chicago, University of Chicago Press, 1961, p.13.

Give ear, O my people, to my teaching; incline your ears to the words of my mouth. I will open my mouth in a parable; I will utter dark sayings from of old, things that we have heard and known, that our ancestors have told us. We will not hide them from their children; we will tell to the coming generation the glorious deeds of the Lord, and his might, and the wonders that he has done. He established a decree in Jacob, and appointed a law in Israel, which he commanded our ancestors to teach to their children; that the next generation might know them, the children yet unborn, and rise up and tell them to their children, so that they should set their hope in God, and not forget the works of God, but keep his commandments; and that they should not be like their ancestors, a stubborn and rebellious generation, a generation whose heart was not steadfast, whose spirit was not faithful to God.

Psalm 78.1–8

4. Moulding and Shaping: Education

DAVID DEEKS AND ANGELA SHIER-JONES

Public debates about the development of children have tended to oscillate between two extremes. On the one hand children are pictured as self-evolving entities, whose patterns of growth and their outcomes (in terms of health, abilities and personality) are determined by their genes. On the other hand, boys and girls are pictured as a thoroughly malleable entity, shaped and directed by the influences of key adults and peers who interact with the child, and by any number of ill-defined environmental influences – cultural, social, economic, religious and climatic, to mention but a few. In the media and in the scholarly world, there are eloquent advocates of both extremes. Neither exposition rings true. Current research has shown conclusively that all human development occurs through a process of dynamic relations involving variables from biological through sociocultural and historical levels of organization. It is now fully recognized that genes, individual behaviour, parental rearing practices, and social policies, for instance, contribute integratively to human behaviour and development. No one set of influences 'can be factually construed as an exclusive, or even prime, impetus to the full development of any organisms.'[1]

The frustrating thing for parents and social planners, not to mention philosophers who strive for precision and tidiness in their accounts of the way things go, is that it seems impossible – both in the case of any individual child and in the case of children in general – to know where the balance is between genetic determinism and environmental influence.

It is, in principle, important to encourage continuing research on genes and their role in the early years of human life, in order to maximize the opportunities for the health and well-being of children.

Wherever geneticists and doctors get to on that issue, it remains clear that huge responsibilities reside with those individuals and organizations that immediately play a part in nurturing – or damaging – a child during the child's development. Who is in mind here? The primary carers of each child, of course, typically the mother, another parent or step-parent, along with members of wider family networks, across the generations. The presumption is that it is the parents and other close companions of a child who are the primary determiners, not only of what a child learns, but of what it fails to learn. In practice, however, 'Sure Start'[2] projects, pre-schools and schools also have a large influence, not least through the adults and the peers that the child encounters in such organizations. Furthermore, child-centred cultural influences bring to bear on child development the taken-for-granted fashions and emphases of each decade in each geographical context. In Britain in the early twenty-first century these include television, the internet, mobile phones and iPods, as well as the fund of traditional games and explorations that have entertained and challenged children for generations past.

Beyond this, generalizations are impossible, as each child's experience is affected by the values and interests of those immediately responsible for the child. Some families, for example, have the resources and interest to stimulate the child in innumerable ways through visits and encouragement to participate in relevant groups and activities (which in a few cases may include Christian churches); other families have neither the resources nor the interest. Immediately, child development becomes a worked example of injustice and inequality.

Even at the point of primary care, the quality of influence on a child is infinitely various. Doubtless education of parents can make a difference to the quality of parental influence. According to Bronfenbrenner, any appreciable, enduring improvement in the child's development can be effected only through an appreciable, enduring change in the behaviour of the persons intimately associated with the child on a day-to-day basis.[3] It would be a general good if parents themselves, as well as government, were to give much greater priority, in the use of time and of public resources, to the improvement of parenting skills. But all training and educative processes have their limits. So it will always remain the case that some parents relax into their role with skill and confidence; others are perpetually exhausted or anxious. Some parents project onto their child their own need to control, while others revel in nourishing the independence and 'otherness' of their child. Some parents unload on to their child their pent-up frustration and rage; others are models of gentleness and patience. Some parents become tense and combative when a child's wilfulness is expressed; others go with the flow of a child's self-expression, confident that negotiation and mutual accommodation will achieve interdependent co-operation. Thankfully, however, recent behavioural genetic studies suggest that differences among parents in their attitudes and behaviours regarding school achievement, reading, leisure-time activities, and so on appear to have no lasting effects on the intelligence of children.[4] In fact, causality between parenting and child behaviour is virtually impossible to determine from studies of parent-to-child effects:

> Because almost all studies of parents and children are correlational in design, it is not possible to establish whether parents' behaviours are affecting the child, the child's behaviours are affecting the parents, the child's behaviour is a product of the parent-child relationship, or the child's behaviour is attributable to familial and extrafamilial factors that are separate from parenting.[5]

Given the difficulty in obtaining objective results concerning the complex set of processes around child development, it might be thought that a vital contribution to the 'success' of raising well-balanced children would be a shared vision of how an 'ideal' of parenthood and child nurture might look. It might sound something like this – if abstractions are allowed: regardless of whether or not it can be objectively proved, a child's life chances are surely maximized when each of the main sources of influence on a child's development is functioning efficiently and effectively, according to their purpose; and all the different influences (parents, family and peers, community groups and organizations, schools, wider cultural and social values mediated through contemporary affordable media and access to participative experience in diverse settings) work together collaboratively and with an eye on fairness of provision for all children. Surely then a child would mature into adolescence and early adulthood with a strong sense of identity and inner security, with a life shaped consciously by adherence to widely shared values, with the skills and learning to master their environment, with a strong incentive to explore and discover the infinite riches of the world around them and with a commitment to share in public debate and collective action for the common good.

Some such vision lies somewhere in the background of public policies, which seek to promote high-quality education and which include either an implicit or explicit induction into responsible citizenship. The devotion of democracy to education is writ large in party manifestos. Governments want the practice of education to reduce criminality, to increase social cohesion in amazingly diverse societies. 'The superficial explanation for this is that a government resting upon popular suffrage cannot be successful unless those who elect and who obey their governors are educated.'[6] Throughout the western world, therefore, initiatives have been set up to address this issue. Following social unrest in three main cities in the UK in 2001, for example, a 'Community Cohesion Review Team' was set up.[7] The findings of their investigations, not surprisingly, highlighted the role of schools as essential in breaking down barriers between young people and in helping to create cohesive communities. A similar example could have been taken from any western democracy as most have broadly utilized the same model for the relationship between education and the state. Governments in developed and wealthy nations increasingly insist on central control of education. The growth of this control has been charted by Dewey from its early Platonic beginnings to the current need of the state to furnish not only the instrumentalities of public education but also its goal:

> When the school system, from the elementary grades through the university faculties, supplied the patriotic citizen and soldier and the future state official and administrator and furnished the means for military, industrial, and political defence and expansion, it became impossible not to recognize the educational aim of social efficiency.[8]

Through the professionalization of the teaching profession according to criteria and codes of practice endorsed by governments, by the fierce regulation of a standardized curriculum in schools and by hands-on management of schools as institutions, governments attempt to produce the outcomes that their particular vision promises, be it social efficiency or community cohesion.[9] In addition, governments extend their control and influence throughout the voluntary and charitable sectors of society – wherever adults work with boys and girls (including churches, of course) in an attempt to safeguard the development of children and protect children from abuse. The pressure for governments to set and police the boundaries of child development now extends much more overtly even into the domestic setting. The majority of western democracies have engaged in some form of debate over whether or not smacking should be outlawed; and have at least raised the question of whether in our open and democratic society, Muslim women should completely cover their faces in conversations with non-Muslims. Within a generation, the mood in these areas of public policy and the administration of them with the back-up of legal sanctions has changed out of all recognition. Rather than explicitly intervening in family life, it is often the case that the state now polices the family through the subtle and pervasive intrusion of experts into familial relationships and structures, thus achieving government *through* families as opposed to the government of families. Governments regulate for a norm of familial 'health' which is achievable only with the assistance of semi-official professionals, such as doctors, lawyers, social workers, home visitors, who are thereby insinuated into family life. By this means, the family today, and therefore the child within it, is more thoroughly governed, albeit in less public fashion, than any of its historical predecessors.[10]

The educational vision and ideal

Faith has played its own part in facilitating, and even encouraging all this. Judaism, of course, was very aware of the link between faith and formation, education and civic responsibility and had developed not only places of learning but the laws and guidelines necessary to oversee them since biblical times. The words of the Shema and the later repeated injunction in Deuteronomy to the people of Israel provided more than sufficient theological basis for the relationship:

> You shall put these words of mine in your heart and soul, and you shall bind them as a sign on your hand, and fix them as an emblem on your forehead. Teach them to your children, talking about them when you are at home and when you are away, when you lie down and when you rise. Write them on the doorposts of your house and on your gates, so that your days and the days of your children may

> be multiplied in the land that the Lord swore to your ancestors to give them, as long as the heavens are above the earth.
>
> Deuteronomy 11.18–21

In his commentary, Norman Lamm points out that by teaching the words of Torah diligently to children, Judaism engenders a confidence in the belief that it will remain devoted to making intellectual, cultural, and spiritual contributions to all humankind.[11]

Christianity, in its turn, absorbed much of this culture of learning from Judaism. The history of the Church records that wherever missionaries travelled to plant churches, they almost always also planted schools, often with the same, albeit less evident, aim as that of the governments today. For example, Ignatius of Loyola, the founder of the Society of Jesus, considered education to be a means of promoting the salvation and perfection of the students. It was his hope that as a consequence of their education, 'they might vigorously and intelligently leaven their social environment with the doctrine and spirit of the Kingdom of Christ'.[12] According to Ganss, Ignatius believed that the lives of citizens in any state would be happy and worthwhile only in direct proportion to the extent to which they were imbued with the Christian spirit. Moreover, since this was dependent on solid and strong intellectual formation, 'Ignatius appropriated the best elements he could find in the educational systems of his day, Catholicized them, and organized them into an instrument truly fit to achieve his purposes in his era.'[13] Christian missionaries and Church-sponsored schools in many parts of the world therefore, actively sought to identify future community and national leaders who were then given unparalleled opportunities for secondary education and for higher education at the best universities in the world.

Throughout Europe and the West, particularly during the last two centuries, the thirst for education was palpable: primary day schools were built in their hundreds; uneducated women and men learned the skills to become autodidacts and then to take up leadership in church and community; and congregations expressed their pride when children in their midst grew out of disadvantaged backgrounds to take their place in universities and teacher training colleges.

How then, in the light of this, should the Church assess the growing imposition of a secular vision of education by the state? Surely, it must admire many of its achievements. Those who belong to minority (as distinct from established) Christian traditions have, after all, tended to benefit disproportionately from state education policies. But even they must also insist that the vision is flawed and that the outcomes, in general, are never likely to reach the fantastical heights aspired to.

Why the doubts? First, we have to look realistically at what we have traditionally called 'human nature' and in particular the nature of children. It is much more ambiguous and stubbornly complicated than current educational doctrine and philosophy dares to admit. Vision is indeed crucial to social progress. But vision has always to mesh with harsh reality. The Church – I trust – dares to look at social engineering projects and in particular at the inner realities of the human heart as honestly as possible. It will insist that, with the best will in the world (which isn't up to all that much), human beings often emerge from childhood deeply tarnished as well as capable of glorious achievement. And these schizoid realities play forward from one generation to another as is accurately narrated in the stories of the families of the Hebrew Bible. How else can the irreverence of Eli's Sons or David's capricious behaviour be accounted for?

So every child, without exception, bears the brunt of some negative influences – influences that are full of contradiction and dislocation. Every child is always the 'victim', to some degree, of the immaturity in the people around them, of prejudice, obsession and addictions, of the resentments arising from the way things have gone in life and from unfulfilled potential, of unhappiness, conflicts, griefs and losses – and therefore of some measure of violence and abuse. Scripture provides us with no shortage of narratives to draw on: Jephthah's daughter, for example, was required to sacrifice her life on account of her father's reckless vow (Judges 11.20–30), and Ishmael was displaced from Abraham's family group because of the jealousy and fear of Sarah (Genesis 21.9–20).

Fortunately, there are also positive influences to celebrate in the life-stories of many children. Through parental love and, say, a school which has embodied humane values and spiritual insights, a child grows up expressing, in the midst of those negative traits, trust, self-confidence, a relaxed attitude to people from different backgrounds and a concern for truth and justice. Perhaps the best biblical illustration of this is Samuel, loved by his mother Hannah, raised in the temple by Eli and who eventually become the great prophet and leader of the people of Israel.

In recent generations, we have become sensitized to the special challenges in the nurture of young children who start out in life carrying some public sign which attracts widespread prejudice or fear. They may become the objects of disrespect and discrimination owing to skin colour or ethnic origin, or to a manifest impairment or disability, or (in more recent consciousness) to the religious commitment and observance of their parents. Vicious rejection and actions that humiliate can so easily create a massive imbalance in what is, in 'normal' childhood, always a troublesome mixture of harmful insecurities or bitter grudges on the one hand and mature moral and spiritual growth on the other. Is it so surprising that relatively young children are responsible for such a large proportion of petty crime and that children from difficult family or community backgrounds are the recipients of so many Anti-Social Behaviour Orders?

The classical response to this is to produce 'appropriate guidelines' such as those found in the books of Ecclesiastes and Proverbs – including, of course, the now controversial advice, 'Do not withhold discipline from your children; if you beat them with a rod, they will not die. If you beat them with the rod, you will save their lives from Sheol' (Proverbs 23.13–14). Such Scriptures, however, are seldom considered appropriate in the contemporary context. Thus the guidelines produced in the United Kingdom to facilitate better education for pupils from minority ethnic backgrounds in predominantly white schools is guided by three philosophical principles; equality, diversity, belonging and cohesion:

Equality

All pupils are of equal value and should have equal opportunities to learn and to be successful. Schools should be proactive in removing barriers to learning and success. The philosophical principle of equality is enshrined in national legislation, particularly the Race Relations Act 1976 and the Race Relations Amendment Act 2000.

Diversity

Since all pupils are of equal value they should be treated equally. But this does not necessarily mean that they should all be treated in precisely the same ways. On the contrary, significant differences of culture, outlook, narrative and experience should be recognized and respected. For example, and particularly obviously, it is unjust to treat pupils new to English as if they are n fact fluent speakers of English already. But also in many other ways pupils' backgrounds and experiences should be recognised and given respect.

Belonging and cohesion

It is important that all pupils should feel that they belong – to the school itself, to the neighbourhood and locality, and to Britain more generally. Belonging involves shared stories and symbols; a shared sense of having a stake in the well-being and future development of the wider community; a sense that one is accepted and welcomed, and that one is able and encouraged to participate and contribute.[14]

The Christian instinct about the 'mixed' or ambiguous outcomes of all human development makes the Church consistently critical of contemporary philosophies or ideologies – which politicians seem so readily to adopt – that claim to be able to 'fix' the subversive undercurrents which threaten government targets on education and crime. At heart, this instinct is a theological conviction. It is integral to the Christian understanding of what it is like to be a human being before God. Human nature, particularly within a child, is not something to be 'fixed' by education, rather it is to be nurtured and perfected. In summary: each and every child is a child of God and therefore to be accorded the status of a human being; each child is a unique individual, so that each child's name and identity are all-important; and yet each child is a *child* and is therefore not to be treated as an adult.

Each child merits the infinite respect that belongs to a human being, and this in spite of the ambiguities in their character and behaviour – which are as characteristic of adults as of children. So a child is never to be considered as pre-human or part-human. Each child is infinitely loved by God, as is each adult. Each child, therefore, is welcomed – in the Church's practice – to all the means of grace that are offered also to adults. In some church practices, the celebration of the truth that children are enveloped by the goodness of God has for generations been expressed in the advocacy of the sacrament of infant baptism. In baptism, where the saving grace of Christ is mediated to the child, the name given to the child by its parents is endorsed. From that moment on this individual child, with its unique identity, will be known in the global community of Christian disciples by its 'Christian' name.

In the last generation the welcome of baptized children into the reception of Holy Communion in some traditions has further enriched the liturgical celebration of the prevenient and universal grace of God. But the child, as child, cannot present itself for baptism or for sharing in the Eucharist any more than Christ could present himself before God in the temple for his circumcision. Children are dependent on their parents – or their primary carers, and this is by God's design. Reference to a 'child' demands always reference to a 'child-in-its-family-setting' (whatever form 'family' takes for each child, with its strengths and weaknesses). Thus the Trinitarian dance of relationships is mirrored in God-created human dependencies. Precisely for this reason the child is to be respected *as a child*. The child's experience, perspectives, vision and needs are not to be evaluated according to adult norms; they are authentically child-like – but nonetheless significant for that. Nor are they any the less important for the well-being of adults, whose world is all too easily cut off from the voice and desires of children. But children, as much as adults, are capable of being mediators of divine grace and God's call to adults and thereby of enriching Church and society. The boy child Samuel mediated God's grace to Eli through his sharing of God's word to him. David, as a child mediated God's grace to Saul and Israel. The youngest child of every Jewish family mediates God's grace at the Seder during Pesach by asking the questions that invite the narration of God's story of redemption. But children often exercise their ministry *differently* from the way adults exercise theirs: through questioning, or playfulness, or an unsophisticated 'saying it as it is' or by the emotive demand to have deep needs met urgently, rather than through careful self-expression, nuanced arguments and wise deliberation on long experience. In the Church, and even more so in wider society, adults are not good at hearing the voice of God through the words and actions of children.

When Christians instinctively built schools alongside churches all round the world they were signalling more than their pivotal understandings about the status of 'the child' before God and before adults, and the adult obligation to provide high-quality educational opportunities. They were also signalling that the moulding and development of children takes place through *institutions* as well as through Christian attitudes, values and interpersonal behaviour. The example set by Christ is clear – both as a child (Luke 2.46–49) and as an adult (Luke 19.47), the institutional places of faith, temples and synagogues, were expected to be places of learning and teaching.

So, to complete the picture, theological convictions were embodied in worked examples of Christian families, as well as Christian churches and Christian schools. No claim can be made that these institutional forms of Christian nurture were inherently superior to comparable institutions built on different foundations. But Christian institutions, for all their weaknesses and unwitting absorption of contemporary mores and cultural assumptions, were proclaimed to be of value for children, for at least two reasons. On the one hand, they gave practical, lived social expression to the convictions of Christian discipleship (including the infinite respect for each individual child as a child of God's with its own name and cluster of gifts waiting to be discerned and developed). On the other, they bore witness to the ambiguities of all human development – full of extraordinary, life-enhancing possibilities, because infused by the grace of God and the prayer of God's people; and simultaneously honest about the limitations and distortions of what was achievable, because locked up in every heart is a well of destructive energies that can be released, to everyone's hurt, in unpredictable and catastrophic ways. This theologically grounded vision of children, child-development and child-nurturing institutions is, I submit, far more realistic and far more challenging than idealized, government-managed educational ideology.

Reflecting theologically

A slightly wider theological reflection is in order here, to fill out the basis of what has just been asserted. Christians expound their faith along three interconnected and mutually illuminating paths.

God is the creator of every child and all the ambivalent influences on their development. God is therefore ultimately responsible for the way things go for children, for good and ill. Faith holds that the long and tortuous path to human maturity, with uncertain outcomes, is a journey that God uses to deliver God's purposes in creating human beings.

God revealed God's self uniquely in Jesus Christ. Jesus' embodied 'godness' clarified beyond question, to the eyes of faith, that God is essentially 'fatherly' in character. Faith declares that God's name and nature is love; and that God is infinitely generous to all that God has made, generous indeed in self-giving, so that Jesus' life – that is, God's life in and for the world – resulted inevitably in suffering, conflict and an untimely, cruel death. But God's promise, which was proclaimed by Jesus in terms of the coming kingdom of God, was not crushed. In and beyond Jesus' crucifixion God's promise retained its power. It is able to generate hope in the human heart and the human family. Flawed human beings, by God's grace and power, can be made fit for God's kingdom. The resurrection of Jesus is witness to this conviction and hope.

God's Spirit is everywhere present in the universe God has created, and therefore in every human heart and community. The Spirit silently mediates to the human heart (to the child as well as the adult!) the love and longing of God that were unveiled by Jesus. Hence, to the insight of faith, all experience in this world is shot through with indications, signs and sacraments of God's grace and righteousness, startling and surprising us at every turn. However, this intimate nearness of God, which is God's gift to humanity, to nourish and mature us in holiness of life, does not remove the epistemic distance of God from human enquiry and research. God is always an unknowable mystery, never the 'object' of human knowledge. Thus, without the gospel message about Jesus Christ, human beings characteristically live and act without reference to God. We behave badly. We allow the worst to emerge in unguarded moments. But the Spirit rescues something moderately good out of our wilful destruction of God's creation and our descent into nothingness – enough for human life to stagger on, enough to sustain prayer and hope – though certainly not on a progressive journey towards ever greater achievements in justice, peace or wisdom.

Through the work of the Spirit and the proclamation of the gospel about Jesus Christ, faith may be born. Faith is best illuminated through the prism of childhood. To expound this vital point, I turn to two passages in the Gospel of Mark: Mark 9.33–50 and 10.13–16. In a nutshell, Jesus' message is this: There are two worlds – an adult world and a child's world. The *adult world* (mainly, in the time of Jesus, a male world) is about control, about restrictions, about defending territory, about denying access to precious things except on terms imposed by powerful gatekeepers: indeed it is about power over other people (especially women and children). Think, for example, of those disciples turning some mothers and their children away from Jesus! The effect of this male power and control is to set up divisions in the human community: 'them' and 'us', the 'ins' and the 'outs'. The 'us' are the disciples around Jesus, privileged and excluding; the 'them' are the mothers and their children. That is the adult world in miniature. And it is not necessary to read much further in the Gospel stories to notice Jesus asserting that an obsession with wealth, and the fantasy that wealth brings security, aggravates this picture of the adult world.

In contrast is the *child's* world. It is about dependence and vulnerability; it is about not knowing about boundaries and conventions and rules, so that the child wanders where she or he wills and explores everything to hand, without discrimination. The child that is secure in its relationships often goes everywhere and anywhere, and puts itself into the company of anyone who is nearby without assessing whether they are friend or foe. Such a child can be recklessly trusting. A secure child often assumes that people and the world around them are like their parents: loving, nourishing and trustable.

Adults often adore what they perceive to be the child's world and can be moved deeply by it. Many adults even 'go a bit silly' in the presence of little children! But, in spite of this sentimentality, adults have structured society. As a child grows it is educated out of a child's world and made ready to enter an adult world. Childhood vulnerability, dependence and trust are best left behind (so adults believe) if growing children and young adults are to survive and flourish in this world. The message to children is clear: Become adults, enter the world of hard knocks, of divisions, conflict and fighting for power and position; enter the world of ferocious competition; make your way through the webs of suspicion and jealousy, of mistrust and betrayal. Visions and dreams are fine – but for goodness' sake keep in touch with harsh reality and the toughness of our environment!

The message of Jesus turns on its head the normal story of human development – that is, the journey from the child's world to the adult world. From Jesus, the message to adults is: Become children! Turn adult, worldly values upside down! You adults, learn afresh about vulnerability, dependence and trust.

But the wisdom of the adult world is underscored by all of human experience: it is a realistic assessment of how hurtful the world can be and therefore of how important are skills of survival and self-defence. Adults cannot be trusted. Adults let each other down, and do each other down, in spite of their sometimes having nobler intentions. So it is crucial to note how Jesus' appeal is to be heard. Jesus' appeal is to trust *God*. God alone is utterly reliable. God alone unequivocally loves. God *is* to be trusted. And the rich, relaxed, purposeful, joyful life God has in mind for human beings ('kingdom life') comes as a gift to people who trust God.

Faith, then, is a transformative response to the Spirit and the gospel message. It establishes a relationship with God; and it enables the life of God (embodied in Jesus Christ) to flow into the world through the heart of the believer. Faith introduces the believer to a taste of the kingdom of God. It does not, however, diminish our need to be worldly wise. The world remains for believers a hurtful and ambiguous, occasionally a bloody, place. But faith and the new life that faith releases in and through the believer significantly change our agenda. Faith shifts the balance – so to speak – so that there is less interest in trying to control people around us, or exercising power over people, or aspiring always to win in competition with our neighbours. There is more interest in being open and vulnerable to other people around us, in discerning and celebrating the gracious working of the Spirit in the lives of other people.

This discernment never happens perfectly. Time and again believers, struggling to survive in this harsh world, express forcefully in words and actions the crudities of the 'adult world'. Their primary objective, however, is to notice with ever greater confidence the wondrous intimations of God's grace in the face of their neighbour. They want to 'see' the Spirit invisibly at work, granting the human family in the most unlikely places (not least in children) the gifts of love, joy, peace, patience, goodness, fidelity and self-control (Galatians 5.22–23). In addition, they want to relate to their neighbour in a radically different way – developing trust, being open and becoming vulnerable. They want to be of *service* to others, as Jesus was the servant of all. So, the followers of Jesus are not naïve about the world; neither are they imprisoned by the culture that adults have developed to manage worldly experience as best they can. They are inspired by the instruction of Jesus: Be innocent as doves *and* wary as serpents (Matthew 10.16).

These theological reflections bring a new insight into authentic human development. Of course, children have to grow out of childhood into adulthood. Of course, children have to be educated; and it is right not only that the state has a large stake in education but also that Christians retain their freedom to engage critically with government in respect of the values and institutional frameworks within which a realistic educational service can be provided with inspiring but attainable (though less than satisfactory) outcomes driving it. But Christians also proclaim a 'reverse' journey, from the defensive and controlling adult world towards a spiritual embrace of child-like virtues – trust, dependence and vulnerability; the humble and costly service of others, especially the stranger; hospitality for all, and initiatives of loving care and patience towards all, including one's enemies.

'The kingdom of God belongs to the child-like'; 'whoever does not accept the kingdom of God like a child will never enter it.'

Jesus was a good as his word. In the face of persecution and danger, so the Gospels proclaim, he was notably not defensive. The author of Mark's Gospel focuses on the strength of character in Jesus, which empowered him to remain non-violent and silent in the face of threats and torrents of false accusations (see especially Mark 14.55–61 and 15.3–5, 29–32). This adult version of child-like trust in God was the *sine qua non* of what I summarized earlier as Jesus' generous self-giving to the point of death (to which Paul often refers, e.g. Philippians 2.5–11).

I conclude here the theological reflection that underpins the Christian critique of overarching governmental policies on education. An obvious question now arises: Could Church or 'faith'-based schools provide a better answer to the educational needs of children than the proffered but unrealistic visions of the state?

Faith schools

Certainly Church schools can add Christian value to the educational experience of children. They achieve this, in contemporary Britain, through Church nominations to the governing body of a school, through the legitimate use of religious education in the curriculum and of collective worship and through the overt Christian ethos of a Christian school. However, faith schools today are not the same as Church-founded schools in the period up to 1870. In the nineteenth century, Church schools were projects under the direct oversight of a Christian congregation, and therefore an integral part of that church's mission strategy. Today's Christian faith schools, where they exist, are generally the result of partnerships between Church and state. The state remains the principal provider and influence in a faith school, most commonly through devising and insisting on a national 'core' curriculum, policed by the state's inspection system. In the United Kingdom, government policies in relation to faith schools since 1944 have been generally benign – not least, in England, because of the government's dependency on the Church of England to provide a large number of schools. In more recent years, however, in keeping with the trends noted earlier, the government has become increasingly desperate to regain or retain social control of young people through schools. Its interventions and demands have, accordingly, become ever more strident and bureaucratic. Is the time near when the churches (minority partners in the provision of faith schools) will feel that all they want to contribute to faith schools is uncomfortably compromised, constrained or marginalized?

If tensions between government and the churches were to increase (and who can guess where government policy will go in the future?), would the churches have the courage to withdraw from an unsatisfactory partnership? Or would they judge that a withdrawal would make the educational experience for children even worse? The churches have offered three emphases that are important in the public agendas about faith schools.

First, they have, on the whole, resisted the easy propaganda which claims that faith schools are *inherently* superior to state-run community schools on the basis that partnerships and human institutions are never rescued from their flawed and ambiguous character simply by virtue of Church involvement. This is not to negate the confidence that the churches have that the truths of faith can add value to the quality of school and education. But it is recognition that this is not automatic. It demands commitment, spiritual maturity and great wisdom. And it does not always work out well.

Second, the churches have proclaimed that faith schools should, wherever possible, have *open* admissions policies. There must be no privileges for families with links to Church – if there is any good from God, it is a good for all or it is no good at all). If there have to be something like entry privileges to a faith school, it will be in the area of excellent and additional provision for children with special needs.

Third, wherever possible, the Church's involvement in education should be *ecumenical* in character. Churches working together in partnership better promote an inclusive vision of a school community where boys and girls from all sorts of backgrounds, culture and ethnic origin learn to live together in tolerable peace and harmony and thereby, with theological resources to hand to support them, are better able to see the work of God in their midst and to praise, trust and love God. And precisely in such a microcosm of the human family, we create the most inspiring and the most realistic environment for the process of education and development. The logical conclusion of this is, if and when opportunity comes, and so long as there is no fundamental compromise of core Christian conviction, that we would join in a *multi-faith* sponsorship of a faith school.

Even though in most western democracies churches are minority partners with the state in the provision of faith schools ('schools with a religious character', to be more precise), they remain very costly for the churches, in money and time. Very few denominations can afford to be involved in a significantly large number of faith schools. Most churches therefore consider it sufficient to be effectively involved in a small number.

The provision of faith schools is not the only useful model of partnership between churches and state education. Much more common than involvement in faith schools is the following: a local church prays for its local community schools and supports them in practical ways to the extent the schools find beneficial. An additional element may be that the church's minister, together with suitably gifted and qualified lay persons from the congregation, make personal contributions in the school (leading collective worship, or giving some classroom support, or offering chaplaincy to the whole school).

Families

I have referred only in passing to the other – greater – moulder of children's development: families. I conclude with some brief reflections on this theme. The Church can no more create a perfect Christian family than it can create a perfect school. In any case, families – in one form or another – are everywhere, and in every era, part of the fabric of society. Families pre-date churches. Churches do not invent families. Families belong to the 'order of creation' (though, to the eyes of faith, they are none the less products of God's creative energy and providential care). So Christians enter into partnership with family forms that are embedded in local cultures, and influence the 'natural' dynamics of families in order to nourish in particular ways what families provide for adults and for children (love, trust, care, loyalty, networks of mutual interdependence across generations, shared interests, responsible participation in neighbourhoods, and the like).

Unfortunately, in the nineteenth and twentieth centuries, by being indifferent to the complex history of family forms, many Christian groups became themselves hooked on an ideology of the Christian family. Ideologies are fantasies that attempt to transcend the messy ambiguities and flawed outcomes of human existence. In some quarters, such an ideology is attached to a 'model' or ideal Christian family – two married parents, each a committed Christian, bonded together in a mutually loving and lifelong relationship of support, loyalty and care, whose children are baptized into Christ and nurtured in the Christian way within the fellowship of a relaxed, respectful and loving congregation. It is proclaimed to be an unambiguous good; it is beyond negative or critical comment. In reality, of course, so-called 'Christian' families are ambiguous – like all institutions. There is no telling what lurks in the human heart and may be released to destroy good intentions and best practice – yes, even in 'model' Christian families.

Fixation on this Christian ideal has not stood the Church in good stead for dealing with what has emerged in the past few generations – a surge in diverse family forms, even among Christians, let alone in society at large. Common developments include divorce, cohabitation, single parenthood, the creation of step-families, and same-sex parents with legal responsibility for the upbringing of children. At every stage these developments have been 'regretted' because they do not match the alleged 'norm' of Christian family life. But, in truth, Christians have to be open to perspectives on child development – positive and negative – in all family forms, rather than assuming that children can flourish in only one normative family unit. Certainly a Christian can bear witness in *any* family arrangement – though sometimes, to be sure, with the greatest of difficulty. And the Church can enter into partnership with a multiplicity of family forms, to establish a creative dialogue which is in the interest of children and therefore of adults. Sometimes this dialogue is facilitated by a local church; sometimes by a specialized Christian agency.

Christian faith opens up relationship with the creator God, who has saved the world in Jesus Christ and who pours out the Holy Spirit to nourish us and nurture us with transfiguring power. The Spirit guides us towards social and personal holiness. Faith and everything that flows from a decision of faith therefore illuminate and affect the moulding and shaping of children, adults and child–adult relationships. Christian faith introduces infinite possibilities into human development through learning and mutual support and care. Christian faith empowers people for service (being a good neighbour to people in need and challenging injustice). Christian faith kindles and perpetually refreshes a vision of God's coming kingdom. In the interim, the promise of the gospel is interwoven with realism about the awfulness into which human beings can sink. Avoiding both cynicism and idealism, challenging complacency and indifference, always encouraging people to push at the perceived limits of knowledge and attainment, Christian faith offers a critique both of schooling (when it is exclusively in the hands of government) and of family life (when it is portrayed in a normative form from a Christian base). At the heart of Christian faith is the adult learning the spiritual maturity of a child, precisely when the adult must carry responsibility for the education and development of the child.

It is ironic that we call on a theology of the child to refresh Christian discipleship in an era when children and young people have chosen not to relate to traditional forms of Church. How can a congregation without children hear the gospel?

Notes

1 Elaine L. Bearer, Cynthia Garcia Coll, Richard M. Lerner, *Nature and Nurture: The Complex Interplay of Genetic and Environmental Influences on Human Behaviour and Development*, Lawrence Erlbaum Associates, 2004, p. 226.

2 Sure Start is a programme of the UK government which aims to achieve better outcomes for children, parents and communities by: increasing the availability of childcare for all children, improving health and emotional development for young children and supporting parents as parents and in their aspirations towards employment. It has a counterpart in Sure-Start Plus which aims to support pregnant teenagers and teenage parents under 18 launched in April 2001. The initiative aims to improve health, education, and social outcomes for pregnant teenagers, teenage parents and their children. A recent academic study of the project, however, indicated that children of single mothers, teenagers and jobless parents who went through Sure Start learned less and were more prone to behaviour problems than those who didn't.

3 U. Bronfenbrenner, 'Motivational and social components in compensatory education programs', in E. Grotberg (ed.), *Critical Issues in Research*

Relating to Disadvantaged Children, Educational Testing Service, Princeton, NJ, 1969, p. 10.

4 See John G. Borkowski, Marie Bristol-Power, Sharon Landesman Ramey (eds), *Parenting and the Child's World: Influences on Academic, Intellectual, and Social-Emotional Development*, Lawrence Erlbaum Associates, Mahwah, NJ, 2002 and Robert Plomin, Heather Chipuer, Jenae M. Neiderhiser, 'Behavioral genetic evidence for the importance of nonshared environment' in E. M. Hetherington, D. Reiss and R. Plomin (eds), *Separate Social Worlds of Siblings: The Impact of Nonshared Environment on Development*, Lawrence Erlbaum Associates, Hillsdale, NJ, 1994, pp. 1–31.

5 P. A. Cowan and C. P. Powell, 'Parenting interventions: A family systems perspective' in W. Damon (series ed.) and I. E. Singal, A. Renninger (vol. eds), *Handbook of Child Psychology: Vol. 4. Child Psychology in Practice* (5th edn, pp. 3–72), New York, John Viley and Sons, 1998, p. 7.

6 John Dewey, *Democracy and Education: An Introduction to the Philosophy of Education*, New York, Macmillan, 1916, p. 101.

7 Community Cohesion Education Standards for Schools: 2004: <http://www.communities.gov.uk/index.asp?id=1502612.>

8 Dewey, *Democracy and Education*, p. 101.

9 See, for example, the Department for Education and Skills report *Delivering Results*: 2006 ESDRS2006R, <http://www.dfes.gov.uk/aboutus/strategy/>

10 See in particular Christopher Lasch, *Haven in a Heartless World: The Family Besieged*, New York, Basic Books, 1977; Jacques Donzelot, *La Police des familles*, Paris, Les Editions de Minuit, 1977, translated by Robert Hurley as *The Policing of Families: Welfare Versus the State*, London, Hutchinson, 1980; David Archard, *Children: Rights and Childhood*, New York, Routledge, 2004.

11 Norman Lamm, *The Shema: Spirituality and Law in Judaism as Exemplified in the Shema, the Most Important Passage in the Torah*, Philadepihia, Jewish Publication Society, 1998, p. 159.

12 George E. Ganss, *Saint Ignatius' Idea of a Jesuit University: A Study in the History of Catholic Education, Including Part Four of the Constitutions of the Society of Jesus*, Milwaukee, Marquette University Press, 1956, p. 18.

13 Ganss, *Saint Ignatius' Idea of a Jesuit University*, p. 18.

14 Source: Derbyshire Education Authority, 2003. As quoted in *Aiming High: Understanding the Educational Needs of Minority Ethnic Pupils in Mainly White Schools: A Guide to Good Practice*: DfES/0673/2003.

‘My child, do not regard lightly the discipline of the Lord, or lose heart when you are punished by him; for the Lord disciplines those whom he loves, and chastises every child whom he accepts.’ Endure trials for the sake of discipline. God is treating you as children; for what child is there whom a parent does not discipline? If you do not have that discipline in which all children share, then you are illegitimate and not his children. Moreover, we had human parents to discipline us, and we respected them. Should we not be even more willing to be subject to the Father of spirits and live? For they disciplined us for a short time as seemed best to them, but he disciplines us for our good, in order that we may share his holiness. Now, discipline always seems painful rather than pleasant at the time, but later it yields the peaceful fruit of righteousness to those who have been trained by it. Therefore lift your drooping hands and strengthen your weak knees, and make straight paths for your feet, so that what is lame may not be put out of joint, but rather be healed.

Hebrews 12.5–13

5. Re-Imagining, Re-Thinking and Re-Doing: Deconstucting our Biblical and Theological Perspectives on the Christian Nurture of Children

ANTHONY REDDIE

In this chapter I want to reflect upon the underlying biblical and theological themes that inform our notions of the nurture of children within a Christian framework in Britain. Building upon and reviewing the research I undertook back in the 1990s, I want to critique some of the assumptions and propositional concepts of God that exist through our reading of particular biblical texts, as a means of delineating how this thinking influences our contemporary practice of nurturing children. This interpretative process will be achieved by means of utilizing a particular theoretical model; namely 'Personal Construct Psychology' (PCP).

Using this tool, initially as means of reassessing my previous work, I hope to show how an understanding of the ways in which human societies construe values and establish truth can assist in explaining how we use particular biblical narratives as a means of establishing the cultural norms for our contemporary practices in nurturing children. In effect, PCP can open our eyes to the often covert ways in which our self-constructed assumptions create frameworks for determining how the Bible is read and what might be learnt from its many narratives, particularly, as these texts affect our understanding of and relationship to children.

This piece is written from a Black theological perspective. In using this term, what I mean to suggest is that the term 'Black' comes to represent God's symbolic and actual solidarity with oppressed people; the majority of whom have been consigned to the marginal spaces of the world solely on the grounds of their very Blackness.[1] I am using a Black theological method as a means of posing a number of political and polemic points about the use and abuse of Holy Scripture and Christian tradition as it collides with contemporary experience and human life. Black theology is committed to challenging the systemic frameworks that assert particular practices and ideas as being normative (normally governed by the powerful), while ignoring the claims of those who are marginalized and are powerless; often demonizing the perspectives of the latter as being aberrant or heretical.[2]

Finally, by way of an explanatory overview of this work, I should say that this essay makes reference to working practices of Black communities, whether African or African Caribbean (in the context of the UK) or African American (in terms of the US). It should not be assumed that my reference to these communities or contexts denotes a specific or particular problem for these groups alone. There is a sense that all communities have their blind spots and examples of poor practice, aided and abetted by even poorer theology (more of which in a short while) in terms of their relationship to children. In highlighting these particular arenas, I am simply seeking to be honest to my own methodology as a theologian and educator; namely that I cannot, nor do I, write for everyone. Instead, I begin from a place that is familiar to me and address my thoughts to the spaces, places and people with whom I share some immediate sense of identity, shared narratives and historic resonances around what it means to be a human being.[3]

Locating myself

For me as a contextual theologian it is very important to locate myself and my work within the particular social or cultural milieu when I begin to explicate my ideas.

I am an African Caribbean male Christian. I was born in Bradford, West Yorkshire in 1964. My parents arrived in Britain in the late 1950s from the Caribbean island of Jamaica as part of the mass migratory movement of predominantly Black people from the so-called 'New Commonwealth'.[4]

Alongside my cultural and ethnic identities (I am at once informed by West Yorkshire sensibilities, the Caribbean and being Black), there are also my religious, denominational and spiritual heritages to be considered in the complex hybridity that is a generic part of what it is to be human.[5] My religious and denominational heritage is located within the Wesleyan Methodist tradition. I was baptized in the Christian Church in the spring of 1965 at Prospect Hall Methodist Church in Bradford. When this church closed, my family and many others decamped to Eastbrook Hall Methodist Central Mission in Bradford town centre. There I spent the next 15 years of my life before I left Bradford in 1984 to read History at the University of Birmingham. In a previous piece of work I have stated that I am much more Methodist than I care to admit and rather too Methodist than is really good for me.[6] My work as a Black British theologian and Christian educator has been and continues to be informed by the denominational and religious tradition into which I have been socialized. This can be seen in my previous work, such as *Growing into Hope*, just as Robert Beckford's work is influenced greatly by his Pentecostal roots.[7]

My own roots and identity have been shaped by Methodism. I was nurtured into and have imbibed Methodist values in my understanding of self, God, education, notions of social progress or advancement and of course, in how one 'does theology'.[8]

Historical and contextual background

To understand the role played by Christianity in the nurture of Black children, one needs to understand something of the development of Black Christianity in the African Diaspora, over the period of the last 500 years. Black Christianity in the Americas and the Caribbean (the sight of my recent ancestry) developed within ongoing struggles of Black peoples to affirm their identity and very humanity in the face of seemingly insuperable odds.[9]

The 'invention' of Blackness, as opposed being 'African' is a construction of the Enlightenment.[10] Although there already existed deep-seated racialized depictions of people of darker skin within the cultural imagination of Europeans, influenced in no small measure by Greek philosophical thought; nevertheless, the construction of an overarching doctrine of racial inferiority ascribed to people of African descent reached its apotheosis during the epoch of slavery, aided and abetted by specious notions of pseudo-science.[11] In short, somewhere across the 'Middle Passage' and the 'Black Atlantic', Africans became 'Negroes'.[12]

Black people in the African Diaspora became Christians in mass numbers during the 'Great Awakening' in the middle of the eighteenth century.[13] The Christianity into which they were coerced and socialized was an exploitative framework that stated that Black people were inherently and divinely sanctioned as being inferior to White people.[14] But Black people were not passive imbibers of a biased and self-serving brand of Christian education. Rather, Black slaves began to 'steal away' from beneath the close confines of their slave masters to worship God in their own existential spaces.[15]

The desire of Black people to form their own ecclesial spaces was the process of a long period of history, arising from the 'Great Awakening' in the middle of the eighteenth century.[16] Black Christianity was born of the existential need to create a safe framework in which the Black self could rehearse the very rubrics of what it meant to be a human being.[17]

Re-assessing my previous work

My early scholarly work was very much located within the area of Christian education and practical theology. In my initial research work I was attempting to create a more appropriate teaching and learning framework for the Christian education of African Caribbean children. This pedagogy was one that would be aware of the cultures, identities, historical and contemporary experiences and expressions of Christian faith within the socio-political and economic realities of inner-city life in Britain.

This work was undertaken between 1995 and 1999 on a research project entitled the 'Birmingham Initiative'.[18] It was an attempt to find a means of providing a culturally appropriate model of Christian nurture and faith formation for Black African Caribbean children in Birmingham, using the insights of Black theology and transformative pedagogy as educational and theological frameworks for the research.[19]

Perhaps the most crucial learning that accrued from my initial research was the inadequacy of cognitive or intellectual frames of reference in terms of religious sensibilities. What I mean by this is that for many marginalized and oppressed peoples, the truths of their experiences (religious or otherwise) are not found in written texts, but instead, are located in the informal and more covert ways in which stories and narratives are passed on between peoples of different generations. This insight was detailed in a subsequent piece of work.[20]

The development of Christian education curricula and accompanying pedagogies for teaching the Christian faith to Black people are more recent innovations in the Black churches. Grant Shockley is of the opinion that formalized, text-based Christian education programmes only came into prominence in the Black Church at the beginning of this century.[21] Prior to that time, an oral tradition that consisted of experience, both individual and corporate, and expressed through storytelling and proverbial wisdom, was the usual means by which the Christian faith was passed on from one generation to the next.

The western over-emphasis upon text seeks to mask the central importance of oral communication and the power within that form to inspire, transform and energize. As Berryman reminds us, the two most influential people in western philosophical thought have been Socrates and Jesus Christ, and neither individual is recorded as having written anything.[22]

The importance of the oral tradition in many communities leads me to a major area of concern in this chapter, namely, how do the often informal and subliminal socio-cultural codes for discerning truth and forms of knowledge (epistemology) inform our ways of reading the Bible, and, as a corollary, affect how we relate to and engage with children within the Church?

In my previous work, given the exploratory stage at which the research was located, I was not in a position to undertake the more deconstructive work of challenging and critiquing Black cultural norms and the biblical interpretation that arises from it. At that point, given the paucity of any substantive Black theology work,[23] I was more concerned with simply trying to create a practical educational and theological framework for the articulation of the Christian faith for Black children and young people in Britain.

In this work, I want to begin from where that work ended and investigate how and in what ways does an often covert form of oral tradition, which can be analysed in terms of 'Personal Construct Psychology', inform and shape our reading of the Bible. Then, as a corollary, I will pose the question: In what ways do our readings of particular texts inform practice and vice versa?

Black Christianity and the Bible

One of the important characteristics of Black Christianity is the centrality of the Bible. This is not to suggest that the Bible is not central to the formulations of other Christian groups or persons, but it is a generalized truth, however, that every branch of Black Christianity across the world holds Scripture to be the supreme rule of faith and the only means by which one can understand God's revelation in Christ.

Despite it radical roots in countering racism and Black dehumanization, many Black churches and the Christians that have emerged from them, whether in the US or in the Caribbean or Britain, have remained wedded to a form of nineteenth-century White Evangelicalism. A number of Black scholars have demonstrated the extent to which Christianity as a global phenomenon has drunk deeply from the well of Eurocentric philosophical thought at the expense of African or other overarching forms of epistemology.[24] Black Christianity has imbibed these Eurocentric, Greek-influenced thought forms, often at the expense of their own identity and African forms of epistemology. This adherence to nineteenth-century biblicism has meant that the blandishments of historical-critical biblical studies have barely penetrated the edifice of the Black Christianity across the world.

For the most part, the heart of Black Christianity in Britain, for example, is built upon quasi-literalist readings of Scripture, in which Jesus and salvation are conceived solely in terms of John 14.6. Again, I must make the point that this particular approach to reading the Bible is not unique to Black people. There are many groups who will not only read the Bible in this way, but will also claim it to be normative of historic Christianity as it has been expressed and propagated over 2000 years. As I have asserted, hitherto, I am using Black Christianity as a particular focus for looking at the overarching concerns that are most probably relevant for every ethnic, cultural or geographical grouping in Britain and beyond.[25]

This adherence to Scripture, like all approaches to reading the Bible, is selective. I have placed the last few words in italics because I think it is of crucial import in the context of this discussion. All of us are selective, idiosyncratic and contradictory in the way in which we handle the Bible.

This can be demonstrated by means of a very simple example. As Miguel De La Torre reminds us, the Bible calls for disobedient children to be executed (Leviticus 20.9).[26] He continues by reminding us that the Bible is not the fullest revelation of God, because Jesus is the 'The Word'. Jesus is the norm by which all the other elements of the Bible are to be interpreted.[27] But the fact is, many Christian communities do not treat the 'Word' as being Jesus, but rather sanction the whole of Scripture as being literally dictated by God and therefore understood as a means of revelation.

The issue of the inconsistency in our reading strategies can be found in the manner in which certain passages of the Bible are taken as literally true (and are to be followed accordingly) while others are not. As I have stated, all people read the Bible in idiosyncratic and contradictory ways, even those who claim to read it literally, as if it were the actual words of God. As Miguel De La Torre reminds us, if the Bible were the literal word of God, then God would be guilty of genocide, infanticide, patricide and regicide.[28]

When Torre points to the fact that the Bible calls for disobedient children to be executed (Leviticus 20.9)[29] he does so in an ironic mode, knowing full well that no right-minded society adhering to Christian values will casually sanction the execution of disobedient children. Many may well believe the Bible to be the literal word of God, but some form of interpretative framework is at work to ensure that, for the most part, catastrophic events like murdering children does not become a regular occurrence.

While most Christian communities have ways of regulating their literal understanding of violent and bloodthirsty texts,[30] I would argue that the underlying constructs people hold about the Bible and the nature of God still inform the overarching values for how we treat and engage with children. In effect, we may not violently assault children as normative practice and then provide it with a Christian/biblical sense of justification, but I will argue that the underlying notions of God and the Bible held by many people provide the substantive framework that makes such cultural horrors possible.

Practical theology and theological reflection

The work of many theorists and practitioners in Christian education falls within the broader theological field of 'practical theology'. Scholars such as Ballard and Pritchard,[31] Forrester[32] and Graham[33] have theorized around the development of practical theology as a model of reflective activity in which the theologian interrogates the connections between the theory and practice of Christianity in a diverse range of contexts and milieux. Practical theology is particularly adept as utilizing interdisciplinary approaches to theological reflection, especially those that are drawn from psychology, which has been proved a durable dialogue partner for those engaged in pastoral theology (which often taken as a synonym for practical theology).

My initial training as a theologian was in the arena of practical and contextual theology, and it is to this work and training that I now return, in order to construct a hermeneutical framework for assessing how Black Christians often read biblical texts as they pertain to their engagement with children.

Personal Construct Psychology

Personal Construct Psychology (PCP) has been used by practical and pastoral theologians as a tool for assessing how all people, but particularly those who profess to be Christians, make sense of God and so undertake their God-talk or theology. PCP originated in the United States in the early to middle 1950s. The originator of PCP was a psychologist and clinical counsellor named George Kelly. Working from the University of Wisconsin, Kelly developed a theory pertaining to the ways in which people construct meaning and attempt to make sense of situations, experiences, images and events as they arise in one's life. Personal construing is a human, meaning-making device. Everyone's construing (construction of meaning) is different and is highly individualistic. Our personal constructs are ways of anticipating and interpreting the world around us.[34]

Some scholars, drawing on Kelly's work, have argued that the Christian faith is not a gift from God, as many believers would assert, but is itself a human construct. The human processes of attempting to create meaning, and an interpretative framework for one's experiences is a human device onto which the overarching structure of Christian faith is placed for authoritative verification.[35]

In effect, using Kelly, some scholars have argued that notions of God and Christian faith are nothing more than personal constructs that human beings have developed in order to provide an overarching framework for understanding and interpreting events in the world.[36]

Not surprisingly, a number of theologians and religious educationalists have found this contention deeply problematic. Given the strongly theistic nature of most Black communities in Britain, for example, this notion would be ridiculed and summarily rejected by a majority of people of African descent. And yet some Black scholars, such as William R. Jones[37] and Anthony Pinn,[38] have argued in favour of the concept, at least on the basis that assumptions surrounding the Christian theism of Black people are unhelpful and often based on an uncritical adoption of unsubtle western supremacist notions of Christian imperialism. Jones, in particular, argues that Black Christian faith should at best be understood as a form of projection of human values and aspirations onto an alleged and speculative notion of the objective reality of a transcendent being named God[39] – that, in effect, that Black religious faith is a form of 'human-centric theism'.

But back to Kelly! Kelly also distinguished between constructs that were 'core' and 'peripheral'. The former are those close to the centre of our whole being and which connote some sense of our humanity and individualistic notions of existence (for example, a belief in God). The latter are of less importance and do not imply anything deeper than a particular phobia or some non-threatening neurosis. 'Peripheral' constructs can be termed as 'permeable', in that they can absorb a multitude of influences and are subject to change.

Moreover, as they are located very close to our conscious self, we can be aware of them, and as a result of this consciousness they can be changed or amended. Counselling, numerous types of therapy and psychoanalysis are just three examples of a number of processes that can attempt to assist people to reflect upon and even change their personal constructs. The corollary of this, however, is the difficulty, some would say impossibility, of even being aware of our 'core' constructs let alone possessing the facility to change them.

Kelly devised PCP as a means of enabling individuals to become increasingly aware of the constructs that confer meaning upon particular aspects of our life. Kelly differed from Sigmund Freud in that he believed that people were not hostages to their past. Through a psychological process such as PCP an individual could gain a greater understanding of a construct that gave rise to a particular problem or issue in their life and be assisted to find appropriate mechanisms to change that construct, and so change their understanding and experience.

Kelly believed that all people are personal 'scientists'. We are regularly testing out new concepts, strategies, and ideas, trying to find new, more appropriate ways of construing meaning of events, experiences and roles. These meaning-making processes are taking place on a continuous basis every day of our lives and we are barely conscious of them. Kelly wanted to find a means of making those processes more explicit so that people could reflect and mediate upon them in order to develop new constructs that might provide greater flexibility and sustenance to one's life. Kelly called this process of attempting to change one's constructs 'Constructive Alternativism'.

Following the early development in PCP, a number of psychologists, educationalists and more latterly theologians[40] have attempted to build upon the pioneering work of Kelly. A number of practical strategies have been deployed in order that the theoretical underpinnings of PCP can be translated into a usable framework for eliciting personal constructs in individuals or groups.

Time does not permit a thorough explication of the various methods available for using PCP in a practical educational and pastoral setting, but there are number of useful texts that offer ample instruction and guidance in this area.[41]

Why is Personal Construct Psychology significant?

The significance of PCP lies in the way in which it has the potential to enable Christian theology to critique the underlying notions of and models of God that influence and shape our attitudes to children.

In this, the final section of the chapter, I want to return to one example from my previous research and re-examine it in the light of PCP. In what ways are particular constructs at work in the ways in which certain biblical narratives are interpreted in relation to children? How do these constructs not only affect our biblical interpretation, but in what ways do they also shape our contemporary cultural practices in terms of nurturing children?

Scholars such as Phillida Salmon have used PCP to investigate the conceptual limits of how we perceive truth.[42] One technique she uses is entitled 'The Salmon Line'.[43] The Salmon Line operates on the basis of individuals (or groups) constructing working paradigms for truth in terms of delineating the extremes of any particular concept. The Salmon Line operates on the principle that you describe the extremes of any particular concept or phenomenon in terms of their polar opposites. So if you wanted to think of constructs of the Bible, for example, you might ask the respondent for two possible polar opposites for how biblical authority is perceived. At one end of the construct might be the phrase 'the Bible is the inerrant'. By definition, the other end of the construct would be the polar opposite to the first statement.

The Salmon Line works by asking individuals to analyse where they would place themselves on the continuum between the two statements (I have usually worked with a number scale of either 20 or 30). When they have placed themselves at a particular place in the continuum, they are then invited to reflect on the reasons for their location. If one is nearer the opposite end to the inerrant pole (which might be exemplified in a statement like 'The Bible is completely relative like all other texts'), then what are the reasons for locating oneself at that point? If you were to move from that position to one further towards the inerrant pole, what changes would have occurred in your thinking?

Using this particular training approach to theological reflection within the framework of practical theology, one can begin to enable participants to consider the factors that influence their particular constructs around certain themes in Christian theology. The fact that we all have myriad constructs means that one could use this method for eliciting our personal constructs for a wide variety of themes or theological concerns. One simply starts with an imaginary line at which there are two opposite poles. The theologian can either ask the participants to construct their own statements that determine the polar opposites for a particular concept or phenomenon (characteristics or attributes of God is a favourite one of many practical theologians and educationists) or propose the form of words themselves with which the group or individuals will work.

Reflecting upon Genesis 22.1–14 in the light of Personal Construct Psychology

I have chosen to reflect upon this text because it is one of those difficult passages that is (for very good reason) overlooked by many people who work with children and has been deemed to be an 'unfriendly text' for children. There is no doubt that once one digs beneath the spiritualized veneer of this text, one cannot help but be appalled at the actions of the main protagonist in the narrative. What are we to make of Abraham's seemingly reckless actions in being prepared to sacrifice his son at the behest of a disembodied voice claiming to be God? I will return to this text at a later juncture in this essay in order to re-read it in the light of PCP and the constructs many Black Christian adults hold in terms of their assessment of the theological value of young children.

It is perhaps, the nature of these 'texts of terror'[44] coupled with the post-Second World War developments in cognitive psychology that led to the growing awareness of the needs of learners, particularly young children. These developments led to an increased appreciation of the role of psychology in the Christian education of children.[45]

The groundbreaking research of Ronald Goldman in developmental psychology led to a wholesale reassessment of the role of the Bible in the Christian education and nurture of children and young people.[46] Goldman contended that the Bible was an adult book and wholly unsuited to the nurture and developmental needs of children.[47] Goldman states:

> I suggest that it is impossible to teach the Bible as such to children much before adolescence, and that we must look for another approach which offers a more realistic alternative to our present ills.[48]

While Goldman's ideas, so fashionable during the 1960s and early 70s have largely fallen out of favour in more recent times, there can be no denying the psychological damage that can be unleashed upon an impressionable mind when they are confronted with a story that uses a child as pawn in a seemingly daring and dangerous game of theological 'Chicken'. Can these actions really be those of a loving God?

How does the framework of PCP assist us in our interpretation of how we read this text? Well, first let me remind you of the route we have taken to arrive at this point. One first needs to understand the historic background and development of Black Christianity in Britain and across the other parts of the African Diaspora. As I have stated previously, Black Christianity emerged as a response to the reality of oppression.[49] One of the main consequences arising from the Diasporan African experience of slavery, colonialism and reconstruction (in the US) was the sense that many Black people learnt very quickly that the world was not a place to be trusted. The world of White people was one in which Black communities lived in terms of fear, trepidation and the constant threat of annihilation.[50] Consequently, many Black communities became cautiously conservative in their socialization patterns and child-rearing practices. Grant Shockley, looking at the Christian education of African American children, reflects upon the conservative and didactic models of pedagogy used in the nurture and Christian formation within many historic Black churches.[51]

The nature of the threat to Black life was such that no concessions were made in terms of socializing and nurturing children into both the contextual struggles of simply trying to stay alive in a hostile environment while also inculcating in them the necessary survival skills borne out through Christian faith as a means of overcoming these very real environmental threats. Janice Hale amplifies this point when commenting on the importance of African derived stories of experience:

> These stories transmit the message to Black children that there is a great deal of quicksand and many land mines on the road to becoming a Black achiever . . . They also transmit the message that it is possible to overcome these obstacles. These stories help Black children de-personalise oppression when they encounter it and enable them to place their personal difficulties into the context of the overall Black liberation struggle.[52]

African Diasporan practices of nurture and formation, which emerged from the fiery furnace of slavery and racism, have alighted on the central importance of Christian faith as the primary means (some might even assert as the only means) by which Black people can survive in a discriminatory and hostile environment.[53] Shockley (who remains the doyen of Black Christian religious education for people of African descent), once again, states that the historic Black

Church[54] in the US has never been noted for its liberal or progressive pedagogy in terms of the training and education it offered for lay people (including children) in the church.[55]

In my analysis of the historic development of Black Christian faith I was anxious to place the development of Diasporan African Christianity in a socio-political context. For in order to understand the ways in which many Black Christian adults, whether parents or informal educators (Sunday school teachers for example) construe meaning from the Bible as a means of informing their practice, we need to understand the historical forces that have influenced their hermeneutical reading strategies.

In preparation for writing this chapter I revisited some of the material that I first garnered when undertaking my doctorate back in the late 1990s. I was particularly interested in the training document 'Getting to Know Yourself', the contents of which are included as an appendix to this essay. This training document was created to utilize some insights of PCP and the 'Salmon Line'. Dusting off that work, I re-introduced it to a group of Black parents and workers with children at the local church level and asked them the questions in the document.

The 'Getting to Know Yourself' document is an attempt to create a practical and accessible resource for helping people to elicit their constructs relating to their work with children, in this case, particularly those of African Caribbean descent.

Of particular import was the way in which many of the adults construed their notions of working with children in terms of the historic factors that have helped to shape Black religious consciousness and identity. Speaking to 12 Black adults (all of whom were of African Caribbean descent – the same as the children),[56] 75 per cent of them, i.e. 9 out of 12 saw their work almost solely in terms of 'bringing children to faith'.[57]

For most of them, it was simply essential that their children have faith. Alternative constructs such as 'sowing seeds', or 'building relationships', which are very much commonplace within the literature of Christian education and practical theology, as displayed in the landmark reports *The Child in the Church* and *Understanding Christian Nurture*, were very much rejected.[58]

As I have intimated on previous occasions in this chapter, I do not want to suggest that only Black adults hold these kinds of constructs. I know from personal experience that many White individuals and communities also exude this form of construction when working with children. For many, working with young children is solely predicated on the notion of helping them to find a personal faith that they can express by means of using the appropriate words, often drawn from the classical lexicon of evangelical Christianity.[59]

It should also be noted that as constructs often converge and overlap, it is probably the case that many of these adults, many of whom would describe themselves as evangelicals, are also working with a binary related notion of 'heaven and hell' and a literal reading of John 14.6 and who can be 'saved'. As I have noted previously in this chapter, for many evangelicals, including those of African Caribbean descent, John 14.6 remains the key Gospel text that spells out the New Testament theological framework for personal salvation in Christ. I believe that other cultural or ethnic groups share this particular construct, although their reasons for doing may be very different. Conservative White Evangelicals, for example, may share a literalist, normative reading of John 14.16, while not having gone through the privations of slavery and colonialism like their Diasporan African counterparts.

The particular dominant construct, which seemed to govern the approach to children's work of these Black Christian adults, was one that sees the acquisition of Christian faith as so necessary that any particular form of pedagogy is valid or justified, so long as the child is guaranteed to accept Christ as their saviour. Half of the Black adults spoke confidently of the need to 'indoctrinate' their children in order that they should come to faith. Some spoke of giving the children 'clear biblical truths' without any sense that the Bible could be read and interpreted in a variety of ways that did not depend upon literalist readings. Nowhere in the conversation was there any talk of the autonomy of the child or the recognition of their 'pre-converted' innate spirituality.[60]

John Hull, the drafting secretary of the highly influential 'Understanding Christian Nurture' is rightly identified as the major innovator in the development of the notion of 'critical openness' in Christian education.[61] Critical openness is a process of nurture and reflection in which the learner is enabled to grow in grace and faith, while being encouraged to be open to plural influences and ideas from other religious traditions and secular philosophies. It is a form of nurture that is open-ended and does not close off or close down other ways of knowing or thinking.[62]

Unlike, say, indoctrination, critical openness preserves and indeed encourages the autonomy of the individual and does not offer a closed system of beliefs and values in opposition to those elements that are considered external to and beyond the fixed parameters of the Christian faith. Clearly, one can deduce that the notion of critical openness takes its cue from many of the frameworks and presuppositions of late nineteenth- and early twentieth-century liberal theology.[63]

In my conversation with these Black Christian adults, I discerned very little in their discourse that could be construed as being sympathetic to Hull's liberal notions of critical openness and the autonomy of the learner.

Rather, it is my belief that the essential nature of Christian faith, not only as the spiritual basis for salvation, but also as a form of oral tradition (to which mention has been made at an earlier juncture in this essay) among African Caribbean people has contributed to an interpretative framework that governs their contemporary practices with children. In effect, this framework believes, to borrow a phrase from (of all people) Malcolm X, 'that by any means necessary' is it essential that their children come to faith.

None of the parents was aware of how their reading strategies of biblical texts, such as Genesis 22 was very much influenced by their personal constructs, which themselves were a product of African Diasporan Christian history.

Re-reading Genesis 22.1–14

Chapter 22 in the Contemporary English Version of the Bible states that 'Some years later God decided to test Abraham, so he spoke to him.' Thus begins this infamous text. The voice of God speaks to Abraham and he, responding, agrees to take his son, Isaac to the land Moriah (verse 2). Abraham gets up early in the morning and begins to chop wood in order to raise a sacrifice to God on an altar (verse 3).

It is interesting to note that nowhere in the text does it say that Abraham sought the opinion of his wife Sarah on this matter. As I have stated in a previous piece of work, there is always an inherent danger in the sole, individual voice responding to what they notionally believe to be the 'voice of God', and acting in potentially destructive ways, later claiming that 'God told them to do it'.[64] The collective and corporate ethic in Christian theology and practice as a means of discerning God's revealed presence and activity, which remains an important theological method within the Methodist tradition in which I work, for example, exists for such dangerous and unrepresentative of occasions as this one![65]

When Isaac asks his father about the seeming absence of a lamb that will be used for the sacrifice, Abraham responds, by stating 'My Son . . . God will provide the lamb' (verse 6). The unmistaken and uncomfortable echoes of substitutionary atonement can be naturally read into this verse. 'God will provide the lamb' can be seen as an early portent of the 'lamb whose death takes away the sin of the world'.[66] Womanist theologians such as Terrell[67] and Williams[68] have critiqued normative atonement theories for their valorizing of the mechanics of suffering, mutilation and death; seemingly as an act of will from a bloodthirsty, patriarchal God.

What is important to note about this text is the seemingly patriarchal collusion between a bloodthirsty male God and a complicit male patriarch. That God should seek to test Abraham using a seemingly 'dispensable' child should invite serious comment; let alone the fact that Abraham does not seem to challenge or question the veracity of the voice and its outlandish command.

While many from a more conservative Evangelical tradition will cry foul at my obvious 'hermeneutic of suspicion' that is clearly in evidence as I read this text, muttering darkly of irreverent and 'unholy' readings of Scripture, I would remind them that if challenging or questioning the voice of God is a wholly illegitimate exercise, then what are we to make of Job, who does that very act and is not reprimanded by God?[69] In actual fact, a close reading of Job shows that it is his so-called friends who give him erroneous advice who are chastised, not Job himself.

If we can allow ourselves the honesty of not sacralizing the text, one cannot but help consider the alacrity with which Abraham appears willing to offer up his son as a sacrifice to God. The frightening aspect of this text is the way in which it is used in much adult Christian education work as a prime exemplar of human obedience. In effect, this becomes a kind of theological and spiritual test case for the kind of sacrificial denying of self that is replete within Christian theology.[70]

This text is clearly one of the most un-child-friendly narratives in the Bible. The fact that it is rarely used when working with children is testament to the dangerous precedents it seems to set around the apparent disposability of children at the whim of God. The dangers of this kind of text are compounded when one considers the constructs that many people carry with them, often subconsciously, when they approach biblical texts. What are the consequences of your interpretation of particular texts if you are already in possession of a set of constructs that do not see children as important agents in their right, but as vessels into which Christian instruction and even indoctrination can be poured at all costs?

In my earlier analysis of a group of Black Christian adults, I argued that by courtesy of history and perhaps also a tendency towards biblical literalism, many of them had constructs that asserted children must come to faith. This sense of unavoidability, inevitably leads to notions of compulsion, which then, as a corollary, find expression in a lack of autonomy or freedom for the child.

It may seem a somewhat wild and speculative form of extrapolation to go from a determination that someone must have faith to notions of punishment and violence, and I do have to confess to not being able to offer any empirical evidence for this hypothesis. But I wonder if this thought is quite so fanciful? If you do work with the notion of children not having any autonomy of their own and that the claims of God (in Christ) are irresistible (it is interesting to note that all the respondents, even the five Methodists[71] were essentially Calvinists) and essential; then it does not take a huge leap of imagination to come to the notion that any form of perceived God-inspired behaviour is acceptable. None of the adults critiqued the Abraham-Isaac abortive-sacrifice narrative. For all of them, it was not unreasonable that God might use such extreme measures to 'teach Abraham and Isaac a lesson'. Some individuals even thought that Isaac's resultant faith may have emerged through this experience of seeing his father's faithfulness to God at first, so to speak!

One can construct a contemporary spin on this thesis by referring to the comments of Bishop Dr Joe Aldred, one of the leading Black Christian figures in Britain, who at the time of writing (2006) is 'Secretary for Minority Ethnic Christian Affairs' for Churches Together in England (CTE, one of the major national ecumenical bodies). In an interview for the *Birmingham Post*, a local newspaper, Aldred is reported to have stated that 'Black Children fail for the want of discipline'. Aldred continues by stating:

> It started a long time ago with all the politically correct stuff about the degree to which parents should control children. In a Caribbean home a good slap on the backside for a child that is misbehaving is seen as nothing wrong. If you do it now, you get reported to the police.[72]

In fairness to my colleague, I must stress that in citing his words I am in no way inferring that Aldred in any sense condones violence against Black children. Indeed, one can cite his recent work in challenging the unrepresentative practices of some Black churches, predominantly in London, in terms of their anti-Christian behaviour to children who are alleged to be demon-possessed.[73]

While I do not believe that Aldred accepts any notion of the acceptability of abusing children in the name of exorcism, I am bound to remark that his easy assumption that the lack of corporal punishment leads to deteriorating academic performance, aside from being a very reactionary and bizarre contention, nonetheless, conforms to the construct I have delineated thus far. The necessity of disciplining children using physical force remains acceptable if you possess a construct that believes that children possess limited agency and that any inferences that might accrue from such actions are more than compensated for if one believes that the resultant learning (particularly in terms of Christian faith) is paramount and a 'price worth paying'.

Aldred assumes that the potentially confused messages we potentially send out to children when we use physical forms of restraint and correction are justifiable if they lead to regulated behaviour and any resultant learning. This view, of course, is predicated on the non-existent evidence that there is any causal link between corporal punishment and learning.

I should stress once again, that I am addressing my reflections to African Caribbean Christian adults and children as a focus for my more generic concerns for how all Christian communities engage with children. I reject any notion that there are systemic pathological forms of behaviour within Black communities whether in Britain, or the Caribbean and North America that are not found in other communities or societies.

Conclusion

It is my belief that particular constructs affect how we engage with and interpret the Bible. This in turn will effect how we then engage with children, in terms of what forms of behaviour are seen as acceptable, normative or permissible. This chapter attempts to highlight the nature of the 'problem'. Clearly, more work needs to be done in this area in order to assess how and with what strategies Christian adults can be enabled to adopt alternative constructs, which will lead to different frameworks for reading the Bible. It is my fervent hope that no Christian adult will ever justify any form of abuse (be it physical or spiritual) even if it is writ large in Holy Scripture. As Kelly reminds, we are not hostages to our past. The future can be remade! Let us have faith in the light of the Spirit of God to banish the darkness of bad practice that so often litters our past. The light awaits! Let us bask in the light!

Appendix

GETTING TO KNOW YOURSELF

* The following sheet has been designed to help you reflect upon the work you do as a Christian educator working with children, or a minister who has pastoral charge of a church in which the ministry amongst and with children is a major concern. There are no right and wrong answers, and this exercise is not designed to make anyone feel inadequate or insecure. It is most helpful if you can be honest with yourself, and to think deeply about your own thoughts and feelings.

* Take your time with the questions. You will not complete the form in the time we have available today. Do what you can now, but go home and reflect further and complete the form in your own time.

---

1 2 3 4 5 6 7 8 9 10 11 12 13 14 15 16 17 18 19 20

1 Above, there is a line from 1 to 20. This line represents a scale of competencies. At no. 20 there is the greatest Christian educator the world has ever seen (excluding Jesus of course). This person is a myth. They do not exist! On a separate piece of paper write

down some of the qualities you feel this mythical person would possess. What would they be like? How would they work? What would be the end product with the children? (What would they be like and what will they have learnt, having been in the presence of this brilliant worker?)

2 Look again at the same line. No. 1 represents the worst Christian educator of all time. Similar to question 1, write down some of the terrible qualities that person would have. What would they be like? How would they work? What would be the end product with the children?

3 Where would you put yourself on the above scale? (Think about how you work? Compare yourself with the two models above.)

4 What do you consider to be your best quality? (E.g. patience, understanding, a good communicator, well organized, enthusiasm, a good listener, keeping discipline, easy going?)

5 What skill/ability/quality do you feel you would need to possess in order to progress further up the line above?

6 What are the 4 main reasons why you carry out the role you do?

6a Of the 4 reasons you have given, which one is the most important? Why?

7 What is your ultimate aim when working with the children in your charge?

7a Assuming your ultimate aim is 20 on the scale above, where would you say the work you do in reality reaches on the scale?

7b Think of one thing you could do, that might raise your second score (7b) further up the scale towards your ultimate aim?

8 The mythical worker knows his/her children intimately, and they score 20. On the scale above, how well do you know your children in comparison? What score would you give yourself? (Think back to the second exercise, 'Do you know this child?')

9 What makes you continue with this role/responsibility?

10 When was the last occasion, whilst undertaking your role/job, you experienced a great sense of joy/happiness/achievement? What caused you to feel this way? How did it affect you?

Notes

1 See James H. Cone, *A Black Theology of Liberation*, Maryknoll, NY, Orbis, 1986.

2 See Kwok Pui-Lan, *Postcolonial Imagination and Feminist Theology*, Louisville, KY, Westminster John Knox, 2005.

3 For an imaginative and incisive exploration of the shared and complex nature of what it means to be a human being see Dwight N. Hopkins, *Race, Culture and Religion*, Minneapolis, Fortress Press, 2005.

4 See Mike Phillips and Trevor Phillips, *Windrush: The Irresistible Rise of Multi-Racial Britain*, London, HarperCollins, 1999.

5 See Emmanuel Y. Lartey, *In Living Colour: An Intercultural Approach to Pastoral Care and Counselling*, London, Cassell, 1997, pp. 9–18.

6 See 'Introduction' in Anthony G. Reddie, *Black Theology in Transatlantic Dialogue: Inside Looking Out, Outside Looking In*, New York, Palgrave Macmillan, 2006.

7 See Anthony Reddie, *Growing into Hope: Christian Education for Multi-ethnic Churches*, vols 1 and 2, Peterborough, Methodist Publishing House, 1998; Robert Beckford, *Dread and Pentecostal*, London, SPCK, 2000.

8 Like the editor of this text, the collective and corporate nature of Methodist theological method has shaped my own particular approach to the doing of theology. See Angela Shier-Jones, *A Work In Progress: Methodists Doing Theology*, Peterborough, Epworth, 2005. See also Anthony G. Reddie, *Dramatizing Theologies: A Participative Approach to Black God-Talk*, London, Equinox, 2006.

9 See Dwight N. Hopkins, *Down, Up and Over: Slave Religion and Black Theology*, Minneapolis, Fortress Press, 2000, pp. 11–36.

10 See Emmanuel C. Eze, *Race and the Enlightenment*, Boston, MA, Blackwell, 1997.

11 See Dwight N. Hopkins, *Being Human: Race, Culture and Religion*, Minneapolis, Fortress Press, 2005, pp. 113–60.

12 See Anthony B. Pinn, *Terror and Triumph: The Nature of Black Religion*, Minneapolis, Fortress Press, 2003, pp. 1–25.

13 See Anne H. Pinn and Anthony B. Pinn, *Fortress Introduction To Black Church History*, Minneapolis, Fortress Press, 2002, pp. 6–8.

14 See Sylvester A. Johnson, *The Myth of Ham in Nineteenth-Century American Christianity: Race, Heathens and the People of God*, New York, Palgrave Macmillan, 2004.

15 Henry H. Mitchell, *Black Church Beginnings: The Long-Hidden Realities of the First Years*, Grand Rapids, MI and Cambridge, UK, Wm B. Eerdmans, 2004, pp. 24–45.

16 See Pinn and Pinn, *Fortress Introduction To Black Church History*, pp. 6–8.

17 Mitchell, *Black Church Beginnings*, pp. 8–45.

18 This research project, which was given the title of the 'Birmingham Initiative', was the brainchild of the Revd Christopher Hughes Smith, the then General Secretary of the Methodist Church in Great Britain's Division of Education and Youth. Having formerly been a minister and District Chairman in Birmingham, he was aware of the deficiencies in the existing Christian education work sponsored by the Methodist Church among Black children. In order to assess the effectiveness of the existing work and to create a mechanism that might attempt to develop a hypothesis for the Christian education of Black children in Britain, funds were obtained to create a research project to that end.

19 See Anthony G. Reddie, *Nobodies to Somebodies: A Practical Theology for Education and Liberation*, Peterborough, Epworth, 2003.

20 See Anthony G. Reddie, *Faith, Stories and The Experience of Black Elders: Singing The Lord's Song in a Strange Land*, London, Jessica Kingsley, 2001.

21 Grant Shockley, 'From Emancipation to transformation to consummation: A Black perspective' in Marlene Mayr (ed.), *Does the Church Really Want RE?*, Birmingham, AL, Religious Education Press, 1989, p. 236.

22 Jerome W. Berryman, *Godly Play: An Imaginative Approach to Religious Education*, Minneapolis, Augsburg, 1991, p. 64.

23 I began my doctorate a few years after Robert Beckford and was very much of the first generation of Black theological scholars in Britain. For an exploration of the development of Black theology in Britain, See Anthony G. Reddie, *Black Theology in Transatlantic Dialogue*, New York, Palgrave Macmillan, 2006.

24 See Robert E. Hood, *Must God Remain Greek?: Afro-Cultures and God-Talk*, Minneapolis, Fortress Press, 1990. See also Gay L. Byron, *Symbolic Blackness and Ethnic Difference in Early Christian Literature* New York, Routledge, 2002.

25 See Kenneth Cracknell, *Our Doctrines: Methodist Theology as Classical Christianity*, Calver, Cliff College Publishing, 1998.

26 Miguel A. De La Torre, 'Scripture', in Miguel A. De La Torree (ed.), *Handbook of US Theologies of Liberation*, St Louis, Chalice Press, 2004, pp. 85.

27 De La Torre, '*Scripture*', p. 86.

28 De La Torre, '*Scripture*', pp. 85–6.

29 De La Torre, '*Scripture*', p. 85.

30 See Renita J. Weems, *Battered Love: Marriage, Sex, and Violence in the Hebrew Prophets*, Minneapolis, Fortress Press, 1995.

31 See Paul Ballard and John Pritchard, *Practical Theology in Action: Christian Thinking in The Service of the Church and Society*, London, SPCK, 1996.

32 See Duncan B. Forrester, *Truthful Action: Explorations in Practical Theology*, Edinburgh: T&T Clark, 2000.

33 Elaine L. Graham, *Transforming Practice: Pastoral Theology in Age of Uncertainty*, Eugene, Oregon, Wipf and Stock, 2002.

34 See George A. Kelly, *The Psychology of Personal Constructs*, New York, Norton, 1955.

35 Those who would assert this argument have often drawn their ideas from the American Practical theologian James Fowler. Fowler's model of 'Faith Development Theory', while not asserting that Christian faith is a construct, does, nevertheless, understand faith as generic to all human being (and that Christian faith is not qualitatively different from other modes of faith construction) and is best understood not as revelation but as a human meaning-making device. See James W. Fowler *Stages of Faith*, San Francisco, Harper, 1991.

36 See James W. Fowler, Friedrich Schweitzer and Karl Ernst Nipkow (eds),

Stages of Faith and Religious Judgement, Birmingham, AL, Religious Education Press, 1991.

37 See William R. Jones, *Is God A White Racist?*, Boston, Beacon Press, 1973.

38 See Anthony B. Pinn, *Why Lord?: Suffering and Evil in Black Theology*, New York, Continuum, 1995.

39 William R. Jones, *Is God A White Racist?*, pp. 4–6.

40 For a number of years there was a small research group at the University of Birmingham School of Education, of which I was a member, who were attempting to look at the theological imperatives of PCP and its usage in practical theology and Christian ministry. The group was chaired by Professor John M. Hull, who was then Professor of Religious Education in the School of Education at the University of Birmingham. The group was disbanded a number of years ago, although some of the scholars in that group have utilized PCP in their doctoral theses. See Peter Hammersley *Adult learning problems and the experience of loss: A study of religious rigidity* (unpublished PhD thesis, the School of Education, The University of Birmingham, 1997). See also Howard Worsley *The inner-child as a resource to adult faith development (Faith in Transition)* (unpublished PhD thesis, the School of Education, The University of Birmingham, 1999).

41 For the definitive rendering of PCP, see George A. Kelly, *The Psychology of Personal Constructs*, New York, Norton, 1955. Practical, worked examples of PCP can be found in P. Dalton and G. A. Dunnett, *A Psychology for Living*, Chichester, J. Wiley, 1992; A. Landfield and F. R. Epting, *Personal Construct Psychology*, New York, Human Sciences Press, 1987; P. Reason (ed.) *Human Inquiry in Action: Developments in New Paradigm Research*, London, Sage, 1988; P. Salmon, *Psychology for Teachers: An Alternative Approach*, London, Hutchinson, 1988; D. Schon, *The Reflective Practitioner*, New York, Basic Books, 1983.

42 See Salmon, *Psychology for Teachers: An Alternative Approach*.

43 See Salmon, *Psychology for Teachers: An Alternative Approach*.

44 See Phyllis Trible, *Texts of Terror: Literary-Feminist Readings of Biblical Narratives*, London: SCM Press, 1992.

45 John Sutcliffe (ed.), *Tuesday's Child: A Reader for Christian Educators*, Birmingham: Christian Education, 2001, pp. 46–71.

46 See Ronald Goldman, *Readiness for Religion*, London, Routledge & Kegan Paul, 1965.

47 Goldman, *Readiness for Religion*, pp. 3–39.

48 Goldman, *Readiness for Religion*, p. 8.

49 See Anthony B. Pinn, *Terror and Triumph: The Nature of Black Religion*, Minneapolis, Fortress Press, 2003, pp. 81–156.

50 See Pinn, *Terror and Triumph*, 2003.

51 See Grant Shockley, 'Historical Perspectives' in Charles R. Foster and Grant S. Shockley (eds), *Working With Black Youth: Opportunities for Christian Ministry*, Nashville, Tenn., Abingdon, 1989, pp. 9–29.

52 Janice Hale, 'The Transmission of Faith to Young African American Children', in Randall C. Bailey and Jacquelyn Grant (eds), *The Recovery of*

Black Presence, Nashville, Tenn., Abingdon Press, 1995, p. 207.

53 Colleen Birchett, 'A history of Religious education in the Black Church' in Donald B. Rogers (ed.), *Urban Church Education*, Birmingham, AL: Religious Education Press, 1989, pp. 76.

54 The term 'Black Church' features prominently in the writings of many Black Christian educators. The term is a generic one, used to described particular faith communities in which Black leadership, culture, traditions, experience and spirituality represent the norm, and from which White, Anglo-Saxon traditions and expressions are absent. These churches are termed 'generic', because unlike in Britain, they are not confined to any one denominational or theological slant. (In Britain, the Black church is still largely synonymous with evangelical, Black majority Pentecostalism.) These churches cut across the whole spectrum of church affiliation and the multiplicity of settings in which Black life is experienced. The development of the 'Black Church' in the United States of America grew out of the racism of the established churches of White, European origin. The worshipping life of these churches displayed discriminatory practices, forcing Black people to leave in order to form their own churches. The denominations most commonly identified with the Black Church are The African Methodist Episcopal Church (AME), the African Methodist Episcopal Zion Church (AMEZ), The Christian Methodist church (CME), The National Baptist Convention Incorporated, The National Baptist Convention of America and The Progressive Baptist Convention. For further details see E. Franklin Frazier, *The Negro Church in America*, New York, Shocken Books, 1964. See also Anne H. Pinn and Anthony B. Pinn, *Black Church History*, Minneapolis, Fortress Press, 2003.

55 Grant S. Shockley, 'From Emancipation to Transformation to Consummation: A Black Perspective' in Marlene Mayr (ed.), *Does The Church Really Want Religious Education?*, Birmingham, AL, Religious Education Press, 1988, pp. 244–6.

56 All the adults were Black African Caribbean Christians. Of the 12, 5 were Methodist, 3 were Anglican and 4 might be broadly described as Pentecostal. Their ages ranged from mid-30s through to early 60s. The group was not chosen under any scientific method, such as random sampling. All 12 were known to me from my previous work as a Christian educator and researcher back in the 1990s. I met with the group once and asked them to go through the questions on the 'Getting to Know Yourself' document.

57 It should be noted that a sample of 12 adults is clearly not a sufficiently representative number on which to construct any overarching generalizations as to the reliability of this research in empirical terms. Rather, I want to suggest that this number and the research of which it is a part is indicative of a general phenomenon that might explain Black hermeneutics in terms of their reading of the Bible as it pertains to children.

58 See *The Child in the Church*, London, British Council of Churches, 1976. See also *Understanding Christian Nurture*, London, British Council of Churches, 1981.

59 For an example of this construction of faith and the idiom I have in mind see 'Christian Jargon' in Anthony G. Reddie, *Acting in Solidarity: Reflections*

in Critical Christianity, London, Darton, Longman & Todd, 2005, pp. 59–67.

60 See David Hay with Rebecca Nye, *The Spirit of the Child*, London, Jessica Kingsley, 2006. See also Jerome Berryman, *Godly Play: An Imaginative Approach to Religious Education*, Minneapolis, Augsburg Press, 1991.

61 *Understanding Christian Nurture*, pp. 4–31.

62 See John Hull, 'Critical Openness in Christian Nurture', Jeff Astley and Leslie Francis (eds), *Critical Perspectives on Christian Education*, Leominster, Gracewing, 1994, pp. 251–75.

63 Hull, 'Critical Openness in Christian Nurture', pp. 251–75.

64 See Reddie, *Acting in Solidarity*, p. 19.

65 See Angela Shier-Jones 'Conferring as Theological Method' in Clive Marsh, Brian Beck, Angela Shier-Jones and Helen Wareing (eds), *Unmasking Methodist Theology*, London, Continuum, 2004, pp. 82–94.

66 See 'Holy Communion For The Easter Season' in *The Methodist Worship Book*, Peterborough, Methodist Publishing House, 1999, pp. 162.

67 See JoAnne Marie Terrell, *Power in the Blood?: The Cross in the African American Experience*, Maryknoll, NY, Orbis, 1998, pp. 17–34.

68 Delores Williams, *Sisters in the Wilderness: The Challenge of Womanist God-Talk*, Maryknoll, NY, Orbis, 1993, pp. 161–7.

69 See Anthony G. Reddie, *Acting in Solidarity*, pp. 22–30.

70 It is worth noting the traditional wording of the 'Methodist Covenant Service' that states 'I am no longer my own but yours. Put me to what you will, rank me with whom you will; put me to doing, put me to suffering, let me be employed for you or laid aside from you . . . I wholeheartedly yield all things to your pleasure and disposal.' Presumably, the last phrase could mean offering up a child for the pleasure and disposal of God? See *The Methodist Worship Book*, Peterborough, Methodist Publishing House, 1999, pp. 290.

71 I make particular note that for Methodists 'Arminianism' (the doctrine that all people can be saved not only those who are predestined by God; a doctrine that asserts the central importance of 'free will') which is antithetical to Calvinistic notions of election, has been one of the defining hallmarks of Methodist theology. See Kenneth Cracknell, *Our Doctrines: Methodist theology as Classical Christianity*, Calver, Cliff College Publishing, 1998.

72 *Birmingham Post*, 31 March 2004. From http://www.corpun.com/uks00403.htm

73 See http://www.wwrn.org/article.php?idd=17775&sec=39&cont=5 for an example of Aldred's leadership on this issue in his capacity as the 'Chair of The Council of Black-Led Churches'.

So he went in to his father, and said, 'My father'; and he said, 'Here I am; who are you, my son?' Jacob said to his father, 'I am Esau your firstborn. I have done as you told me; now sit up and eat of my game, so that you may bless me.' But Isaac said to his son, 'How is it that you have found it so quickly, my son?' He answered, 'Because the LORD your God granted me success.' Then Isaac said to Jacob, 'Come near, that I may feel you, my son, to know whether you are really my son Esau or not.' So Jacob went up to his father Isaac, who felt him and said, 'The voice is Jacob's voice, but the hands are the hands of Esau.' He did not recognize him, because his hands were hairy like his brother Esau's hands; so he blessed him. He said, 'Are you really my son Esau?' He answered, 'I am.'

Genesis 27.18–24

6. Maturity, Delinquency and Rebellion

SHERYL ANDERSON

Introduction

> I would there were no age between sixteen and
> three-and-twenty, or that youth would sleep out the
> rest; for there is nothing in the between but
> getting wenches with child, wronging the ancientry,
> stealing, fighting . . .[1]

In this essay I want to explore some of the theological issues raised by what appears to be a particular human tendency for rebellion and defiance, which typically occurs as our children make the transition from childhood to adulthood. Traditionally, such behaviour has been seen as evidence for the inherent sinfulness of humanity, the inevitable consequence of the disobedience of Adam and Eve when they ate of the fruit of the tree of knowledge of good and evil. Such a view is exacerbated by the fact that this life stage is distinguished by the onset of puberty, so the link between rebellion and sexual activity is readily established. The behaviour of young people, with their disobedient and dissolute ways, is experienced by adults as threatening, dangerous and in need of control. It is popularly believed that this view is firmly supported by Scripture, especially the Book of Proverbs. Even those who have never read the Bible are able to quote, 'Spare the rod and spoil the child'[2] in order to justify the discipline and punishment that is seen as necessary to keep the young on the straight and narrow; although probably few would recommend the somewhat extreme measures recommended in the book Deuteronomy which prescribes the death penalty for incorrigible sons.

> If someone has a stubborn and rebellious son who will not obey his father and mother, who does not heed them when they discipline him, then his father and his mother shall take hold of him and bring him out to the elders of his town at the gate of that place. They shall say to the elders of his town, 'This son of ours is stubborn and rebellious. He will not obey us. He is a glutton and a drunkard.' Then all the men of the town shall stone him to death. So you shall purge the evil from your midst; and all Israel will hear, and be afraid.
>
> Deuteronomy 21.18–21

Is it the case, however, that Scripture upholds this conformist view? Does the Bible consistently and actively favour obedience and chastity over and against wilfulness and corruption? I want to suggest that it does not, and that actually Scripture understands anti-social and rebellious behaviour in a somewhat different way. I further want to suggest that this alternative view may in fact be helpful to us if we are seeking to engage in meaningful discourse with the secular views of childhood and adolescence offered by twenty-first-century post-modern western culture.

In the beginning

The Hebrew Scriptures – Genesis

The Book of Genesis is an extraordinary account of the origin of the world and of the human race, of humanity's struggle with suffering and sin, and of the history of the early ancestors of the Israelites. It attempts to give an account of the human condition and, by inference, of the God who brings all things into being.

In the second, older, narrative of the creation story (Genesis 2.4b—3.24), the woman succumbs to the temptation offered by the serpent to eat of the tree of the knowledge of good and evil, and gives some of the fruit to her husband, who is with her. The consequence of this action is that, 'The eyes of both were opened and they knew that they were naked' (Genesis 3.7). According to the traditional western interpretation of the episode, this is how sin and death enter an otherwise perfect world. The gullible woman – a secondary and derivative creation – is lured by the wily serpent (subsequently identified as the

Devil) and intentionally goes against an express instruction from God and eats from the tree. The man is complicit in this action, although not the actual instigator of it. However, he makes matters much worse by blaming first the woman and then God for the situation. On the traditional reading, the primary sin is one of disobedience; the woman deliberately chooses to take the fruit from the tree and the man deliberately chooses to take the fruit from the woman. The secondary sin is that of an awareness of sexuality; because the man and the woman now possess the knowledge of good and evil, they are able to perceive that they are naked. The notes in the *New Jerusalem Bible*, for example, suggest that Genesis 3.7 is to be understood as, 'The arousal of lust, as first manifestation of disorder introduced into the harmony of creation.'[3] Disobedience therefore, leads to exposure, guilt and shame.

However, an alternative interpretation might suggest that actually Adam and Eve were set up. The text states that the serpent was *arum* – shrewd, subtle, clever – more so than any other wild animal. The serpent enquires about God's interdiction, and the woman replies correctly that she and the man are forbidden to eat, or even touch (her own embellishment) the fruit of the tree in the middle of the garden, or they will die. The serpent says this is not so, they will not die, which turns out to be the case. For as we subsequently discover, the serpent tells more of the truth than God does. Is the serpent challenging the veracity of God's statement because he believes God to be a liar, or does the serpent know something about the situation, or more importantly about God, that is hidden from the woman and the man and, at this stage, from the reader? It appears that God may have an ulterior motive, one that the serpent is aware of.

Notice what influences the woman's decision: the tree is good for food, it is a delight to the eyes, and it will make one wise: nourishment for the body, the soul and the intellect. Contrary to her later claim, the woman is not tempted by the serpent but by the fruit. She is the inquisitive one, the seeker of understanding, the tester of limits; her curiosity overcomes the divine prohibition and she takes the fruit and eats it.

In the general thrust of the story, we are not surprised. As many a parent will testify, the minute you show something to a child and tell them they cannot have it, you are asking for trouble. In the tradition of all cultures, commands such as Genesis 2.17 exist to be broken; this is the whole point of the story. Out of curiosity, the woman takes the risk and chooses self-awareness and knowledge, over obedience and innocence. Thus she demonstrates what is arguably the epitome of being human. One could even speculate that it is all part of God's intention; human beings have to be put in a position where they can freely choose to exercise free will.

On the traditional reading of the text, this is the defining moment in which humanity chooses to disobey the command of God, and has been suffering the consequences ever since. It could, as Paul Tillich might express it, simply seek to describe the separation of the finite being from the infinite ground of all being. Alternatively, it could be seen as a story that seeks to explain the process that we all go through, of developmentally appropriate differentiation until we reach maturity. As human beings grow up they are supposed to accept cognition, choice, and moral responsibility, so what we have here is the development of independence at the expense of innocence. Interestingly, there is Hebrew word play at work in the text, for the word for naked is *arummim*. Humanity becomes more serpent-like (*arum*) as things previously hidden become exposed (*arummim*). However, being revealed brings with it the possibility of revelation. It cost us our innocence, but there is a sense of something gained as well. Almost as though rebellion is a part of God's nature.

Part of the basis for this view is what happens throughout the rest of Genesis, especially the stories of the patriarchs. Israel is founded on dubious, marginalized characters, applauded for their ingenuity, resourcefulness, and downright cunning – their *arum*. So many of the ancestors of Israel demonstrate an ability to trick their way into what they want or need, it is clear that compliant obedience is not a necessary qualification for success. Lack of power or the requirements of culture and tradition are no barrier to achieving the purposes of God or of the individual. In some senses, delinquency pays.

Much of the first part of Genesis is about choice and promise. Humanity chooses autonomy and has to learn to live with the consequences. God chooses one offering over another, which prompts a jealous rage that ends in murder. As a result, God protects the murderer with the promise of retribution on any who should harm him. God later chooses to destroy all life on earth, however, God also promises to safeguard Noah and makes a long-term pledge of protection to him and his descendents that becomes the basis for the covenant relationship. This relationship in itself is one of choice and promise. In Genesis 17.7 God says to Abraham, 'I will establish my covenant between me and you, and your offspring after you throughout their generations, for an everlasting covenant, to be God to you and to your offspring after you.' Children are a central feature of this covenant. God promises to bless Abraham and to make of him a great nation, by giving him descendants. However, the actual line of succession is fraught with difficulty. As the book progresses, a theme develops; individuals in families act in ways that clearly oppose the accepted moral code or social convention. More interestingly, God seems to collude with this behaviour, as it enables God's promises to be fulfilled.

Cain and Abel, Ishmael and Isaac, Esau and Jacob, Leah and Rachel: the book of Genesis contains a series of stories about sibling rivalry in which the younger child is preferred to the elder, and the consequence of that preference is behaviour that is at best irresponsible and anti-social, and at worst downright criminal.

What makes the narrative of Cain and Abel particularly shocking is that it is God who is doing the favouring. For reasons that are unclear, God prefers the offering of the younger son, Abel (a shepherd) to that of the older son, Cain (a farmer), and appears annoyed at Cain's fury and sense of rejection – an attitude guaranteed to increase the friction between the brothers. Following the murder, Cain is condemned to a hand to mouth existence of nomadic exile, and this establishes a pattern. In the case of Ishmael and Isaac: despite the fact that Sarah has God's promise that it is through her son Isaac that the covenant will be fulfilled, she is jealous of Hagar and Ishmael, and requests Abraham to banish them. It seems that God is willing to collude with this behaviour and encourages Abraham to acquiesce to her demands. According to Genesis 16.12 Ishmael is predicted to be 'a wild ass of a man, with his hand against everyone, and everyone's hand against him; and he shall live at odds with all his kin.' Again the older son is doomed to develop what could be described as extreme antisocial behaviour, although in 17.20, there appears to be some future allowed for Ishmael, as he is destined to become the father of twelve North Arabian tribes.

Similarly with Esau and Jacob, the case of the feuding twins. Isaac clearly prefers Esau, who is a hunter and the eldest, but Rebekah prefers Jacob, who is a quiet man, and a shepherd who can cook! Esau, with the casual arrogance of the entitled, has no regard for his birthright and sells it to Jacob for some red lentil stew, 'a mess of pottage'! To make matters worse, Rebekah conspires with Jacob to obtain Isaac's blessing by fraud. Basically, Jacob lies, cheats and steals the blessing that is rightfully Esau's. He compounds the lie by implicating God in the conspiracy (27.20), which is surely tantamount to blasphemy. Nevertheless, the narrative implies admiration, if not actual approval, for Jacob's cunning. Furthermore, Esau and his descendents are condemned to a future of subjection to Jacob and his descendents, and to survive as outlaws, through a bandit's life of plunder (27.40). By way of manipulation and deceit, Jacob gets the inheritance – a double portion, and the blessing – prosperity and dominion. Naïve interpretations of the story try to exonerate Jacob and make Esau the bad son and Jacob the good son; but the original writer was more sophisticated than that. Scholars suggest he (and it almost certainly was a he) wanted to offer a story that reflected and explained the political and social realities of the world that he inhabited. Later I will suggest that it also reflects and explains the realities of ordinary family life and that, in such circumstances of favouritism, rebellion and delinquency are almost inevitable, but not necessarily bad. Delinquents are invariably disadvantaged people, which can make them skilful, courageous and ingenious, as well as scheming liars.

Most of the siblings recorded in Genesis are brothers, with the notable exception of Rachel and Leah. In this instance Jacob prefers Rachel – interestingly also a shepherd – to Leah her elder sister. Jacob falls in love with Rachel, and agrees to work for Laban, her father, for seven years in order to marry her. However, Laban tricks Jacob into marrying Leah before Rachel, with the excuse that the custom in Haran is for elder daughters to marry first. Jacob loves Rachel more than he loves Leah, so God compensates Leah for Jacob's lack of favour by providing her with sons. There then follows intense sexual rivalry between the two women (including the involvement of their maidservants), which is acted out through the naming of the children. These titles are used to explain the origins of the ancestors of the tribes of Israel. Eventually Rachel bears Jacob a son, Joseph, and subsequently Benjamin (the birth of whom kills her). Joseph becomes the favoured son of Jacob, and thereby hangs another tale.

The arrangement for the handing on of inheritance to sons is significant. The authors of Genesis need to account for why the patriarchal line is passed on through sons other than the firstborn. The fact is that in Genesis, no hero worth his salt is born under usual circumstances. Reflecting on these passages, writers often comment that God does seem to choose the most unlikely people for God's service. This does seem to somewhat understate the case. The founders of Israel are in fact conniving, deviant, law-breakers. They come from families that in this day and age would be referred to social services as dysfunctional and delinquent. Even Joseph, who is portrayed as morally superior, is not above deception and exploiting his power to frighten his siblings. Yet God keeps on choosing them, and the perversity of this is not lost on the narrators of Genesis.

There is an interesting, final touch. In chapter 48, as Jacob lies ill, Joseph brings to him his two sons, Manasseh and Ephraim, to be adopted and to receive a blessing. This meeting is very carefully described in the text. Manasseh, the elder, is presented to Jacob's right hand and Ephraim, the younger, to Jacob's left; but Jacob crosses his hands and places his right on the younger boy and his left on the firstborn. Joseph is displeased and tries to correct this saying, 'Not so my father! Since this one is the firstborn, put your right hand on his head' (48.18). It is as though the narrator wants to make quite sure that the reader gets the point. Being the firstborn matters, it gives superior status and entitles one to a double portion of the inheritance. Despite all the evidence in the whole of the preceding 47 chapters, a preference for the younger over the firstborn is highly irregular and so when it happens it happens for a purpose.

Scholars have long since agreed that Genesis – in fact the whole of the Pentateuch – is the result of several different sources of traditional narrative being woven together by one or more redactors. At least four strands are identified, and they each have particular emphases and use of language; they each also have a particular model of God. It is not possible to go into the detail here, but in editing the strands, the redactor(s) enable the stories to become more than the sum of their parts. By weaving these strands together, Genesis produces a remarkable model of God, and because Genesis is the first book in the Bible and because it is about foundational things, that model is profoundly influential.

The combination of two strands, in Genesis 1 and Genesis 3, has a remarkable effect. The story of the Garden of Eden never suggests that humanity is made in God's image, but because the other (Priestly) story comes first the reader knows that there is something special and different about humanity that is of God, that God has intentionally put there. It is no wonder then that humans are readily persuaded by the news from the serpent that, 'when you eat of it your eyes shall be opened and you will be like God, knowing good and evil' (Genesis 3.5).

There is a tension between justice and mercy evident in Genesis, as the different traditions emphasize different aspects of the deity. The Priestly tradition never once uses the words mercy, or grace or repentance and God is depicted as a cosmic and transcendent being meting out remote justice. God commands and it happens. According to this view, God is orderly and controlling: you get what you deserve; obedience is rewarded, transgression is punished. There is no possibility of throwing oneself on the mercy of the divine judge. The other traditions, however, are completely the opposite. God is personal and persuadable: hand-making humanity from the dust of the earth, walking in the garden in the cool of the evening, debating with Abraham over the fate of the cities of Sodom and Gomorrah. God is gracious and merciful; wrongdoing can be forgiven, repentance is possible. The words mercy, grace and repentance occur about 70 times in these strands. God is also faithful and long suffering. For example, in Exodus 34.6–7 God is speaking:

> The LORD, the LORD, a God merciful and gracious, slow to anger, and abounding in steadfast love and faithfulness, keeping steadfast love for the thousandth generation, forgiving iniquity and transgression and sin, yet by no means clearing the guilty, but visiting the iniquity of the parents upon the children and the children's children, to the third and fourth generation.

Historically, for all sorts of cultural, psychological, political and social reasons, the Priestly model of God seems to hold sway in our minds, over the alternatives. Yet the redactor combines the traditions in such a way that God is both universal and personal, and justice and mercy are held in balance in such a way as to create a new understanding of God that resonates both theologically and socially. I imagine that virtually all parents can identify with the need for compassion, sympathy, and forgiveness on the one hand, and justice, discipline, and control on the other – in relation to the raising of children. According to the Hebrew Bible, the stick and the carrot as a means of developing character are resources equally available to God. God is depicted as loving and faithful, but sometimes angry. In fact God is as torn as any loving parent, seeking to raise their children into decent, responsible adulthood.

Adam and Eve's disobedience of God mirrors our children's disobedience of us as parents. Like God we are fearful that they will fall outside of our direct control by eating of the tree, by acquiring knowledge before they have the maturity to use it wisely. Similarly, the preference of the younger over the older, against the natural order of things, provokes situations in which rebellion and delinquent behaviour are inevitable. Nevertheless, parents do have preferences, and even if we do not, our children think that we do, with similar consequences. Parents can also collude with their offspring's antisocial behaviour. Just like God, we can sometimes see that, if only they would come to their senses, the future lies more positively in the hands of our clever, devious, resourceful, disobedient, children, than in those of our well-behaved, boring, over-adapted ones.

Is now

Sin and adolescence

There are those who would argue that adolescence is a late twentieth-century phenomenon, and the whole notion of teenage rebelliousness and disobedience a modern, post-World War II invention. In truth, the concept of childhood itself appears to be a cultural construct that is subject to change and is relative to time and place. For this reason, critics argue, Scripture, which is so culturally distant from where we are today, is the last source to which we should turn for help in dealing with our errant youngsters.

It appears, however, that from the earliest of times societies have struggled to manage the behaviour of the young, particularly young men.

> I see no hope for the future of our people if they are dependent on the frivolous youth of today, for certainly all youth are reckless beyond words.
>
> When I was a boy, we were taught to be discrete and respectful of elders, but the present youth are exceedingly wise and impatient of restraint.[4]

Even Augustine of Hippo (AD 354–415) recounts activities that can be seen as typically adolescent antisocial behaviour. In the *Confessions*[5] he records, with shame, that when he was 16 he joined his peers in boasting about sexual exploits, and engaged in petty pilfering (some pears from a neighbours garden) simply for the excitement of it, and for the sense of bonding to his peers and belonging to the group.

> My pleasure in it was not what I stole but, rather, the act of stealing. Nor would I have enjoyed doing it alone – indeed I would not have done it! O friendship all unfriendly! You strange seducer of the soul, who hungers for mischief . . . so that, when they say 'Let's go, let's do it,' we are ashamed not to be shameless.[6]

Augustine viewed children as inferior, and believed that adults must break a child's blind and sometimes belligerent will to prepare the way for the manifestations of God's grace. However, he did understand childhood as a progression towards maturity; that as children grow physically, so they also assume greater accountability for their actions. Augustine had an interesting view of adolescence, which for him began at puberty and brought with it not only increasing moral accountability but also an increasing sense of guilt. After recounting the exploit of the theft of pears, Augustine berates himself with a list of vices, which he perceives as sinning just for the sake of it. The increasing accountability of adolescence therefore, is evidenced by the increasing willingness of young people to challenge accepted norms, simply because it is human nature to do so. For Augustine, human nature is incorrigibly corrupt and fallen, part of a single mass of sinning that envelopes all the descendents of Adam.

According to Martha Ellen Stortz,[7] Augustine argued this point on the basis of Romans 5.12. In his version of the Latin text, Adam's sin penetrated [*intrare*] the world. For Augustine, the word *intrare* had profound significance because of its sexual connotations. The fact that Adam and Eve had covered their genitals with fig leaves after they had eaten the fruit was more than enough evidence. Here lies the root of original sin. No wonder that adolescence, with all its explosion of sexuality, is seen as a sinister, frightening and unpredictable condition, which has to be kept strictly under control.

The legacy of Augustine lives on. Although today we would understand the narcissism of infants differently and, as Methodists, would balk at the notion of a human nature so inexorably turned toward corruption that only through baptism can forgiveness of sin be attained; still the wilful misbehaviour of youth encourages theology, not to mention social policy, to adopt a punitive and controlling attitude. Only through obedience can salvation be obtained. Forgiveness comes only once we have atoned for our wrongdoing: but what is wrongdoing and how does one atone?

According to Richard Swinburne,[8] there are four components to atonement – repentance, apology, reparation and penance. By privately and publicly disowning the wrongdoing (repentance and apology) and eliminating as much of the effects of it as possible (reparation) – preferably restoring the status quo – and compensating the victim for any harm done (penance), the wrongdoer effectively distances him- or herself from the wrong act. Thus repentance entails recognition by the wrongdoer that he or she did the act and that it was a wrong act to do. It also involves a determination to amend. Apology is the process of publicly expressing this repentance to the victim. Reparation is the means by which the wrongdoer can endeavour to eliminate the consequences of the harm done; and penance a way for the wrongdoer to demonstrate the sincerity of their apology by making it costly.

Much public rhetoric about the iniquitous behaviour of young people deplores the fact that they seem to be unable to tell right from wrong. If Swinburne's account of atonement is accepted then this is a key feature in our efforts to restrain and direct our wayward children. In order for repentance to occur, the wrongdoer must be able to distinguish a right act from a wrong act. Contrary to popular opinion, it is my contention that young people are perfectly able to differentiate right from wrong. They know that theft, assault, insolence, vandalism, and so forth are morally (and in some cases, legally) wrong acts: it is just that, in their opinion, what they did in those particular circumstances did not actually count as theft, assault, insolence, vandalism, etc. In this respect younger people are no different from older people. Human beings have a remarkable capacity to deny and redefine certain acts in order to reframe them in a less morally reprehensible way. Even leading politicians and world leaders are not exempt.[9] This predilection was not lost on the author of Genesis; 'The woman whom you gave to be with me, she gave me the fruit from the tree, and I ate' (Genesis 3.12).

Thus, one of the issues to be determined in relation to adolescence and sin is their capacity to make moral decisions. At what point can somebody be held morally responsible for his or her actions? Certainly the Church tends to view young people as insufficiently mature to be 'proper' Christians, and often seeks to police their behaviour and activities in ways that adults would find intrusive and offensive. The potentially disruptive nature of adolescents makes adults anxious, but insufficiently to inspire us to provide adequate theological support and education. Marcia J. Bunge[10] notes that although many churches offer religious education for children, it is often theologically weak with material uninteresting to children: particularly true for the material devised and offered to adolescents. She suggests that this seems to be for two reasons: (1) reflection on spiritual development and religious education of children is seen as not proper theology; and (2) such theological reflection on children and childhood as does exist, narrowly focuses on the sinfulness of children and their need for obedience and instruction.

We live in a culture that is basically secular, where God is allowed free rein in the private world of spirituality, morality and personal values, but is excluded from virtually every other discipline of interpretation, analysis, explanation and action. You may believe that delinquent and antisocial behaviour are the product of original sin, but there is no room in public discourse for such a discussion, and little space for it within the Church. Currently, we do not have an adequate theology of childhood, still less one of adolescence. The tendency for secular psychological and social development theories to view human life as a series of progressions, where life phases are stages to be achieved before one goes on to the next level, is not readily compatible with a view that we are all made in God's image, presumably at all ages in our lives. Jesus Christ may have been without sin, but he was not without childhood and, if the incarnation means anything, presumably he went through all the upheaval of adolescence too. Thus, I concur with Rahner's view,[11] that a person's relationship with God is operative at every stage of human growth and development, so it is inappropriate to view childhood and adolescence as simply preparation for the greater part of life that occurs sometime in the future. To suggest that it is really only adult life that counts is condescending towards children and young people. It is as if childhood and adolescence is understood to be a time when one is capable of only a partial relationship with God, as though God's grace is limited only to those who can make mature attachments.

And shall be for ever

So what do we know about delinquency and rebellion? Is there a case for arguing that there is something of God in opposition and disobedience, and rebellion can serve a creative function?

One of the important things we do know about young people is that during adolescence the influence of peers becomes highly significant, and the peer group plays a key role in the development of values and behaviour. Sociologists argue that persons exposed to delinquent associates are likely to acquire the same traits and that the importance of peers, the amount of time spent with them and loyalty to peers are substantial enough to exert a strong effect on the behaviour of adolescents. Even Augustine discerned that his own adolescent bad behaviour owed as much to his need to be accepted in the group, as to his innate sinfulness.

However, despite the large number of studies that have examined the effect of delinquent peers, the issue of the nature and quality of peer relationships and their connection to delinquency remains unresolved. It does seem to be the case that membership of a delinquent peer group is a strong predictor of subsequent increases in delinquent behaviour, but there is a consensus among researchers that chronic antisocial behaviour generally starts much earlier in life. In other words, mixing with the wrong crowd can lead one to get into trouble, but staying in trouble long term is caused by factors that are deeper rooted than simply a poor choice of friends. Adolescents who develop strong mechanisms of self-control (conscience) are far less likely to get into trouble than those who do not. One of the factors that encourages the development of such internal control is the strength of the emotional attachment to their parents. Antisocial tendencies are inhibited by empathy, which develops from parental warmth and loving relationships.[12]

To complicate matters even further, rejection by a peer group has also been identified as a factor that can contribute to the development of deviant behaviour. A rebellious youngster is likely to look out for similar troubled peers with whom to hang out, thus re-enforcing a sense of alienation and social isolation. Groups matter; when the author of Genesis 2.18 has God comment, 'It is not good that man should be alone', he is stating a fundamental truth about human nature.

However, groups are not totally random, unpredictable entities.

Those who study them note that they follow certain social patterns, develop in particular social ways, and serve specific social functions. Individuals in groups adopt particular roles, whose purpose is to keep the group operational and stable. Groups have a developmental sequence: in the initial stages people come together as relative strangers; there then follows a period of struggle and conflict, as boundaries and limits are tested; the group is then able to establish values and standards for behaviour; finally the group is able to serve its purposes, which may include an actual clear task (play a football match) but may often incorporate something more nebulous (hanging out together). This developmental sequence is sometimes referred to as forming, storming, norming and performing, an expression coined by Tuckman[13] in the 1960s. What is interesting for our purposes is that the crucial stage in this process is the storming one. Groups that are unable to cope with the struggles around power and control, consistently fail to perform as social entities. It appears that one of the essential ingredients for creative human social development is the capacity radically to dissent and to have that tolerated and managed within the group.[14] Many so-called reality television programmes rely on this process to create a series worth watching. Without this ability, social groups never become cohesive and inevitably collapse. In order to flourish, human beings need to live in dynamic groups, where limits and boundaries can be challenged and changed, and norms repeatedly established and re-established, so that they can be owned collectively.

It is possible to argue therefore, that certain forms of rebellion are a necessary part of growth. Without the potential for defying power and challenging social norms, humanity stagnates. At the present time when there is much debate on the notion of social inclusion, it is important to remember that although human beings have a fundamental need for a sense of identity and belonging, this is not achieved through simple obedience to cultural norms, but is actively created through social interaction, some of which has to be conflictual if it is going to be healthy.

If this is the case then one can reasonably assume that Scripture would reflect the reality of human experience, which I have argued it does. Furthermore, a Christian could make the proposition that Jesus, in his teaching and preaching, would make reference to the potential for salvation in rebellious and delinquent behaviour, which of course he does.

The Good News

Jesus, and all those who listened to him, would have intuitively understood the implications of a preference for the younger child as revealed in Torah. As already noted, the accounts in Genesis demonstrate a decided tendency for the patriarchs to gain advantage by subverting power and defying cultural norms. Judaism proudly traces its heritage back through rebellious individuals who systematically undermine the status quo. Telling a story that begins, 'There was a man who had two sons. The younger of them said to his father, "Father, give me a share of the property that will belong to me." So he divided his property between them . . .' (Luke 15.11–32), inevitably raises certain expectations in the minds of the audience. Jesus would know that the people would be anticipating a tale of adversity overcome through cunning and guile. What he actually tells is a story about a rebellious son who makes a sharp break with his father, his brother and the community in which they live. The younger son's request is tantamount to wishing his father dead. To make matters worse, the foolish father agrees to his greedy son's request, and the brother acquiesces, accepting his double-share of the inheritance at the same time. This behaviour breaks all the cultural values of respect and honour and would have alienated the family from the entire village. What we have here is not just a rebellious son but a rebellious family. No wonder the younger son runs away.

In the far country the younger son squanders his money in reckless, delinquent living, and soon finds himself destitute. When famine strikes he ends up with a job looking after pigs – just about the most degrading occupation a Jew could undertake. Then he has an idea. This is the point at which the anticipated cunning plan begins to develop. The younger son decides to swallow his pride and see if he can return home as a hired servant. Notice that this decision is entirely driven by economic necessity. His father's hired servants eat, but he does not. He is not remorseful, there is no evidence whatsoever in the text that he (in Swinburne's terms) wishes to express repentance, or make apology, reparation, or penance. He does rehearse a little speech that he will make to his father, 'Father, I have sinned against heaven and before you; I am no longer worthy to be called your son; treat me like one of your hired hands.' So, on a generous reading, it could appear that he acknowledges his wrongdoing, but there is no suggestion of real regret at his sin. He is primarily motivated by his stomach.

So what we have is the delinquent son of an irresponsible family returning to the village where he and his kin have caused disruption and unrest in the community. Village hostility is such that when his father sees him coming, he runs out to greet him because the son is in danger from hostile neighbours and needs his father's protection. His sense of urgency is made all the more apparent because older men in the Middle East do not run, except in a dire emergency. Greeting his son with a kiss and an embrace, the father forestalls any angry village reaction, indicating that the boy is still under his protection – all of this before the young man utters a word. Eventually when he does speak, he is not able to complete the rehearsed speech, and now, in the context of his father's acceptance, the words sound remorseful.

Given that the family has now seriously alienated the entire village, throwing a party and inviting everyone to it is a sensible ploy to restore relationships. A fatted calf would feed a lot of people. If no one comes, the family's reputation in the village is lost, but if they do come, then they are indicating their acceptance of the younger son back into the life of the family and the community.

The parable could end here quite satisfactorily. The family and the village are celebrating and relationships are being restored. However, the older son ruins everything by flatly refusing to join in. The elder son remember, has done quite nicely out of this. On the back of his younger brother's request he took his double portion of the inheritance. He did not protest or respectfully decline, to protect his father's honour, and he now publicly insults his father by refusing to join the feast. His father pleads with him (a deeply undignified thing for a father to do) pointing out that there is nothing else to give the older son, since he already has given him all of the estate that remains.

The behaviour of the older son and the squabbling going on outside the house would have confirmed in the minds of the villagers that this family are dysfunctional, antisocial and not to be trusted. In fact it is the resentful greed of the older son that will irreparably damage the family's relationship with the community. Delinquency is not just acting up and running away, sometimes it is also remaining bitterly obedient and stubbornly staying put.

The significance of the behaviour of the family, and the individuals within it, would not have been lost on those listening to the parable for the first time. Remember that Jesus tells this story in response to some Pharisees grumbling about him eating with sinners, and follows it with the parable of the Shrewd Manager, where he seems to be encouraging people to make friends by deception and dishonest wealth. Is Jesus implying that delinquency and deviousness are acceptable? Like the accounts in Torah, there is a hint in the narrative that God values obedience and conformity a lot less than the powerful and respectable members of the community would have us believe. On this reading, the Prodigal Son is an account of a family where all the norms are turned upside down. The older son is more delinquent than the younger one, and the father, in order to protect his children, behaves in ways that are disruptive to the community and offensive to his dignity. What seems to matter to the father is that the runaway has returned safe and sound; that which was lost has been found. Immediately preceding this, Jesus has told the parable of the Lost Sheep where he emphatically states that, 'There will be more joy in heaven over one sinner who repents than over ninety-nine righteous persons who need no repentance' (Luke 15.7). The question is, why? What is it about a repenting sinner that generates 99 times the joy in heaven than a righteous person?

One theory of the human personality suggests that as part of our socialization as children we learn to adapt to the social and cultural norms expected of us, usually by following the customs and rules of behaviour laid down by our parents.[15] We learn that in order to be acceptable we have to behave in certain ways. As we grow up, we internalize all these rules and ways of behaving, often to the extent that they become subconscious. Some rules are about social niceties, how we speak to our elders, for example; others are less obvious. When you are an infant, you might discover that making your big brother laugh is a good way to stop him bullying you; or you might learn not to get angry about anything, because when you do your mother disapproves. These can become rules of behaviour in exactly the same way as greeting people by shaking hands or not climbing on the furniture. These rules can stay with us all our life.

Of course, children do rebel against the rules and expectations that their parents or parent-figures appear to be setting for them. I might resist letting aunty kiss me when she visits, or refuse to share my sweets politely with the children next door. When the grown ups are not around, I might deliberately stand on the furniture in my shoes, or say rude words, or yell at the neighbours. Sometimes, when I am feeling fed up with having to make jokes to keep my brother from bullying me, I might scribble on his book or carelessly drop his favourite toy so that it breaks. There might even be times when I feel so angry about not ever being angry around my mother, that I sulk all day, just to show her. When children behave in these ways it is as though they are taking the parental rules and turning them around, deliberately acting in opposition to them.

People who are very careful in their behaviour, who avoid doing anything for fear of causing offence, who are tentative or anxious in social situations, who are unable to make decisions, and always defer to others, are said to be overly compliant. That is, in an extreme way, they continue in adult life, to behave in the ways they decided on as a child, in order to please the grown ups and fit in.

People who persistently challenge all the boundaries, who invariably resist taking instruction, who continually argue about structures or regulations, or who are unable to stick to any agreements, are said to be oppositional. That is, they are engaging in rebellious behaviour in adult life that comes from childhood decisions to oppose childhood rules.

By the way, there is no inherent value judgement attached to these ways of behaving. Sometimes adapted child behaviours work positively for us. If you look both ways before you cross the road, you probably do so unconsciously because you were taught to from a very young age, and by replaying this rule-following pattern you get safely to the other side. Sometimes these behaviours work negatively. Someone may have discovered at a young age that an effective way to get attention from the grown-ups was to sulk. As an adult they may still sometimes sulk in the hope of getting what they want, ignoring other adult options of simply asking directly or negotiation.

What is important for our purposes is to recognize that both these sets of behaviours come from the same source. Non-reflective, habitual obedience and rebellion are two sides of the same coin, and our decisions as adults to engage in either behaviour may have more to do with our experiences as children than what is going on here and now. The notion of overly compliant or oppositional adult behaviour being responses to childhood decisions about perceived social and interpersonal norms is interesting because it helps to explain something puzzling in human experience. Testing the limits can be rebellious or creative, oppositional or inspirational. Similarly, obedience can be due to self-discipline or passivity, a sense of responsibility or simply going along with the crowd. The concept of 'adapted child' behaviour may help us to decide which.

In the parable of the Two Sons (Matthew 21.28–32) Jesus describes a situation where a father tells his elder son to go and work in the vineyard and the boy responds by saying he does not want to, but later changes his mind and goes. On being given a similar instruction, the younger son initially agrees, but does not go. Jesus makes the point that the tax collectors and prostitutes are going into the kingdom of heaven ahead of the chief priests and the elders because they are behaving like the elder son, who initially adopts a rebellious position and then changes his mind, choosing to do what his father wishes. The younger son, however, at first appears compliant but then actually moves into an oppositional position, so is still making an adapted child response. The crucial distinction seems be whether one is making an active choice or simply following a parental instruction – or going against it if one is being oppositional. If it is a choice then presumably Jesus made such decisions himself.

The story of the boy Jesus in the temple (Luke 2.41–50) is a wonderful example of rebellious behaviour on the part of Jesus. Here we have a 12-year-old boy who runs away from his parents so that he can spend time listening to and questioning the Jewish teachers in the temple. It takes Jesus' parents three days to find him. Jesus must have known that they would be beside themselves with worry and that his behaviour was highly disruptive. Travel was an extremely dangerous business in those days and was only undertaken for certain specified reasons. For security, people travelled with extended family or trusted neighbours and this detour meant that Mary and Joseph would now be some days behind their group on the way back to Nazareth, and therefore in a much more vulnerable position. So Jesus has not only caused his parents anxiety, but he will also have put them to some considerable personal risk. Jesus would have been perfectly well aware of what a delinquent thing it was that he was doing, and yet his behaviour is not interpreted (either at the time by his parents, or by us reading the text now) as deviant or oppositional. He is not being naughty, mischievous, or unfeeling. He is, however, making it clear that in some matters of social and interpersonal behaviour he may well choose to go against the mainstream and act autonomously in accordance with his understanding of what God requires. A choice that is so obvious to him that he is surprised it not obvious to his parents. What matters is the choosing.

In conclusion

It is worth noting that there are two clear examples where Scripture does not condone or in any way appear to favour the rebellious or offensive behaviour of the delinquent. The first story appears in the book of Samuel where the author writes:

> Now the sons of Eli were scoundrels; they had no regard for the LORD or for the duties of the priests to the people . . . Thus the sin of the young men was very great in the sight of the LORD; for they treated the offerings of the LORD with contempt.
>
> 1 Samuel 2.12–17

The second story occurs in the second book of Kings where Elisha is 'taunted by some small boys [who] came out of the city and jeered at him, saying, "Go away, baldhead! Go away, baldhead!"' (2 Kings 2.23–24).

In both instances it is made clear that delinquent behaviour will not be tolerated: the entire household of Eli, we are informed, was punished forever, 'because his sons were blaspheming God, and he did not restrain them' (1 Samuel 3.13) and 'two she-bears came out of the woods and mauled forty-two of the boys' that had taunted Elisha (2 Kings 2.24). So what is it that makes some delinquent behaviour acceptable and others not? In both these instances it is noticeable that what is 'sinned against' is set apart as being sacred to God rather than just human society. Rebellion against the sacred would appear to have different consequences than rebellion against the secular.

In every other way, however, it would seem that obedience is not necessarily all that it is made out to be. It can come from an erroneously compliant part of our personality, which reacts in unthinking ways more appropriate to experiences from the past. Similarly, rebelliousness is not necessarily 'all bad' or 'irredeemable'. It can be a creative and potentially constructive part of human interaction and behaviour, out of which God can encourage and engender new ways of being. Challenge, difference and dispute are an essential part of the development of human groups and enable us to adapt and function resourcefully and productively. Furthermore, some antisocial behaviour, but not all, can be understood as a natural God given part of growing up, as individuals determine for themselves the significance of social norms and behavioural constraints.

All of these themes can be identified in Scripture. Genesis is riddled with acting out, antisocial, dysfunctional families and individuals who, nevertheless, manage to achieve God's purposes in their lives and for the world. In the New Testament, Jesus tells stories about similar situations, where rebellious behaviour becomes the means by which the grace of God is made evident. One reason why there might be 99 times the amount of rejoicing in heaven over one sinner who repents is because that individual consciously makes a different decision. The prodigal son, the older son in the Parable of the Two Sons, Rachel, Jacob, Isaac, Cain, they all rebelled against the culture and tradition of society and yet, by the grace of God, that rebellion in itself became the opportunity for transformation.

It could be argued that both Eve and Jesus acted out of the same motives, not oppositional defiance, but a creative resourcefulness that would bring about the possibility of salvation. The end result being that redeemed humanity will be greater than a humanity that never experienced the choice to do right or wrong. Or, as Mark Twain is purported to have said, 'If the Lord didn't want them to be rebellious, why did he create them in his image?'

Notes

1 William Shakespeare, *Winter's Tale*, act 3, scene 3.

2 Proverbs 13.24, King James Version.

3 *New Jerusalem Bible*, Standard Edition, London, Darton Longman & Todd, 1985, note 3b, p. 21.

4 Hesiod, eighth century BC.

5 *The Confessions of St Augustine*, translated and edited by Albert C. Outler, New York, Dover Publications, 2002.

6 Augustine, *Confessions*, 2.9, 29.

7 Martha Ellen Stortz, 'Where or when was your servant innocent?' in Marcia Bunge (ed.), *The Child in Christian Thought*, Grand Rapids, MI, Eerdmans, 2001.

8 Richard Swinburne, *Responsibility and Atonement*, Oxford, Clarendon Press, 1989.

9 On 26 January 1998 President Bill Clinton famously declared on national television 'I did not have sexual relations with that woman, Miss Lewinsky.' It later transpired that this statement was only correct if one used a very specific and narrow definition of 'sexual relations'.

10 Bunge, *The Child in Christian Thought*, particularly note 12 on p. 4.

11 Karl Rahner, 'Ideas for a theology of childhood' in *Theological Investigations*, vol. 8: *Further Theology of the Spiritual Life* 2, translated by

David Rourke, New York, Herder & Herder, 1971.

12 There is an ever-growing body of research on the causes of adolescent delinquency. See, for example, R. Agnew, 'Interactive effects of peer variables on delinquency', *Criminology* 29 (1991), pp. 47–72.

13 B. W. Tuckman, 'Developmental sequence in small groups', *Psychological Bulletin*, 63 (1963), pp. 384–99.

14 See also J. A. Garland, H. E. Jones and R. L. Kolodny, 'A model for stages of development in social work groups' in S. Bernstein (ed.), *Explorations in Group Work: Essays in Theory and Practice,* Boston, Boston University Press, 1976, pp. 17–72.

15 For a more detailed account of transactional analysis see, for example, I. Stewart, and V. Joines, *TA Today: A New Introduction to Transactional Analysis*, Nottingham, Lifespace Publishing, 2000.

Then Jesus said, 'There was a man who had two sons. The younger of them said to his father, "Father, give me the share of the property that will belong to me." So he divided his property between them. A few days later the younger son gathered all he had and travelled to a distant country, and there he squandered his property in dissolute living. When he had spent everything, a severe famine took place throughout that country, and he began to be in need. So he went and hired himself out to one of the citizens of that country, who sent him to his fields to feed the pigs. He would gladly have filled himself with the pods that the pigs were eating; and no one gave him anything. But when he came to himself he said, "How many of my father's hired hands have bread enough and to spare, but here I am dying of hunger! I will get up and go to my father, and I will say to him, 'Father, I have sinned against heaven and before you; I am no longer worthy to be called your son; treat me like one of your hired hands.'" So he set off and went to his father. But while he was still far off, his father saw him and was filled with compassion; he ran and put his arms around him and kissed him. Then the son said to him, "Father, I have sinned against heaven and before you; I am no longer worthy to be called your son." But the father said to his slaves, "Quickly, bring out a robe – the best one – and put it on him; put a ring on his finger and sandals on his feet. And get the fatted calf and kill it, and let us eat and celebrate; for this son of mine was dead and is alive again; he was lost and is found!" And they began to celebrate. Now his elder son was in the field; and when he came and approached the house, he heard music and dancing. He called one of the slaves and asked what was going on. He replied, "Your brother has come, and your father has killed the fatted calf, because he has got him back safe and sound." Then he became angry and refused to go in. His father came out and began to plead with him. But he answered his father, "Listen! For all these years I have been working like a slave for you, and I have never disobeyed your command; yet you have never given me even a young goat so that I might celebrate with my friends. But when this son of yours came back, who has devoured your property with prostitutes, you killed the fatted calf for him!" Then the father said to him, "Son, you are always with me, and all that is mine is yours. But we had to celebrate and rejoice, because this brother of yours was dead and has come to life; he was lost and has been found."'

Luke 15.11–32

7. Being and Becoming: Adolescence

JOCELYN BRYAN

Introduction

Children grow up and during this process they reach a stage when they are no longer children but they are not adults either. This is the phase of development that is generally known as 'adolescence'. It is a transitional phase, which manifests itself in physiological change: as the body continues to develop beyond the point of fertility at puberty and psychological change: as the adolescent makes the journey from dependency to independence and responsibility. More than any other phase in childhood, this last stage concerns 'becoming'. What it means to 'be' in adolescence is generally associated with strife, confusion, and loss as one 'becomes' an adult. But from within this struggle to develop from child to adult, a new identity and sense of self emerges, shaped by the experiences of childhood. This new sense of identity constitutes not only a new awareness of 'being' but also a sense of purpose and role. The adolescent emerges with an understanding of what they have 'become' and are to 'become'.

Theologically, it makes sense for a reflection on adolescence to draw upon understandings of identity and selfhood. It is the stage which is marked by the end of one identity, that of a child and the adoption of a new identity, that of an adult. But what does the child 'become' as an adult? How does our theological understanding of being created in the image of God relate to this particular stage in life? Moreover, how does it relate to human development in more general terms? How does the image of God as parent inform the theological discourse of adolescence? In the journey from childhood dependence to adult independence, how does the theological understanding of freedom and responsibility contribute to a theology of adolescence? What is the Christian understanding of 'becoming' and is there an end point to the process in adulthood or is the end point something which is beyond reach in the human lifespan?

These are some of the many questions which arise when we begin to reflect theologically on adolescence. At its centre is the relationship between the self as a unique being in a specific time and space created in the image of God and the changing self whose 'being' is constantly in a state of ' becoming'. The discovery of self-identity and the person God has created one to be is one of the fundamental quests in the Christian journey of discipleship. For many theologians it is essential to the ultimate goal of discovering ones self within God. Augustine suggested that the search for God required an inward search for one's true self. The inner presence of God within the individual self is a foundational understanding in Augustine's writings most notably in his *Confessions*.

Fraser Watts has suggested that the concept of the self and, by association, identity provides an opportunity for a rich dialogue between psychology and theology.[1] Without engagement with the contemporary understandings of adolescence and the development of identity, any theological reflection runs the risk of ignoring significant insights into human nature and development. These are held in the domain of the social sciences and psychology in particular. Therefore, throughout this chapter I will draw upon recent research in developmental psychology and adolescence to set up a dialogue between the disciplines of theology and psychology from which the principle themes for a theology of adolescence will emerge.

Background to adolescence

Childhood, adulthood and old age have always been recognized as principle stages in the human life cycle, but not adolescence. For centuries children were assumed to leave childhood and enter adulthood without any acknowledgement of a transitional stage between the two. Today, however, adolescence is seen as a notoriously difficult phase in the development of an individual surrounded by numerous myths. In 1904, Hall described this stage of life as a time of 'storm and stress'.[2] Erik Erikson believed it to be a necessary time of identity crisis from which one emerged with a sense of identity, by which he meant a commitment to an occupation, an ideology and an understanding of social roles.[3] Studies of adolescence have held consistently to the notion that this is a difficult stage of development in which self-identity is formed. Hence, the implicit and explicit agenda has been the examination of problematic behaviour and the emergence of identity. For any adolescent individual, it appears that the challenge is to negotiate the passage from adolescence into adulthood avoiding the many problems and crises that characterize these years.

So the enduring image of this final stage of child development before attaining adulthood remains one of disruption and crisis. Parents dread the 'teenage years' – they are to be endured rather than enjoyed. But, like all the preceding stages of childhood, this is a stage of considerable change: physiological, psychological and social. However, the nature of the change from child to adult is associated with a change in 'being' as the child 'becomes' an adult person. The child leaves behind their child identity and through this transitional process takes on the identity of an adult. During this transition, relationships change and new relationships are formed. There is a gradual loss of the closeness of the parent–child relationship and the establishment of other close relationships both within a peer group as well as intimate relationships with the opposite gender. It is a letting-go stage of life, but also a stage of exploration and discovery, leading to the establishment of a different sense of being. During this time the adolescent acquires a different sense of who they are, and is able to organize their understanding of their identity.

The relationships that the young person has, both within the family and with peers, are highly influential in this process of change and development. These relationships shape not only who they are, but also who they will become. It is this particular aspect of adolescence which this chapter explores. It will examine the influence of relationship in adolescence both from a biblical and psychological perspective to inform our theological understanding of being and becoming in this final stage of childhood.

The concept of adolesence and identity formation

As already indicated, it is perhaps surprising that it is only within the last century that the concept of adolescence has been defined as a life span phase and most of the research into these years has been in the social sciences. Adolescence is understood as a sociological construct, which has arisen from the gap opened up by the average age of puberty decreasing because of better health care and diet, along with the introduction of compulsory education and the rising age of marriage, financial independence and adulthood.[4] Santrock recently defined adolescence as beginning in biology and ending in culture, indicating that it is not a phase of the life span marked by a fixed age, like many of the other stages in childhood.[5]

However, long before this century there are references to youthfulness that would most likely be classified as referring to adolescence. Aristotle is quoted as seeing young people as passionate, irascible and apt to be carried away by their impulses. Others trace the concept of adolescence back to the Enlightenment with its affirmation of the individual and the resulting emphasis on self-determinism. Following the Enlightenment, one's identity was no longer regarded as a matter of fate but individuals had more choice regarding their future social roles and these choices were exercised during the years that would now be classified as adolescence.[6]

There has undoubtedly been a significant shift in the development of individual identity in western society which has influenced adolescence and our definition of it. Children no longer gain their identity and adulthood simultaneously with an assumed economic role by marriage, beginning a trade or taking on an inherited property.[7] Instead, the increase in personal choice through the greater availability of education and major political, ideological and sociological developments has changed the nature of the formation of identity dramatically in the last century and also altered the length of time over which this takes place. This has led to confusion regarding the end point of adolescence. To say that it ends in culture is not necessarily a helpful marker. What is clear is that the distinction between a child and an adult is easier to discern than that between an adolescent and an adult.

Historically, the marker from childhood to adulthood has included rites of passage and training in preparation for new responsibilities and a new identity, for example, the Jewish rites of Bar Mitzvah or more recently Bat Mitzvah. But for the majority of adolescents in contemporary western society the predominant marker is reaching the age of either 18 or 21 years, which is accompanied by defined legal responsibilities and privileges. However, many adults who are many years older than 18 or 21 behave in ways that would be classified as adolescent. Age serves as an empirical marker, but it is inadequate as a means of defining the end of adolescence and the attainment of adult maturity. The question remains, what is an adequate and helpful definition of the end point of adolescence? Or to put it another way, what are the defining characteristics of adulthood that a young person is to attain at the end of the transitional processes of adolescence? When children progress through childhood into adolescence and then on to adulthood, what is the goal they are moving towards? What have they 'become' at the end of this stage? In other words, what do we understand by responsible adulthood? If this question can not be answered it has serious implications for young people and their motivation to take on the responsibilities and behaviours that are assumed in adulthood.

Maturity and the developmental goal of adolescence

In the 1950s Erik Erikson[8] was the most influential theorist regarding adolescence. He defined it as a time of identity formation in which young people had to resolve their identity crisis and develop an integrated self-identity. His influence has faded, but the debate concerning the goal of adolescence continues. Elkind describes adult psychological maturity as 'a healthy sense of identity and self, developed during the teen years' this is characterized by 'an inner core of consistency and stability that allows them to deal with new situations in terms of past experiences'.[9] But what is the definition of a 'healthy sense of identity'? Loder refers to the end point as being 'becoming one's own person',[10] which assumes the development of independence and distancing from the security and comfort of the parental care. Again, this seems inadequate; there is surely more than independence that is achieved by adulthood.

In the different psychological accounts of development the evaluation and definition of the goal of development remains problematic and variable. This is the case not only in current academic psychology but also within the various schools of therapeutic psychology, so that for Freud the goal is the individual's sense of psychic unity, for Jung it is the individuated self and growth in consciousness and for humanistic psychology it is self-actualization. Piaget set the goal of cognitive development as abstract thought and manipulation and Kohlberg examining the moral development of individuals set an end point of attaining personal ethical principles. It is a fragmented picture, which indicates the complexity of human nature and the vast array of approaches and emphases which are applied to the study of it.

However, what can be said is that the current understanding of identity formation suggests that it is a lengthy process, which is complex and more gradual than theorists such as Erikson suggest. Identity formation begins with the early attachment of the infant to its care giver, continues with the development of a sense of self and the growth of independence and responsibility, and reaches a final stage of life review and integration, which can take place as late in the life cycle as old age. However, it is evident in adolescence that the child has reached a point where they can begin to synthesize their childhood identities and identifications to construct a psychological pathway to adult maturity.[11] But the identity formed at this point is not necessarily stable for the rest of life. Indeed, a healthy identity is described as adaptable, flexible and open to changes in society, relationships and ideologies. So implicit in identity formation is the likelihood of change.

Christian understanding of development

Having identified the variety of psychological approaches to development, it is important to explore the Christian understanding of development, which provides the overall context for the exploration of a theology of adolescence.

Christian accounts of human development have tended to focus on personality development and spiritual maturity. This is predominantly directed towards what we are to be rather than what we are. That is not to exclude what the biblical narrative says about human nature and the human state of being. However, from the perspective of the development, accounts describe what we strive to become. The becoming rather than the being dominates. Consistently Christian theories of development describe a progression towards God. The incarnational model of Jesus presents Christians with the ultimate goal of what they strive to become; we are to grow into the likeness of Christ (Ephesians 4.15). Within these accounts of growth towards God, growth in holiness and growth in Christ, there is an acknowledgement of the significance of the relationship with God and others which is grounded in love.

Unlike psychological perspectives then, there is more general agreement on the goal of development, although the theological language and emphasis differs between accounts. Hence Kierkegaard suggests the goal is for the self to become transparent before God, and Augustine proposes that the over-riding goal is the quest for God and this orders all other desires and needs. John Wesley expressed development in the Christian life as growth in grace and holiness which is part of the Methodist understanding of the doctrine of Christian Perfection. But how are these measured? What are the marks of such growth?

The evaluation of development in Christian accounts includes various criteria. Moral behaviour, relationship with others and faith and commitment to God are commonly expressed as characteristics of developing discipleship. Growth in moral behaviour is discerned in the decisions and choices that determine behaviour. In the Methodist understanding of growth in grace and holiness, the nature of the relationship between God and humanity is exemplified and actions and spirituality are related. The experience of God's love and grace leads to a response of living in a way that reflects this love in what we do and are. Growth in love and concern for the well-being of others are viewed as important signs of this development. Christians respond to God's grace in order to be perfected in love. In a similar vein, Thomas Merton emphasized that God, as revealed in Christ, returns us to the material world and to love others, and Teresa of Avila regarded movement towards God and the experience of God as moving us to service in the world and our responsibility towards others. Growth for her is evidenced by 'the birth always of good works, good works'.[12]

Commitment to God is characterized by the degree to which someone surrenders themself to God. What is interesting is that such writers as Augustine of Hippo and Thomas Merton see the search for God and for the true self as one and the same. Hence, as we grow in our knowledge and commitment to God we develop in our understanding of our selves and our self-identity.

It is important to note that the Christian approach to personal development discussed here is not to be confused with approaches to faith or religious development, although there is some degree of overlap in issues and questions. Growing in faith is part of Christian development and absolute faith a goal referred to above. Studies in this field have described religious development in stages of faith,

James Fowler being the most influential. However, there is a danger that this is isolated from the rest of personal development and the integration faith into personal identity formation is given insufficient attention. A theology of adolescence requires engagement with identity formation during this stage of development acknowledging that one's sense of being and becoming is informed by ideological and theological understanding.

Theological approach and biblical motif

Given the history of the concept of adolescence, the paucity of theological reflection and engagement on the subject is not surprising. There are few, some would argue, if any, references in Scripture to adolescence as a legitimate phase of the life span. Research in youth ministry has attempted to engage in theological study of adolescence and this has yielded significant insights into ministerial practice, but in the majority of cases this has not been grounded in theology but rather looked to the social sciences to direct the Church's work with young people and develop a practical theology.[13]

As discussed previously, the theme of adolescence emerging from the social sciences literature is the formation of identity. It is the stage when the child breaks away from their parents, gains a sense of independence and forms their self-identity. The foundations of individual identity and personhood are understood to lie in the nature of our relationships.[14] It follows that one of the most fruitful approaches in the construction of a theology of adolescence is in the conversation between the theological understanding of relationship and personal identity and the insights from the social sciences. The focus of this conversation will be in reflecting upon the parable of the Prodigal Son in Luke 15.11–31 from both a theological and psychological perspective.

The Prodigal Son has been called 'a gospel in miniature', an indication of the theological richness of the parable. But it offers psychological riches too! Within the story, the network of relationships between the two sons and the father presents the opportunity to develop a theology of relationships and identity which can inform our theological understanding of adolescence. The character of God as Father, encompassing compassion, patience, infinite love and forgiveness is at the parable's heart. The younger son's desire to free himself from his father and form his identity constitutes the main story line, raising the question of his relationship with his father and the place of freedom within it. The way in which this freedom is managed by the younger son poses the question of morality, sin and forgiveness and their place in identity formation. How does one develop from an irresponsible young person to a responsible adult? Through the younger son's experience of lostness and sin can he be described as growing in holiness? Finally, how does the younger son's relationship with his father influence and shape his sense of being and becoming? The main question for this chapter is: what can be distilled from this parable concerning the formation of human identity during adolescence which will contribute and direct a theology of adolescence?

There have been few attempts to engage with texts in this way. However, the growth in theological reflection and practical theology has brought with it a recognition of the value of an interdisciplinary approach. Watts has frequently highlighted the benefits of the dialogue between psychology and theology including how psychology can contribute to systematic theology and biblical interpretation as well as the more obvious topics of religious experience and creation.[15]

My intention, therefore, is to conduct a conversation between theology and psychology regarding the development of identity and its place in the developmental process of graduating from childhood to adulthood. I will use the relationship of father and son within the story of the Prodigal Son as a biblical framework around which to construct this dialogue.

Personhood and identity: a theological perspective

Before the development of identity through relationship is explored in the parable of the Prodigal Son, it is necessary to set this reflection in the context of the Christian understanding of personhood and identity. The Christian faith grounds identity in the notion that human beings are created in the image of God (Genesis 1.26–27) and live in relationship with each other and with God. It is through these relationships that we develop our identity and sense of self. This formation involves both understanding our place in the world and also how we are called to respond to or behave in the world which constitutes our morality. Hence what we do as well as who we are is integrated in our identity.

Central to this understanding of human identity is our relationship with God. We are engaged in a personal relationship with God through which God calls us into a relationship of love and service. Within this relationship we learn that we are valued and loved by God and this has been revealed to us in the life and person of Jesus. Hence, our understanding of ourselves as persons is grounded in God, who calls into being and makes us in his image. This, according to Wolfhart Pannenberg,[16] underscores the Christian relationship to the world, relating to it as gift and a calling from God. The effect of this is to develop identity focused on an openness to the world, to God and to each other. In other words, it is through our relationships that we develop an understanding of our identity. Being in relationship with God and others influences that way in which we develop a sense of who we are, our role and responsibilities and our motivation and goals.[17]

Human identity is developed and nurtured in relationship but it is grounded in our creation in the image of God. From this it follows that we are created to carry God's image or perhaps wonderfully to be representatives of God in the world. This gives us our sense of purpose: we are called and created to be signs, or to portray God in the world. Identity and purpose are therefore related in the created image of God, which we bear as human beings. So, in order to carry out this purpose we are dependent on our relationship with God and the relationship we have with others; both of which form and shape our understanding of our personal identity.[18] Within this theological framework 'being' and 'becoming' are clearly related and the function of relationship within the development of an awareness of identity can be understood.

The significance of this God-centred identity is that the person is located in the on-going life of God. The biblical narrative offers example after example of those who found the source of their identity in their relationship with God and the claim God made on their lives. In contemporary culture where self-identity is shaped not only by relationships but by the media and individualism, the Christian tradition offers the adolescent an enduring narrative in which to locate their personal narrative and source their personal identity through their relationship with God and others. A theology of adolescence seeks to bring understanding to the emergence of identity within the theology of the human person as created in the image of God, called a child of God and called to grow into the likeness of Christ.

Disengagement from parents

The younger son in the parable of the Prodigal Son fulfils most of the characteristics of a contemporary adolescent. Indeed I want to suggest he is one. The parable gives no indication of his age, but we can infer from the story that he is in late adolescence rather than early. The parable's story line can be seen as essentially the adolescent younger son leaving home, breaking away from the security he has known with his father and attempting to realize his independence. To leave home in this way, the younger son required his father to split his land in two so that he could sell off his half of the land for cash. This would bring shame on the family but, furthermore, by requesting this before his father's death, it would be interpreted as essentially saying to his father 'I wish you were dead'. This is a dramatic way of leaving home, but it illustrates starkly the strength of the desire that the younger son had to forge his independence and identity. In the parable there is no indication of the father's hurt, anger or distress. He obliges his son and lets him go. He affords him the responsibility to spend or invest his inheritance as he wishes and so permits him to find his personal identity away from his home and the security of his father's presence.

Adolescence is a period when the tension between autonomy and attachment is felt acutely by both parents and their children. It is often a source of conflict and stress within family relationships. Parents see their influence and control slipping away and adolescents become frustrated by the hold parents wish to retain over them. The result of this tension is conflict, often poor communication and mutual frustration on both the part of the parent and adolescent.

Viorst describes this stage of separation from parents as a loss which is both frightening and sad.[19] Besides the loss of closeness brought about by the growing independence of the adolescent, there is the loss of the self as a child and with the onset of puberty the loss of the former familiar body. Adolescence can be described as a 'letting-go' stage of life. Parents have to learn to let go of the high-dependency relationship they have, up to this point, shared with their child and the adolescent has to let go of their dependency on their parents, along with their child-self and their physical self as they move through puberty. These are significant changes in the adolescent's relationship with their parents and how they experience themself. Their self-identity as a child is no longer appropriate and has to assimilate these changes and adapt to them.

The younger son's identity development: stage 1

By applying a psychological perspective on the younger son's behaviour, Marcia's[20] analysis of Erikson's theory provides some significant insights. Marcia suggested that during adolescence the individual is to some extent either in a state of crisis or commitment. During crisis the adolescent is choosing among meaningful alternatives and during commitment the adolescent shows a personal investment in what they are doing. He also suggested that there are four main identity states in Erikson's theory: identity diffusion, identity foreclosure, identity moratorium and identity achievement. Identity diffusion is described as when the adolescence has not experienced a crisis or shown any commitment to alternatives. They are undecided about occupational matters and ideological choices and likely to show little interest either. This is commonly associated with young adolescence.

Identity foreclosure is the state when the adolescent makes a commitment but they have yet to experience a crisis. I suggest that this is exactly where the younger son is before the beginning of the parable. Up to this point the younger son will have been committed to his duties fulfilling the role he has been brought up to follow, but for some reason his acceptance of this has gradually declined and he wants to explore the possibility of different vocations and ideologies and live in a different place in a different way. So he is now in the state of identity moratorium; in the midst of a crisis with only vaguely defined commitments. What is remarkable in this parable is his father's response to his son's crisis. He shows outstanding generosity not only with his estate but also in granting his son the freedom to spend his inheritance as he chooses. The father is willing to let go of his son, he allows him the freedom to find his identity away from his presence. Freedom and the financial benefit of half the estate are both gifts from his father.

Freedom and letting go

MacFadyen offers an understanding of freedom which is based upon the nature of our relationship with God.[21] He describes the 'provision of space for free human response to the divine address'. Fundamental to this understanding is the special significance of the personal relationship human beings have with God. A personal relationship can be described as an encounter between two or more characters who are different and who have some independence and autonomy in the relationship and can therefore relate to each other on the basis of freedom rather than coercion.[22] Human beings are in partnership with God, they are co-creators. Humanity is made in God's image and is involved in an active relationship with God. The Word calls us into being and we respond to the Word. The model of dialogue partner is fundamental to our understanding of the nature of this relationship. Because it is this partnership that enables us to be free to respond to God and that response may include rejection. MacFadyen suggests that in the doctrine of creation, creation begins with 'letting-be' and it has autonomy as an independent order of being. He claims that 'the Word of creation precedes any demand: the "let us make" precedes the "be fruitful". This is a mark of God's grace. Our responsibility before God is "not first of all a task, but a gift".'[23] He goes on 'even where the Word has the character of call or obligation, it has to be understood within the context of this primary letting-be of the divinely chosen dialogue partnership'.

Genesis 1.1—2.3 reinforces this as it shows God to be the risk taker, who first blesses human beings with fertility and then entrusts them to rule over the creatures of the earth, giving them power then letting them go. In other words, God establishes a relationship with human beings, which grants them freedom. Middleton describes God in Genesis 1 as 'like no one as much as a mother, who gives life to her children, . . . and takes the parental risk of allowing her progeny to take their first steps, to attempt to use their power to develop toward maturity'.[24] God is a generous creator who shares power with humanity and offers them the freedom to participate in the creative process. Without freedom maturity would not be achieved.

Generosity and freedom are characteristics of God and they shape the nature of the relationship God has with God's children. God in God's generosity grants us autonomy and apparently demands nothing from us in return. In the parable of the Prodigal Son, this is clearly illustrated in the father's response to the younger son's request for his inheritance. The risk-taking, generous father lets his son go in order that he might develop his identity and grow in maturity. Making choices and taking decisions are part of the maturation process. It is precisely this gift of freedom that enables humankind to choose whether to seek the will of God and to grow more into the likeness of Christ. Adolescence normally involves increasing the degree of freedom children receive from their parents to foster independence. There is risk on behalf of both partners in the parent/adolescent relationship, but freedom is necessary for the process of maturation. Therefore a theology of adolescence must include an understanding of the freedom God gives humanity in order that we might develop towards maturity. This is modelled in the father/son relationship in the parable of the Prodigal Son.

The younger son's identity development: stage 2

In the distant country the younger son squandered his money on a life of debauchery until he had spent it all. At this point the son has entered the state which Marcia terms 'identity moratorium'. He is in the midst of a crisis and his commitments are absent or only vaguely defined. The gap between the security of his father's home and the autonomy of adulthood is apparent. Freedom and responsibility have been difficult to adjust to. He has not invested or spent his wealth responsibly and the transition to independence has become psychologically and physically painful. But it is within this situation that he begins to develop his self-awareness and identity and he achieves this by reflecting on his home situation. He realizes that even his father's hired men are better off than he is. It is the process of recalling his parental home and the relationship he has with his father, which facilitates and enables him to move forward in his identity formation.

One of the significant findings regarding the development of adolescents is the importance of the role of parents. Parents are responsible for the emotional climate in which a child grows up. Psychological studies have indicated that it is not just what parents do that matters, but the emotional context in which this takes place. One of the main findings is that an authoritative style of parenting is most likely to lead to healthy adolescent development.[25] This style is characterised by warmth, firmness, and psychological autonomy granting. Firmness acts as an effective deterrent against delinquency and problems such as drug and alcohol abuse, warmth associated with positive affirmation builds self-esteem and, along with psychological autonomy granting, is seen to act like a protective shield reducing anxiety, depression and other forms of internal distress.[26]

Studies suggest the reason for the effectiveness of authoritative parenting is because of the emotional context associated with its set of specific parenting practices.[27] This is because actions take on different meanings depending on the emotional climate in which they occur. In the family context this is determined by the style of parenting. Three things are worth noting regarding the effectiveness of authoritative parenting: the nurturing and involvement of the parent make the child more receptive to parental influence and this helps the child/adolescent to develop effective social skills and integrate well within society (socialization); the way in which the parent provides both support and structure enables the child/adolescent to develop self-regulatory skills such as self-awareness and an appreciation of their limits. These facilitate the process of developing independence, competencies and responsibility. Finally, the verbal negotiations and give and take, help both cognitive and social functioning, particularly in relationship formation. It therefore seems important to take note of not only what parents do but how they do it.[28]

Henri Nouwen describes the younger son as being 'held and blessed by the father'.[29] The holding and blessing of the father characterize the warmth and the positive nurturing, which the son has received from his father and which continues even though the son has chosen to leave and go to a distant country. The human exercise of freedom and choice is always held within the divine embrace of God. Holding provides warmth and security. The vulnerable lost younger son can only contemplate his acute sense of who he is and what he has become because of the love and support he has known throughout his life from his father. If this had been absent he would never have acknowledged his emptiness, sinfulness and defeat. The paradox he faces is that in his bid to free himself and become the person he was created to be, he is trapped. Trapped by poverty, he is hired out to feed the pigs and is even denied their food; trapped by loneliness, those around him shun him, and trapped by his sense of guilt and sinfulness.

Loder describes the adolescent as 'a person for whom all previous solutions from the last ten years of life undergo an upheaval that thrusts the developing person into the abyss of nothingness . . . and that calls the person into transformation'.[30] This is a point of 'coming to the senses'; when reason and reflection lead to change and integration. The younger son's words 'I will leave this place and go to my father and say "Father I have sinned against heaven and against you; I no longer deserve to be called your son; treat me as one of your hired men"' (Luke 15.18–19) indicate that the younger son has reached Marcia's identity achievement. He has undergone crisis and reached commitment. Nouwen[31] suggests that 'it was the loss of everything that brought him to the bottom line of his identity'. Identity formation becomes even more evident as he turns to face his father and his home.

Moral development and responsibility

The younger son in his 'crisis' squanders his wealth and engages in a life of debauchery. This is not a responsible way to live. There is no doubt that in the story his behaviour is sinful. A number of questions arise from this. The first requires reflection on the relationship between sin and responsibility and maturity. When an adolescent becomes a responsible adult what does that mean? How does irresponsible behaviour in adolescence affect relationships and influence identity formation?

Responsibility is that which holds us as accountable for our actions. It is part of the moral discourse and determining responsibility is one way in which behaviour is evaluated. The law states at what age an individual can be deemed responsible and accountable for their actions in this country, it varies from 16 years of age for some actions and 18 years of age for others.

Psychology has described the moral development of the child as unfolding in stages. Kohlberg[32] is one of the main theorists who offers a cognitive perspective. He saw internalization as fundamental to this developmental process. Internalization is a developmental change from behaviour which is externally controlled to behaviour which is internally controlled. Kohlberg's levels begin with behaviour being controlled by external rewards and punishments at Level 1. Level 2 is the intermediate stage of internalization whereby the child abides by the standards set which indicates that they have been internalized, but these standards are not their own, they are external, coming from parents, teachers, the laws of society. Finally, the highest level is when morality is entirely internalized and not based on others' standards. At this point morality is integrated with identity, but will have been shaped by external factors such as upbringing, religious convictions, and the moral culture and laws of society. However, the highest level of moral development has been shown to be elusive, with very few adults reaching the final stages.

There have been many critics of Kohlberg's theory. One problem is that it does not recognize the significance of the parent–child and other family relationships in the moral development of the child. The effect of culture is also missed in the theory. Gillian[33] criticizes it for inadequately recognizing the care perspective of moral development, by which she means the view of morality that considers people in relationship, with concern for others.

It is clearly evident that our development in understanding personal responsibility depends upon our relationship with others and God. These not only shape and inform understanding but it is in the impact of our actions upon our relationships for which we stand accountable. Sin corrupts relationships, both between people and with God. The younger son's confession 'Father, I have sinned against heaven and against you' (Luke 15.18) indicates that both the corruption of the personal and the divine relationship are realized. The younger son recognizes his responsibility and sees that he is accountable for his actions. This indicates his level of self-awareness and maturity. His sense of morality is evident and this indicates a development in his sense of identity.

Facing and forgiveness

The younger son can be seen at this point to have reached the point when he is prepared to face his father. The theme of the face has grown in significance in philosophy and theology recently.[34] It is the embodiment of the way in which the interpersonal communication takes place and is therefore central to the process of forgiveness. The face is the principle site for communicating and showing emotion. It is also of importance in the formation of relationships and identity, and the awareness of self and other. As well as it association with the self as being, it is also associated with presence. Hence, the face becomes the focus of who I am and my presence. In relationship it is the other's being and their presence that is experienced through the face.

Early in development, the face is significant in the formation of sense of self and sense of other. From three months infants respond to their parent's faces. In these early stages of infancy the face is foundational to the knowledge of a nurturing presence, a loving other. This gives rise to what is termed intersubjectivity.[35] Stern describes how parents respond to their infants and children out of their own 'subjective' states which vary in the quality of responsiveness and empathetic tuning.[36] This moves the psychology of development from one person to two persons, reinforcing the significance of others in who we are and what we become. It suggests that we develop our self-awareness and our awareness of the impact of our actions (our agency) when we are faced and recognized by another. Within these relationships there is a degree of emotional resonance between the two individuals and this is part of the development of empathy.

In deciding to face his father, the younger son chooses to return and enter his father's presence. He is willing to take responsibility for what he has done and who he is. One senses that this holds for him both a longing and a fear. Loder suggests that the human face is a 'personal centre that is innately sought by a child and the focus of the earliest sense of one's humanity'. He goes on to say that 'the original face-to-face interaction is the child's sense of personhood and a universal prototype of the Divine Presence'.[37] Here the early experiences of the original face-to-face interaction take on a new significance as within them lies the models for forgiveness and reconciliation.

Confession and repentance are interesting with reference to the concept of the self and identity. There is a facing of ones past self and present self in the presence of another for the sake of one's future self and what one desires to be. In this process, there has to be an acknowledgement of the present self being continuous with the past self, even though that is painful. However, at the point of judgement we desire a disassociation of the past self from the present and trust in the changed self and new identity. For this change in identity to be secure, grace and forgiveness are essential. It can be argued that each moment of confession is a point of identity formation, when one appraises who one is before God. The self-awareness and disclosure, which culminate in repentance, indicate an openness and trust in the relationship with God which continues to shape and inform the continuing development of one's identity.

The principle virtues in the process of forgiveness are empathy and compassion. Empathy serves to reduce the psychological distance between the individuals and enlarges the context in which the relationship is present. It is unsurprising that empathy is a characteristic of partners in a healthy and secure relationship. The Christian faith recognizes the intimate knowledge and understanding that God has for each of God's children. Empathy and compassion resonate throughout the Scriptures as part of the very nature of God. The younger son turns to face his father, trusting in his empathy and compassion. He has found the courage to begin to realize his identity and takes responsibility for who he is and who he will become. The experience of the secure, warm and loving relationship throughout his childhood has enabled him to make this decision. Here, the emotional climate set in the nature of relationship is seen to enable a reflection on his past and present self but also given him a new sense of responsibility for who he is and will become. His being and becoming come together in a more coherent manner.

The younger son's identity development: stage 3

The father identifies his son even though he was a long way off, he runs to embrace him. Immediately a celebration is ordered, for 'this son of mine was dead and is alive' (Luke 15.24). The son's return to his father indicates he has attained Marcia's identity achievement, defined as an adolescent who has undergone a crisis, the insecurity and state of lostness is passed for the time being and he has made a commitment. The celebration and words of his father affirm his identity. He is now ready to work with his father and brother. Through the process of crisis and changing commitment he has developed a sense of who he is and a new sense of purpose.

Jean Vanier[38] suggests that 'a moment of grace, in a gentle ray of light, in a moment of awareness of who we really are', provides us with the inspiration and strength to make clear choices and commitment. The parable of the Prodigal Son reveals such a moment of grace, when the younger son is acutely aware of who is. His sense of being as his father's son is affirmed by the father's overwhelming response of grace and love and it is this which inspires his commitment to his discovered purpose and identity.

The nature of the relationship between the son and the father is a key influence in this developmental phase of the younger son. Theologically, this indicates the way in which our growing sense of being and what we are called to become is dependent upon the 'vertical dimension' of our personhood, namely our relationship with God. The return of the son offers a rich metaphor for the search for God and self, meeting in a moment of extraordinary grace and forgiveness. The search for self and the search for God overlap and, for some Christian thinkers, become the same. To find one's self in God, is to discover one's true identity. Adolescence is the stage in the life span when this process begins.

Emerging themes for a theology of adolescence

The formation of identity is seen as one of the major psychological developments during adolescence. A growing awareness of who one is, how one fits into the world and one's purpose in the world, characterizes this last stage of childhood. Contemporary understanding of adolescence indicates that it is a time which includes 'letting go' and loss as a necessary part of the development of independence and self-awareness. But it also a time of discovery and integration as relationships change and new relationships are established. In the growing appreciation of who one is the concept of the self becomes better organized. This is achieved through the ability to integrated the past sense of being with the present changing sense of being and from this, a template for the future emerges which is shaped by a sense of purpose and who one is to become.

The Christian faith roots the formation of the person in the concept of human beings created in the image of God. This development of the person takes place through their relationship with God, others and the world. It is primarily through these relationships that a person develops their sense of being and their self-awareness. There is an inter-relatedness between God and the self, which is fundamental to human identity. What characterizes this relationship and how this influences the formation of identity and leads to responsibility and maturity are significant questions for this last stage in childhood.

How identity is revealed or discovered in theological understanding is a matter for discussion. One perspective suggests that our God-given identity is something that we already are, but we have to enable ourselves to 'be' it. Another perspective is that the true self and identity is only achieved in union with God so that as one grows closer to God more of one's true self is revealed. If adolescence is the stage when identity emerges, what enables this to take place or how does growth in holiness manifest itself at this stage in the life span? This has been examined within the relationship between God and the individual using the motif of parent/adolescent relationship in both theology and psychology.

The dialogue between a psychological understanding of the emergence of identity in adolescence and the story of the Prodigal Son has raised many theological questions about the meaning of becoming an adult and how it is attained. The nature of freedom is important here, since it has been proposed that freedom is necessary for maturity and responsibility. It is therefore essential that theological understandings of freedom and grace are woven into a theological understanding of the last stage of childhood. However, this freedom is seen as held in the love of God, the source of security and indeed freedom.

The question remains, what is the end point of this developmental process? How do we define adulthood? From a theological perspective the overall goal of development is expressed in a variety of ways, for example, Christian perfection, growth in holiness, to grow into the likeness of Christ. Alternatively, a generalization of Christian theories of development can be summarized as essentially a progression towards God, with Christ as the model of for development. Here, the emphasis is on the 'becoming' rather than the 'being', which leads to the eschatological perspective of our becoming part of the new creation when we will be 'made perfect'.

During this exploration of adolescence the influence of relationships in the formation of identity has been recognized as of primary significance. The main focus of this enquiry has been the relationship between the parent and adolescent resourced by the parable of the Prodigal Son. I suggest that the very nature of the relationship of God with his children in the process of identity formation is revealed here. God is characterized by love, grace and freedom in the person of the father. Within such a relationship, the adolescent is able to grow in self-awareness and form a deeper understanding of who God created them to be and to become. Being and becoming are integrated and formed as the process of growing into the likeness of Christ continues during the human life span.

Notes

1 Fraser Watts, *Theology and Psychology*, Aldershot, Ashgate 2002, p. 73.

2 G. S. Hall, *Adolescence*, New York, Appleton, 1904.

3 Erik Erikson, *Identity, Youth and Crisis*, New York, Norton, 1968.

4 Robbuins Duffy, *This Way to Youth Ministry*, Grand Rapids, Zonderman, 2004, p. 176.

5 J. W. Santrock, *Adolescence*, Dubuque, Iowa, William C. Brown, 4th edn 1990, pp. 28–9.

6 C. Clark, 'The Changing Face of Adolescence: A Theological View of Human Development' in K. Dean, C. Clark and D. Rahn, *Starting Right: Thinking Theologically about Youth Ministry*, Grand Rapids, Zondervan, 2001, p. 41.

7 K. R. Dean, *Practising Passion: Youth and The Quest For a Passionate Church*, Grand Rapids, Eerdmans, 2004, p. 82.

8 E. Erikson, *Identity, Youth and Crisis*, New York, Norton, 1968.

9 D. Elkind, *All Grown up and No Place to Go: Teenagers in Crisis*, Reading, MA, Addison-Wesley, 1984, quoted in Dean et al., *Starting Right*, p. 47.

10 J. E. Loder, *The Logic of the Spirit: Human Development in Theological Perspective*, San Francisco, Josey-Bass, 1998, p. 286, quoted in Dean et al., *Starting Right*, p. 47.

11 J. W. Santrock, *Life Span Development*, Mcgraw-Hill College, 7th edn 1999, p. 372.

12 Quoted in P. Morea, *In Search of Personality*, London, SCM Press, 1997, p. 177.

13 K. C. Dean, 'Proclaiming Salvation: Youth Ministry for the Twenty-First Century Church', *Theology Today* 56 (2000), p. 525.

14 A. McFadyen, *The Call to Personhood: A Christian Theology of the Individual in Relationships*, Cambridge, Cambridge University Press, 1990.

15 Watts, *Theology and Psychology*, passim.

16 W. Pannenberg, 'Person' in *Die Religion in Geschichte und Gegenwart*, Tübingen, J. B. Mohr Paul Siebeck, 2nd edn, 1961, pp. 5, 230–5, cited in P. Hefner, 'Imago Dei: The Possibility and Necessity of the Human Person' in N. H. Gregersen, W. B. Dress and U. Gorman, *The Human Person in Science and Theology*, Edinburgh, T&T Clark, 2000, p. 86.

17 P. Hefner, 'Imago Dei', p. 87.

18 P. Hefner, 'Imago Dei', p. 89.

19 J. Voirst, *Necessary Losses*, New York, Fireside, 1998.

20 J. E. Marcia, 'Optimal Development from an Erikson Perspective' in H. S. Freidman (ed.), *Encyclopedia of Mental Health*, vol. 3, San Diego, Academic Press, 1998, quoted in Santrock, *Life Span Development*, p. 372.

21 McFadyen, *The Call to Personhood*, pp. 20–3.

22 McFadyen, *The Call to Personhood*, p. 18.

23 E. Brunner, *Man in Revolt*, p. 98 quoted in D. Cairns, *The Image of God in Man*, London, Collins, 1973, p. 155.

24 J. R. Middleton, *The Liberating Image*, Grand Rapids, Brazos Press, 2005, pp. 294f.

25 M. Gray and L. Steinberg, 'Unpacking authoritative parenting: Reassessing a multidimensional construct', *Journal of Marriage and the Family*, 61, 1999, pp. 574–87.

26 L. Steinberg, 'We Know Some Things: Parent-Adolescent Relationships in Retrospect and Prospect', *Journal of Research on Adolescence*, 11(1) 2001, pp. 1–19.

27 N. Darling and L. Steinberg, 'Parenting style as context: An Integrative Model', *Psychological Bulletin* 113 (1993), pp. 487–96.

28 Steinberg, 'We Know Some Things', p. 1.

29 H. J. M. Nouwen, *The Return of the Prodigal*, London, Darton, Longman & Todd, 1994, p. 45.

30 J. E. Loder, *The Logic of the Spirit*, San Francisco, Jossey-Bass, 1998, p. 204 in Dean, 'Proclaiming Salvation', p. 525.

31 Nouwen, *The Return of the Prodigal*, p. 49.

32 L. Kohlberg, 'Moral Stages and Moralisation: The cognitive development approach' in T. Lickona (ed.), *Moral Development and Behaviour*, New York, Holt, Rinehart & Winston, 1976.

33 C. Gilligan, 'The centrality of relationships in psychological development: A puzzle, some evidence and a theory' in G. G. Noam and K. W. Fisher (eds), *Development and Vulnerability in Close Relationships*, Hillsdale, NJ: Erlbaum, 1996.

34 See J.-L. Marion, 'The Face: An Endless Hermeneutics', *Harvard Divinity Bulletin* 28/2 (1999), pp. 9–10, quoted in F. Leron Shults and S. J. Sandage, *The Faces of Forgiveness*, Grand Rapids, Baker Academic, 2003.

35 J. E. Loder, 'The Logic of the Spirit: Human Development in Theological Perspective', San Francisco, Jossey-Bass, 1998, p. 90, quoted in Shults and Sandage, *The Faces of Forgiveness*.

36 D. N. Stern, *The Interpersonal World of the Infant: A View from Psychoanalysis and Developmental Psychology*, London, Karnac, 1985.

37 J. Loder, *The Transforming Moment*, Colorado Springs, Helmer & Howard, 2nd edn 1989, p. 163, quoted in Shults and Sandage, *The Faces of Forgiveness*.

38 J. Vanier, *Becoming Human*, London, Darton, Longman & Todd, 1999.

To what then will I compare the people of this generation, and what are they like? They are like children sitting in the marketplace and calling to one another, 'We played the flute for you, and you did not dance; we wailed, and you did not weep.' For John the Baptist has come eating no bread and drinking no wine, and you say, 'He has a demon'; the Son of Man has come eating and drinking, and you say, 'Look, a glutton and a drunkard, a friend of tax collectors and sinners!' Nevertheless, wisdom is vindicated by all her children.

Luke 7.31–35

8. Collecting Memories: Identity, Nostalgia and the Objects of Childhood

TERRY J. WRIGHT

Introduction

If confession is as good for the soul as its advocates suggest, then I will tell all without reserve or hesitation: I like toys – and I buy those toys I especially like. Highlights over the past few years include amassing a collection of about 300 *GI Joe* action figures and buying a Darth Vader helmet and lightsabre in anticipation of 2005's cinematic release of *Star Wars Episode III: Revenge of the Sith*; and I am not above obtaining the occasional *Transformers* toy or model dinosaur or even DVDs of my favourite programmes from my childhood in the 1980s. I confess, then, that I have bought more toys than is probably expected of a man who is now in his early thirties; but I do so unashamedly and without repentance.

This admission will no doubt raise a few eyebrows and prompt mutterings concerning my state of mind; but without even needing to mention my wife's own increasingly extensive *Sylvanian Families* collection, I can say that I am not an isolated phenomenon. A quick search on the Internet for *Star Wars* unearths around 101,000,000 results; for *GI Joe*, 7,910,000 results; and for Optimus Prime of the *Transformers* range of toys, 2,080,000 results.[1] Many of these websites are constructed by fans – people like me – almost as shrines at which to pay homage to those idols of childhood that command devotion even some twenty years after the original epiphany.[2] All of which invites the question: why do some people – why do some *adults* – collect toys, things more typically associated with those of a younger age?

Given the question, it is not inappropriate to suggest that collecting is fundamentally an issue of human identity and the way in which that identity is expressed and upheld, which for the adult collector of toys is manifested and expressed through the accumulation of objects relating to or inspired by childhood memories. Through buying action figures, plastic dolls and the like, the adult in a sense images the child, embodying the desires of childhood with the potency of adulthood in one flesh. The adult does not literally become a child again, but the decision to indulge in nostalgia and to re-create a childhood with all the meaning that adulthood can ascribe to it retrospectively is a subversive rejection of the expectations society places upon the adult's role. Dedicating time, effort and money to building a collection of any kind thus reveals something of the values of the person collecting;[3] indeed, collecting also indicates how the person interprets the world around them by the value it assigns to the time, effort and money dedicated. At times, the passion that collecting inspires and channels adopts an almost religious quality in its search for the lost and in its desire for completion. Collecting the objects of childhood remembers the past and seeks to establish a somewhat idealized continuity between that past and the present. To collect, therefore, is an expression of human identity.

The aim of this chapter is not to address issues of childhood *per se* but to look at the way in which the imagery of childhood as portrayed in Scripture – particularly the father–child imagery applied to the relationship between God and humanity – demonstrates that human identity is properly constituted by God alone, to whom all other formative relationships are subordinate. I will also be concerned to look at issues of nostalgia in so far as this is very often a key factor in the decision of many adults to collect once more the objects of their childhood and so a significant influence on the formation of their identity. Crucially, we will suggest that despite the many parallels between collecting and practising faith, the latter itself acts as a critique of the former: human identity is formed aright only when its basic orientation is towards the God and Father of Jesus Christ (1 Peter 1.3).[4]

Collecting memories of the 1980s

If collecting adopts religious features, then indoctrination begins at childhood. As a young boy growing up in the 1980s, I had a number of *Star Wars* action figures – Han Solo in Bespin outfit, Darth Vader, Boba Fett, Jedi Knight Luke Skywalker, and so on – but nothing that would amount these days to anything approaching a 'collection'. That honour would first be given to *Transformers*, toy robots that at the manipulation of certain features would be changed from their mostly humanoid forms into a variety of vehicles and machines. During a period of three to four years, I had either bought or been given a total of around 120 *Transformers* toys of all shapes and sizes (and prices). However, my commitment to this expression of faith wavered as, approaching my early teens, I became increasingly interested in *Action Force* figures. These were the 3.75 inch scale *GI Joe* toys imported from the United States and repackaged to be more marketable on British soil. Now in secondary school, these were my toys of choice: although I still enjoyed *Transformers*, the idea of shape-shifting giant robots could not compare to the idea of a specialist group of soldiers committed to the eradication of the terrorist organization Cobra. *Action Force* was simply a more realistic concept. By the time I finished collecting *Action Force* toys – the first time around! – at about the age of 14 or 15, the size of this collection dwarfed that of my *Transformers* and included some comparatively rare figures that could be obtained only by searching relentlessly through toy shops or mail order.

Transformers and *Action Force* each had an elaborate story behind the toys themselves that was explicated through comics and television cartoon series (though these were often produced for a North American market and so imported into the United Kingdom with appropriate editing). The *Transformers* were a race of mechanical beings from the planet *Cybertron* who had been embroiled in an age-old civil war between the heroic *Autobots* and the evil *Decepticons*. *Action Force* was the codename for an elite anti-terrorist organization seeking to extinguish the threat of Cobra and its Hitleresque leader Cobra Commander. These comics and cartoons acted almost as a kind of liturgy, introducing complex and diverse narratives to establish characters that, until that point, had been nothing more than moulded, coloured plastic. Placed alongside 'file cards', the set texts that accompanied each toy to provide information about the character's personality, motives and fears, the media enabled the devout child to respond reverently and commit so much more to the toys by recognizing the life infused in them. As each newly acquired robot or soldier adopted its role in the play-ritual stimulated by the media-liturgy, the child was invited to enter into the stories themselves and so encouraged to re-enact them – or to devise new plots inspired by them – with the assortment of toys in possession. Playing with action figures required the ability to make sense of the liturgy and to interpret its sequence of events from one medium to another, which in so doing helped to develop the imagination; but this worthy activity could not happen without some degree of financial commitment.

True, many of the comic and cartoon stories were opportunities for the latest toy to be plugged, but this form of advertising was usually in the service of the story rather than vice versa.[5] Essentially, the toys were popular not because of the media in which they appeared but because they were good, mostly inexpensive toys that engaged the imagination. Although the toys required no indwelling of the narrative, no following of the liturgy of comics and cartoons, they did prompt at least this boy to collect a wide range of characters and accessories by appealing to his desire to gather, to order, to dramatize and exercise his own imagination.[6] My collections were less about 'owning' than about unleashing creativity. This creative power was mine alone, but I chose to interact with those charged to my care by respecting their integrity as they acted in the world I provided for them. They were not subjects over which my demigod sovereignty was proven but rather tools used to express my ideas about the world and my own role within it.

Generally, figure-based toy ranges – whether *Transformers*, *Action Force/GI Joe*, *Star Wars*, *Barbie*, *Sylvanian Families* or *Bratz*, to name but a few examples – feature a large number of characters and accessories and at times promote the purchasing of multiples to 'army build'.[7] For the buyer of toys, the ultimate challenge is to collect all items available in a given range, to find completion. Collecting toys is a form of consumption. Granted, children themselves are seldom in a position to buy vast quantities of toys, certainly from their own reserves; but many are capable of wringing extra funds from relatives as is possible through persistent, fervent prayer. Children are consumers by proxy; that is, they 'possess a form of "pester power" that exerts a significant influence on the purchasing decisions of others in the household'.[8] A child's 'power to consume . . . is almost entirely in the hands of adults'.[9] Indeed, whatever is bought 'must appeal to both children and to the adults who pay out on their behalf'.[10] As Patricia Holland observes of 'the promotional image', children are given context not by 'familial constraints' but by 'commerce alone. The parents or other adults who are expected to pay for the goods are invisible, taken for granted, replaced by financial symbols.'[11] In so far as a child is often taken implicitly to 'belong' to its parents,[12] the child's own ability to reverse this relation and so to extract from its parents what is needed for its own self-assertion is perhaps an inevitable corrective to ideas of what counts as 'product'. Despite the pleasure I took from additions to my collections, I look back now with regret at the manipulative tactics I used in procuring many of them. While children may not be consumers as typically understood, their lack of financial clout detracts not at all from their consumer mindset and parents are unlikely to respond negatively to their enthusiastic petitioning.

Collecting and recollecting

That said, many mothers and fathers will no doubt do their best to frustrate their children's attempts to rule the household purse; but a significant proportion of adults with the disposable income to empty Toys R Us suggests that companies such as Hasbro or Mattel will not necessarily be alarmed by the restrictions imposed by financially cautious parents. Away from the nest, the adult now has no need to cajole others into satisfying his or her desires to spend, spend, spend (though the bank manager may well demand appeasement). This returns us to our earlier question: Why do some adults collect toys? The question may be rephrased: Why do people collect anything at all? Marjorie Akin writes:

> I would argue that there are five major reasons individuals collect things: to satisfy a sense of personal aesthetics, to gain a sense of control or completion, to connect themselves with history, for profit (real or imagined), and for, as one avid collector described it, the 'thrill of the chase'.[13]

It is not too hard, then, to understand the motives of a collector. People collect the objects they do because the objects first appeal to them; because in hunting missing items (the 'thrill of the chase'), it promotes the collector's sense of control over his or her environment; because certain items are connected with the past and possession of those items helps the collector to integrate with that past. Sometimes objects have monetary value, though most collectors would not claim to be investors.[14] Of particular interest to us is the idea that collecting can make connections with the past. There is, of course, an appeal to owning something that connects us with history. Owning a piece of the past situates us in that history as though we were there: thus those 'collectors [who] seek out coins from the reigns of historically significant rulers, such as Henry VIII or Ghengis Khan, [do so] because they like the personal connection with the famous past that such ownership gives them'.[15] Inevitably, this connection is stronger when the collection is based upon an actual, experienced past. To hold once more an action figure not handled for over a decade can be a powerful experience, evoking memories of childhood and merging those recollections with fresh remembrances of the hopes and dreams also held at that time. Faith is rekindled.

Perhaps this is why so many people collect objects from their childhood, even though in the case of a toy collector it means engaging in a form of consumption at which society in general mocks. Adults are not meant to spend their Saturday mornings worshipping at the local toy shop, combing the shelves for the latest releases. Here, though, is again the interesting reversal of roles that we saw earlier in our brief discussion of the child as consumer. 'Childhood' is understood first by how we understand 'adulthood';[16] 'children are defined principally in terms of what they are *not* and in terms of what they *cannot* do.'[17] Thus, Holland comments, childhood 'is not only different from adulthood, but also its obverse. In this view,' she continues,

> childhood should be everything adulthood is not: children are powerless and dependent on adults; they are without knowledge and need to be educated; economic and sexual activity is prohibited for them – and so on. Yet these negative definitions allow abstract 'childhood' to become a depository for many precious qualities that 'adulthood' needs but which are incompatible with adult status; qualities such as impulsiveness, playfulness, emotional expressiveness, indulgence in fantasy, sexual innocence.[18]

The relation between childhood and adulthood is, however, a false dichotomy; rather, it is 'a variety of fluctuating states, constantly under negotiation',[19] as the child refuses to be domesticated to preserve adult dominance. Indeed, the child's emergence as a consumer trespasses onto what is traditionally an adult domain and thus opens the way for an adult once more to engage in childhood. For some adults, this takes the specific form of toy collecting, not necessarily to play with them as they would have done as a child but to offer a means of finding childhood calm in a world of adult disorder. By holding an object of the remembered past in the present, the memory of what we once were and the awareness of what we are now are meshed together in a seamless identity that contributes to what we hope to be in the future. Collected objects are given a meaning that then induces nostalgic recollection of childhood,[20] which in turn forms part of the basis for adulthood.

This means that nostalgia is far more than the romanticizing of the past. Originally a diagnosable disease of homesick soldiers,[21] nostalgia (from *nostos*, 'return home', and *algia*, 'pain' or 'longing')[22] is extremely difficult to define. Ostensibly, 'it is longing for a place, but actually it is yearning for a different time – the time of our childhood, the slower rhythms of our dreams.'[23] On this account, the homesickness felt by many is not necessarily spatial or geographical but temporal, a feeling that time has been lost, even misused, which results in the past being mythologized.[24] Nostalgia is more than simply longing for the past; it aims to provide some form of roots for the displaced. It is the longing for a home. As Svetlana Boym writes:

> To feel at home is to know that things are in their places and so are you; it is a state of mind that doesn't depend on actual location. The object of longing, then, is not really a place called home but this sense of intimacy with the world; it is not the past in general, but that imaginary moment when we had time and didn't know the temptation of nostalgia.[25]

For this reason, as Janelle Wilson argues, 'nostalgia can be seen as an intrapersonal expression of self which subjectively provides one with a sense of continuity',[26] a home away from home. 'Nostalgia may facilitate *continuity of identity*, allowing people, through narrative and sometimes vicarious experience, to "place" themselves in time and space' so they can better understand 'who and where [they] have been'.[27] Appropriating the various liturgies and set texts of the past reminds the nostalgist of how he or she once lived and encourages similar, contemporary practice. It is inadequate, however, simply to yearn for childhood, for the adult's actual childhood may not have been quite as charming as memories suggest. What matters is the contemporary recollection of childhood, sanitized and shaped to ground the present in a vestige of the past. Thus the apparent fragmentation that affects contemporary society reshapes the more traditional forms of community, enabling nostalgia and the objects that cause nostalgia to support new communities or subcultures based on networks of people with shared memories and similar interests rather than on spatially located groups. Collecting objects of the past, even if the past itself was not shared, reveals the type of community and values held and endorsed by the collector, first through the forging of that community based on the collective memory and then through the continuation of that community in which the collector participates.

All this suggests that when an adult actively seeks to buy toys, there is far more involved in that consumer choice than the choice to be a consumer of these particular products. Nostalgia is not a cry for help in the face of a shaky present or an uncertain future; it *is* the help, wearing the clothes of childhood. Simply to dismiss an adult who buys toys as someone trying to recapture a lost childhood by wallowing in the nostalgic mud of his or her memory therefore misses the point: the sought-and-bought objects have a contemporaneity that denies the common idea of nostalgia merely as a mnemonic sedative but enables the forming and perpetuation of a particular identity in the present.

Transforming identity

In so far as it is a matter of human identity, the act of collecting unconsciously adopts an almost religious significance. For the adult collector of toys, the persistent stimulation that comes through engagement with the personal past, the thrill of the chase, the anticipation of once more entering into the childhood narrative that should so long ago have been rejected are all too powerful to ignore and undesirable to resist. Continuity of identity is affirmed through the act of collecting and its recollection of an ancient rite now updated and revised becomes the means by which the world is engaged. However, it is at this point that those parallels with religion become problematic and they do so because it is at this point that collecting sets itself up as a false alternative to that which truly affirms and constitutes human identity: the God and Father of our Lord Jesus Christ (1 Peter 1.3).

We see this problem emerge in Luke 12. Here, someone expresses a strong desire to have a proportion of the family inheritance and seeks Jesus' help in procuring it (Luke 12.13). Jesus refuses (12.14) and tells the crowd to shun greed, 'for one's life does not consist in the abundance of possessions' (12.15). The parable of the rich man who horded his material goods and wealth (12.16–19) to no avail stands as a stark reminder of this: 'God said to him, "You fool! This very night your life is being demanded of you. And the things you have prepared, whose will they be?"' (12.20) Effectively, the man sought his identity in the wrong thing: he was storing up treasures – literal treasures! – for himself but was not rich towards God (12.21). Only when people realize that their lives are constituted fundamentally by God and so first seek his kingdom will they be in a position not to worry about their identity or how it is formed and upheld. Jesus, all the time presupposing that their relationship with God should have priority and reflect his graciousness, tells his disciples that they need not worry about their lives or strive after things because God knows what they need and is prepared to give to them (12.22–34).

This passage, however, is notable also for its use of certain imagery to portray the relationship between God and his people. He is their Father; the corollary is that they are his children, to whom will be given the Father's kingdom (12.30, 32). That this identification of God as Father is linked to a parable concerning material possessions and an exhortation to trust in the sheer goodness of the Father rather than in those possessions is surely no coincidence: as a child is obliged solely to depend on its father's security, so are the people of God required similarly to place unswerving trust in their Father. However, whatever father–child imagery Luke employs to portray the relationship between God and his people is secondary to the prior use of the same imagery to portray God's relationship specifically with Jesus. The story of the young Jesus in the temple is the first instance in Luke of Jesus' own reflection upon his identity. Upon finding Jesus missing from their convoy, his parents eventually find him at the temple in Jerusalem:

> When his parents saw him they were astonished; and his mother said to him, 'Child, why have you treated us like this? Look, your

> father and I have been searching for you in great anxiety.' He said to them, 'Why were you searching for me? Did you not know that I must be in my Father's house?'
>
> Luke 2.48–49

Crucially, Jesus prioritizes his relationship with God – whom he designates 'my Father' – over his relationship with his parents. He recognizes that his identity is formed ultimately by his relationship with God and then by all other formative relationships, such as those with his parents. Again, the paternal imagery used of God implies that Jesus is his child; but there is something here that expresses a more fundamental relationship between God and Jesus, a relationship that would be diminished if we were not to accept that the imagery itself is empowered by the reality to which it points. Luke's account of Jesus' baptism shows God declaring Jesus to be his Son (3.22). What Jesus intimated as a boy in the temple, God now acknowledges explicitly to be true: that he, God, is Jesus' Father and that the man Jesus is God's Son. Thus when Jesus teaches his disciples to pray to God as 'Father' (11.2), he does so knowing that his identity is secured by his Father's affirmation and the Spirit's anointing (3.22). The disciples may also call God 'Father' because they are called by Jesus, the Son of God, and so may share in the intimacy he has with God.

This Christological emphasis is the heart of the scriptural presentation of divine–human relations. It uses father–child imagery to stress that all human persons stand in relation to God as his children; but they do so truly only by relating to him through his Son, Jesus, the incarnate Word. The Old Testament, of course, does not and can not make such explicit claims: here, father–child imagery is used powerfully instead to affirm the people of Israel as the 'children of the LORD' (Deuteronomy 14.1). God is Israel's father not only because he brought his children into the world (Deuteronomy 32.6; Isaiah 64.8; Malachi 2.10) but also because he liberated his 'firstborn son' (Exodus 4.22) from Egypt and carried his people in the wilderness 'just as one carries a child' (Deuteronomy 1.31).[28]

The fatherhood of God is mediated through that of Israel's own fathers: God introduces himself to Moses as 'the God of your father Abraham, the God of Isaac, and the God of Jacob' (Exodus 3.6). With this statement, God makes it clear to Moses – and through him to Israel – that Israel's status as 'firstborn son' is conditioned by the promises that he made to Israel's ancestors (Deuteronomy 7.8), and in particular to Abraham, that Abraham's descendents will be as numerous as the stars (Genesis 15.4–5). Israel, the children of Abraham, is the child of the LORD because the LORD is intimately connected with her father Abraham. Ultimately, Israel's identity *as* Israel is formed by her relation to the LORD.

We approach the christological nuances when this father–child imagery is applied to specific Israelites rather than to Israel as a nation. In 2 Samuel, God says of David's offspring that he 'will be a father to him, and he shall be a son to me' (7.14). Psalm 2.7 speaks of the LORD's anointed in terms of a begotten son, imagery that is, of course, repeated in the New Testament conviction that Jesus is God's only begotten son (John 3.16 KJV). Indeed, the New Testament's affirmations of God as father are expressed primarily through his being the Father of Jesus Christ; the imagery of divine–human, father–child that characterized the relationship between God and Israel becomes flesh in the relationship between the man Jesus and his heavenly Father. Thus Matthew's genealogy describes Jesus as 'the Messiah, the son of David, the son of Abraham' (1.1); as God is portrayed as the God of Abraham, again the implication must be that Jesus is the Son of God, a fact confirmed by his baptism and God's affirmation that Jesus is 'my Son, the Beloved' (3.17). Similarly, Mark's Gospel immediately identifies Jesus as the Son of God (1.1), and John's Gospel leaves us with no doubts whatsoever as to the intimacy between God the Father and Jesus the Son (10.30; 14.6b–11a). It is an intimacy that, in the Johannine letters, can only impact positively upon human fellowship (1 John 1.3) as believers are called the children of God on the basis of the Father's love, which is manifested supremely in God's Son (1 John 1.3; 3.1a; 4.9–11; cf. 2 John 3b).

Outside the Gospels and the Johannine literature, the other New Testament writings also build upon the relation between God and Jesus, drawing out the implications that believers are God's children if they are associated with Jesus in much the same way as the people of Israel were associated with God through their father Abraham. Thus Ephesians states that God 'destined us for adoption as his children through Jesus Christ', described as 'the Beloved', a reference, of course, to Jesus' baptism (1.5–6; cf. Matthew 3.17); and in Colossians, Paul tells of thanks given to 'God, the Father of our Lord Jesus Christ' (1.3), a phrasing echoed by Peter (1 Peter 1.3). Perhaps the keenest declaration of our status as the children of God is found in Galatians: '[I]n Christ Jesus you are all sons of God (*huioi theou*) through faith' (3.26).[29] In his letter, Paul aims to convince his Galatian audience that the Mosaic Law ought to play no part in their lives. Essentially, a group of Jewish-Christian missionaries[30] had been presenting the Galatians with what Paul sees as 'a different gospel' (1.6); evidently, these missionaries required the Galatians' circumcision and their total obedience to the law (as suggested by 3.10 and 5.2–4). However, Paul is concerned that in so doing they have misunderstood completely the centrality of Christ in God's new dealings with his creation; the law belongs to God's former way of dealing with his people, because now all who are counted as God's people are so because they are 'in Christ' (3.26) rather than 'under the law' (3.23). Thus any attempt to relate to God under the law effectively bypasses Christ and so is doomed to failure.

The crucial image in Paul's argument is that of the Mosaic Law as a *paidagōgos* (3.24), that is, a person, usually a slave, responsible for the protection and discipline of a child as it grew into adulthood. By using the *paidagōgos* as an image for the law, Paul intimates that Israel is a child needing to submit to the authoritative guidance of the *pater familias*, the male head of the household. Indeed, the imagery is telling: for families in the upper socio-economic groups, where children were expected to carry on the family name and business,[31] the *paidagōgos* was

> charged with the supervision and conduct of one or more sons in the family. He . . . gave no formal instruction but administered the directives of the father in a custodial manner, though, of course, indirectly he taught by the supervision he gave and the discipline he administered.[32]

Depending upon the maturity of his charge, the *paidagōgos* would guide and punish as necessary; but by embodying the father's standards, he would expose the shortcomings of the child and thus stimulate development in the appropriate, desired way until the child, too, embodied those standards. The effect was to produce a mature adult capable of acting responsibly and making wise decisions without custodial supervision.[33] Although Paul's suggestion that Israel is a child clearly affirms that she is genuinely the child of God her father, there is also the lingering judgement that she has yet to grow to represent him faithfully as a fully responsible, adult child. Israel was given the law to mark her out as God's people; thus her faithful observation of that law would enable her to embody her Father's standards and so be identified as his child. Now Paul reasons that the identity of God's children is no longer conditioned by the law. Does he mean by this that Israel has finally reached adulthood? No; instead, Jesus has come, representing Israel as her messiah to offer to God the appropriate, mature response on her behalf. Thus the faith of which Paul has spoken consistently throughout Galatians (2.16, 20; 3.14, 22–26) is the faith or faithfulness of Christ himself: his faithfulness to the law, to the commandments of God, to God's calling that saw him crucified (3.13).[34] All humanity is to relate to God not through the law but through Christ, who embodies the law in his flesh and in whose maturity others share by the Spirit. Accordingly, Christ supersedes the law, or, as Paul phrases it, '[N]ow that faith has come, we are no longer subject to a disciplinarian, for in Christ Jesus you are all sons of God through faith' (3.25–26).

Paul then presses home his point: while the Israelites were under the law and so under the watchful eye of the *paidagōgos*, they could not receive their inheritance until the time of majority. The imagery Paul uses at this point – that of 'heirs' and 'minors' – indicates that the inheritance would be received when the proper time comes; until then, the Israelites are 'no better than slaves' (4.1). All this changed, however, with the coming of the mature Israelite, Jesus Christ, the Son of God, 'born under the law, in order to redeem those under the law' (4.4–5a). Enslaved under the *paidagōgos*-law, the people of Israel had no right at that time to receive the inheritance undoubtedly promised to them; but through participation in the Son of God they may rightly be considered as God's adopted children (4.5b) and so in receipt of the promise (3.22), the Spirit of God's Son (4.6). This adoption implicates the Gentiles, too, who are also God's children if they are 'in Christ' – it is because they have been accepted into God's family as his adopted children that the Jews have received the Spirit (4.6). God is the Father of Jesus Christ, the one true Israelite and thus the one true Son of God; but in so far as Jews and Gentiles may be found 'in Christ', they are also God's sons and so true heirs of the promise of the Spirit. If the Galatians' identity as God's people is being questioned, as seems to be the case (1.6–9; 3.1–5), then the fact that God's children – the Galatians included – have received the Spirit of his Son (3.2; 4.6) means that their identity as God's children cannot be denied (4.7).

Paul's interpretation of the role of the law as a *paidagōgos* that portrays Israel as a young child essentially comments on the formation of Israel's identity in relation to Christ, God's Son. There is no judgement here that the status of a child is something to be despised or contrasted unfavourably with that of an adult; Paul's imagery simply builds upon the everyday phenomenon that a person of a certain age will one day be an 'adult' with all the responsibilities that accompany that transition. The imagery serves Paul's contention that God's covenant people are defined by their relation to Christ. Thus, it is no exaggeration to say on the basis of Paul's argument in Galatians that human identity is shaped fundamentally by whether or not a person is 'in Christ'. Undoubtedly, there are other factors that contribute to the formation of human identity – we have already claimed that collecting is one of these – but their influence cannot provide the basic orientation towards God that is directed through the Spirit's enabling of human participation in Christ's own sonship.

We see, then, that Scripture continually builds upon the idea of God as Father standing in relation to his human children and in so doing stresses the centrality of Jesus in those relations. First and foremost, Jesus Christ is the Son of God (*huios theou*) through whom, secondly, human persons may become sons of God (*huioi theou*). The emphasis falls upon the importance of the relation of all people to God through Christ: we may be the children of God because, by the Spirit and through Jesus, the Son of God, we also are God's 'sons'. Scripture thus demonstrates that human identity has its basic orientation towards God and does so by utilizing imagery that depicts the divine–human relation as a father–child relation. This is not to say that Scripture does not utilize childhood imagery in any other way,[35] but that the imagery of father–child relationships has a fitting potency for our discussion. As we have seen, a collector's identity in large part is formed by the objects of collecting and reveals the values held by the collector; a toy collector's identity excavates an additional stratum of meaning by assigning value to the continuous play between adulthood and childhood that is expressed in the material form of toys. In so far as the status of adulthood is thrown temporarily into confusion, the adult collector of toys becomes a child again without necessarily losing the maturity that comes with adulthood. However, as with any human person, the collector's identity must first be formed by his or her relationship with God, who has revealed himself to be the Father of Jesus and, through him, the

Father of all humanity. Thus, God stands in relation to all, whether all acknowledge it or not, and so the divine-human relation must qualify and impact all other relations within the created order, including that between collector and collection and nostalgist and past. Whenever the practices of collecting mirror those rituals by which the believer approaches God, they always have a tendency to deny the 'object' to which these rituals point, namely, Jesus, the Son of God, through whom alone we, by the Holy Spirit, have access to God the Father (Ephesians 2.18).

Memory and identity

It is at this point that the act of collecting is critiqued by the religious dimension it mimics, particularly as it relates to the evocation of the past and its appropriation of that past to constitute self-identity in the present with the intention of moving into the future. Acts of remembrance are vital components for both the person who accepts that human identity is formed primarily through relating to God through Christ and the nostalgist-collector whose identity is very often shaped by the collected objects of childhood. The point of departure between the two lies in the nature of the object remembered and the reasons for the importance of its remembrance for constituting human identity.

I said earlier that to hold once more an action figure not handled for over a decade is often a powerful experience. This act recalls childhood: memories of visiting toy shops, transfixed in awe before the array of icons displayed, contemplating which should be the next to be placed reverently in the sanctuary of the bedroom. These meditations in turn open the door to further recollections: sacred thoughts of a new character's placement within the collection, of its interaction with the other figures already present, of how the overall narrative changes with its introduction, of how *this* narrative was created by *this* boy at *this* age, *this* boy who, away from his toys, read *this* book, took *these* subjects and sat *these* exams, conversed with *these* people, had *these* dreams, hopes and aspirations and, with *all these together*, is now *this* man writing *this* chapter about *these* very things, trying to provide some kind of rationale for why he collects as he does. Of collecting, we have said that it is a way for the collector to maintain a sense of control over his or her environment and that, in collecting items connected with the past, the collector is enabled to cope with the present and move into the future through the memory of continued identity stimulated by the collected objects. Memory is a powerful motivator of action and collections of historical objects remind us of where we have been, both individually and communally, and suggest paths for where next to tread. Fundamentally, this is a question of identity: Who are we? From where have we come? Where are we going? Material culture can help us to address these questions; but it can do so only in a limited way.

In Scripture, remembering the past, especially the past actions of God, is a recurring exhortation intended both to justify and to spur action (see, for example, Deuteronomy 8.1–10 [note the further father–child imagery of 8.5] and 24.17–18, 21–22). Remembering the past is not meant to result in despondence or rebellion (as in Numbers 11) but to enable positive self-awareness of continued identity in the present and so into the future (as in Luke 15.17–18). Given that human identity is shaped primarily by God through Christ, the key act of remembrance for Christians is the Eucharist or Communion. Paul in particular makes the connection between its institution by Jesus and the importance of its continuation for those who accept that their identity derives from him:

> For I received from the Lord what I also handed on to you, that the Lord Jesus on the night when he was betrayed took a loaf of bread, and when he had given thanks, he broke it and said, 'This is my body that is for you. Do this in remembrance of me.' In the same way he took the cup also, after supper, saying, 'This cup is the new covenant in my blood. Do this, as often as you drink it, in remembrance of me.' For as often as you eat this bread and drink the cup, you proclaim the Lord's death until he comes.
>
> 1 Corinthians 11.23–26

Participation in Holy Communion is an act whereby the community of the Church meets with God as it remembers Christ. It is therefore an act of worship and not the act of idolatry that collecting can so often become in its elevation of the material. The communicant does not control the Holy Communion ritual, for the efficacy of the sacrament is entirely outside his or her powers. Thus, the act of remembrance to which the liturgy gives form is not simply an expression of nostalgia that dwells on the past in order to consolidate the present with the intention of using that past to move into the future. Fundamentally, Communion is an act that focuses not on the self but on him who forms the self, that is, Jesus; and in so doing, each communicant is open to *his* past, *his* present and *his* future. Thus Communion is no mere recollection but both a remembrance of Jesus's sacrificial death and the risen Christ's promised return; as the liturgy puts it, 'Christ has died, Christ is risen, Christ will come again.' For this reason, the Christian's act of remembrance in Communion critiques the collector's nostalgia because the former is based upon the divine promise that Christ will return, that he will remember his people and some day return to them in the flesh. As worthy as collecting may be for some, it does not and cannot link the present with the past and the future in the way as does participation in Christ. By reflecting on the death of Christ, by acknowledging his current position at the Father's side and by eagerly awaiting his physical return, the Christian has a framework in which to place his or her past and present and so can move into the future freely without the past negatively conditioning that future. Perhaps this is why Paul says to those Galatians balanced precariously on the edge of slavery that '[i]t is for freedom that Christ has set us free' (Galatians 5.1 NIV).

Concluding remarks

At the beginning of the chapter, I asked this question: Why do some people – why do some *adults* – collect toys? Certainly, the status of the adult collector of toys *as* an adult is not jeopardized by such an activity, and buying toys does not mean that the adult suddenly forgets his or her responsibilities as an adult and can no longer be trusted to act in an adult manner. The decision to obtain the objects of childhood is a particular expression of human identity that derives its meaning from the collector's own past; but it cannot hope to be the definitive expression of the collector's past, for that, as with all human persons, is found only through participation in Christ.

I have sought, therefore, to provide an account of why many adults collect toys, that is, of why many adults allow themselves to be associated with those things more typically linked with those of the younger generations. Collecting objects of history enables the collector to connect with the past, to be assigned a 'place' in history and so to preserve an identity; collecting toys is simply a particular instance of this more general enabling. However, the adult collector of toys enters into the world of the child deliberately in order to preserve his or her identity; the accumulation of the material objects – images, even – of childhood becomes the way in which the adulthood and the values he or she accepts with it are expressed. In so doing, the collector adopts a reverential posture towards his or her past and engages with the activity of collecting as though it had near-religious significance. Scripture does not condemn this practice as such, but it does critique its idolatrous leanings by making clear that the basic orientation of human identity is towards God and does not consist solely of those secondary activities such as toy collecting by which we might define ourselves. Despite the religious undertones we might discern in the practice of collecting, the very religion it parallels critiques and subordinates it to the power of the gospel message and does so on the basis of the import of the childhood imagery used throughout Scripture. The casting of an adult as a child is overwhelmed by the affirmation of the human person as a child of God through participation in the life of the Son of God. Scripture thus makes much use of father–child imagery and shows that those who are 'in Christ', 'in' God's Son, stand in proper relation to God as his sons and so have their identity formed aright. This is consolidated through Communion, the act of remembrance *par excellence* that is more than simple nostalgia due to its continuous witness to the risen Christ, who has promised to remember those who, through him, strive for his Father's kingdom (Luke 12.31). Human identity thus finds its ultimate expression not in material wealth or in remembering one's roots, however either of these may be conceived, but in witnessing to the one in whom all human activity is given shape and meaning, Jesus Christ.

What has been said here cannot, of course, be the final word – certainly not the final *theological* word – on matters of identity, nostalgia and collecting. Nor is this the definitive account of how Scripture uses the imagery of childhood: I have looked briefly – perhaps too briefly – at a few relevant texts in particular in order to say what I have said about the adult's past childhood. Yet what *can* be said, to conclude, is that being an adult by no means forbids us from being a child. By this, I do not mean that we may be child*ish*, that we may act irresponsibly and without wisdom; but we *are* free to engage with one another playfully, free to remember our past with fondness, free to indulge our creativity. If standing firm against slavery permits me to buy action figures, to enjoy watching DVDs of 1980s cartoons or to find perverse pleasure in 'rearranging' my wife's *Sylvanian Families* collection in bizarre ways, then I will celebrate my freedom without reserve or hesitation.[36]

Notes

1 These results are from a Google search made on 16 September 2006.

2 *Star Wars* merchandise is ever-popular, not least because of the recent prequel trilogy that has introduced a new generation of fans to its universe. Production of *GI Joe* figures – known as *Action Force* in the United Kingdom for a significant part of the 1980s – ceased for a while during the mid- to late 1990s before a re-launch in the United States in 2000. The *Transformers* range has had a succession of theme changes – *Beast Wars*, *Armada* and *Heroes of Cybertron* are but three – to maintain its presence in toy shops, a presence I expect to become even more noticeable with the forthcoming *Transformers* live-action movie (at the time of writing, scheduled for cinematic release in the summer of 2007). Although specific details may be found by any cursory search on the internet, in particular I recommend www.starwars.com, www.yojoe.com and www.transfans.net

3 Marjorie Akin, 'Passionate Possession: The Formation of Private Collections' in W. David Kingery (ed.), *Learning from Things: Method and Theory of Material Culture Studies*, London, Smithsonian Institution Press, 1996, pp. 104, 107.

4 I make no apologies for employing the scriptural language of God as 'Father' here, though by using the term I do not wish to imply that God is 'male' or favours or legitimates 'male' over and against 'female'.

5 See David Buckingham, *After the Death of Childhood: Growing Up in the Age of Electronic Media*, Cambridge, Polity Press, 2000, pp. 155–9 for an absorbing account of the relation between children's television and merchandising.

6 Cf. Akin, 'Passionate Possession', p. 108: 'Collecting seems to be part of the very human urge to put the universe in order, to categorize and name things.'

7 Many collectors will buy multiples of the same figure – for example, a Cobra Viper (*Action Force/GI Joe*) or an Imperial Stormtrooper (*Star Wars*) – to build vast 'armies'.

8 Buckingham, *After the Death of Childhood*, p. 147.

9 Buckingham, *After the Death of Childhood*, p. 165.

10 Patricia Holland, *Picturing Childhood: The Myth of the Child in Popular Imagery*, London, I. B. Taurus, 2006 reprint, p. 66.

11 Holland, *Picturing Childhood*, p. 66.

12 John Wall, 'Fallen Angels: A Contemporary Christian Ethical Ontology of Childhood', *International Journal of Practical Theology* 8:2 (2004), pp. 160–84, 166.

13 Akin, 'Passionate Possession', p. 108.

14 Akin, 'Passionate Possession', p. 113: '[P]eople who accumulate goods that are secured and maintained with the primary goal of eventual resale are, by my definition, investors, not collectors. How do collectors differ from investors? A collector may occasionally sell an item to secure funds for another purchase that will improve the quality of the collection overall, or because of some personal financial difficulty, but the intention is to permanently preserve the material.'

15 Akin, 'Passionate Possession', p. 111.

16 Buckingham, *After the Death of Childhood*, p. 7.

17 Buckingham, *After the Death of Childhood*, p. 13, italics original.

18 Holland, *Picturing Childhood*, p. 15.

19 Holland, *Picturing Childhood*, p. 16.

20 Janelle L. Wilson, *Nostalgia: Sanctuary of Meaning*, Lewisburg, Bucknell University Press, 2005, p. 110.

21 Svetlana Boym, *The Future of Nostalgia*, New York, Basic Books, 2001, pp. xiv, 3.

22 Boym, *The Future of Nostalgia*, p. xiii; Wilson, *Nostalgia*, p. 21.

23 Boym, *The Future of Nostalgia*, p. xv.

24 Wilson, *Nostalgia*, p. 23.

25 Boym, *The Future of Nostalgia*, p. 251.

26 Wilson, *Nostalgia*, p. 147.

27 Wilson, *Nostalgia*, pp. 61, 84, italics original.

28 The imagery of Israel as God's 'firstborn son' is not as exclusive as it sounds, for it implicates all other nations as his children, too, though Israel stands in special relation both to them and to God. See also Exodus 19.5, where Israel is described as God's 'treasured possession' although, says God, 'the whole earth is mine'.

29 We cannot hope to offer here a thorough exegesis of Galatians 3.23—4.7. It is enough for us to see the basic use to which Paul puts the *paidagōgos* metaphor and what this means for understanding how a human person is constituted. The more contentious issues such as the phrase 'works of the law', the precise role of the law and how *pistis* is used throughout Galatians must be set aside.

30 James D. G. Dunn, *A Commentary on the Epistle to the Galatians*, London, A&C Black, 1993, p. 11.

31 D. L. Stamps, 'Children in Late Antiquity' in Craig A. Evans and Stanley E. Porter (eds), *Dictionary of New Testament Background*, Leicester, IVP, 2000, p. 197.

32 Richard N. Longenecker, *Galatians*, Word Biblical Commentary, Vol. 41, Nashville, Thomas Nelson, 1990, p. 148.

33 For a comprehensive account of the role of the *paidagōgos* as depicted by Greco-Roman literature, see David J. Lull, '"The Law was our Pedagogue": A Study in Galatians 3:19–25', *Journal of Biblical Literature* 105:3 (1986), pp. 481–98, 489–94.

34 The phrase *pisteōs Iēsou Christou* (Galatians 2.16,20; 3.14, 22–26) may be translated either as 'faith in Jesus Christ' (objective genitive) or 'the faith [or

faithfulness] of Jesus Christ' (subjective genitive). Our reading assumes the latter, that *pisteōs Christou Iēsou* refers to Christ's own faithfulness and therefore to divine action in contrast to human action.

35 Texts such as 1 Kings 3.7, Jeremiah 1.6–7, Hosea 1.3–11 and Matthew 18.3 are but a few examples of childhood imagery used to portray adults – in the case of the Hosea passage, the children themselves image the nations of Israel and Judah.

36 Thanks to those at the www.joebattlelines.com message forums for their confirmation of my view that nostalgia is an important factor in the motivation of adult collectors of toys.

About this we have much to say that is hard to explain, since you have become dull in understanding. For though by this time you ought to be teachers, you need someone to teach you again the basic elements of the oracles of God. You need milk, not solid food; for everyone who lives on milk, being still an infant, is unskilled in the word of righteousness. But solid food is for the mature, for those whose faculties have been trained by practice to distinguish good from evil. Therefore let us go on toward perfection, leaving behind the basic teaching about Christ, and not laying again the foundation: repentance from dead works and faith toward God, instruction about baptisms, laying on of hands, resurrection of the dead, and eternal judgement.

Hebrews 5.11—6.2

9. The Never-Land of Religion and the Lost Childhood of the Children of God

ANGELA SHIER-JONES

Introduction: the child without a childhood

The mistaken assumption that childhood as a stage of human development did not exist until the seventeenth century owes much to the work of Phillippe Ariès and his monumental study *Centuries of Childhood*.[1] In fact, as has been conclusively demonstrated in more recent studies,[2] childhood has been recognized as something distinct from adult life in every age, but not always in the same way or as it is currently understood. The concept of childhood has changed over time to take account of different attitudes towards, and understandings of, the human child. It would be reasonable to assume that the same would be true of the nature of Christian childhood[3] and that it should be possible to recognize changes in the understanding of Christian childhood corresponding to changes in the understanding of what it means to be a child of God. What becomes apparent, however, on looking for evidence to support this assumption is that Ariès' thesis is more tellingly applied to the children of God than it is to its original subjects. This is all the more puzzling when the influence of religion on concepts such as childhood is taken into consideration. Arguably, the main reason for this is that Christianity has for centuries provided confusing and contradictory statements of what it means to be a child of God – and almost no definition or conception of Christian childhood.

A child and a child of God are not the same, yet the distinction between them has often been blurred by images of Jesus surrounded by children, blessing children and – most importantly – being a child. In religious art and literature, for example, children are invariably depicted as being closer to God, more pure, innocent and undefiled. Angels and cherubim are frequently drawn in the image of children. The so-called 'slaughter of the innocents' in the Gospel of Matthew is a reminder that innocent is synonymous with child. St Paul certainly associates being a child of God with being 'blameless and innocent . . . without blemish in the midst of a crooked and perverse generation, in which you shine like stars in the world (Philippians 2.14–15). Yet Augustine was convinced that infants and children possessed an innate depravity, such innocence as could be ascribed to them was, he believed due to their physical weakness alone. Calvin also considered the whole nature of a child to be 'a seed of sin'.[4] The doctrine of original sin, on which such beliefs are based has scriptural warrant outside of the narrative of the 'fall' in, for example, the words of the Psalmist: 'Indeed, I was born guilty, a sinner when my mother conceived me' (Psalm 51.5).

In spite of evangelical claims for those who are 'born again' it is far too simplistic to state that the natural child is sinful whereas the child of God is not. The relationship between the two is more complex and perplexing. Though they are not the same, they are clearly interdependent. Scripture presumes, for example, that certain attributes of the natural child are not only desirable but essential to becoming a child of God. Hence the texts, 'Truly I tell you, unless you change and become like children, you will never enter the kingdom of heaven' (Matthew 18.3) and 'Whoever becomes humble like this child is the greatest in the kingdom of heaven' (Matthew 18.4). But these texts, so often used to justify the suppression of human intellect for the sake of faith, need to be set alongside such verses as 'The wicked go astray from the womb; they err from their birth, speaking lies'(Psalm 58.3) or God's declaration that 'the inclination of the human heart is evil from youth' (Genesis 8.21).

As this volume has already shown, Scripture contains several stories of children which provide a myriad of possible interpretations of what it means to be a child. When those stories are taken seriously they speak profoundly to this day and age. The murder of James Bulger[5] and the fact that up to 50 per cent of those who sexually abuse children are themselves children[6] must be a part of the backdrop for our reflections on childhood. The newsworthy children of the twentieth and twenty-first centuries, Damilola Taylor and Stephen Lawrence;[7] the prevalence of bullying, the necessity for ASBOs,[8] and the experiences of child soldiers,[9] all actively stifle any idealized and spiritualized notion of children as completely innocent and pure.

One of the problems seriously hindering reflection on what it means to be a child of God is the fact that Scripture fails to provide any clear guidelines as to what a child is. Is the youth referred to in the Genesis text still a child – or is 'youth' a whole different category of being altogether? How old must a child be before they cease to be the sort of child that a child of God should seek to become? Is an infant also a child? For that matter, is being a child something that is purely biologically and chronologically determined, or is there something else? These questions merely highlight the obvious: children, whether of natural descent or born of God, are far too complex to be able to caricature or summarize them neatly and accurately on the basis of either age or idealized characteristics. Any attempt to do so is bound to end in failure or contradiction or both. The only means of doing justice to the complexity of the nature of a child is to explore the distinctive context in which a child exists and develops, namely childhood.

There have been few studies of childhood *qua* childhood in either the natural sciences or theology. Perhaps this is due to there being so little in the canonical Scriptures about the childhood of Christ,[10] or perhaps it is because children have historically had such a low status in society. Whatever the reason, the end result is the same – a universal acknowledgement of Rousseau's statement:

> Childhood is unknown. Starting from the false idea one has of it, the farther one goes, the more one loses one's way.[11]

For the theologian, however, the journey is not optional. In order to obey the biblical imperative to become like a little child, without throwing away personal integrity or losing touch with reality and earning the scorn and ridicule of those who insist that such obedience is nothing more than 'escapism', the richness and complexity of childhood must be explored. Neither can the task be undertaken as a theological abstraction. If it is to have any lasting value, the exploration must take full account of the interdependency noted earlier between the childhood of the human or natural child, and that of the child of God. For this reason, the following section draws heavily on David Archard's study of childhood[12] to examine in what way the theories and concepts of social and biological maturing can help in the development of a coherent theology of Christian childhood.

Biogenic law and developmental theologies of childhood

The advent of psychology in the second half of the nineteenth century engendered the first serious scientific explorations of childhood as a stage in human development. Charles Darwin's paper entitled 'A Biographical Sketch of an Infant' published in *Mind* in 1877 was of fundamental importance to the idea of childhood as a developmental stage in human maturity and evolution.[13] Given his study of the processes of evolution, it was natural for Darwin to expect to see developments in his child as he observed him grow during the first few years of his life. Darwin also compared these observations with those he had made of the higher animals: 'He understood one word, namely, his nurse's name, exactly five months before he invented his first word mum; and this is what might have been expected, as we know that the lower animals easily learn to understand spoken words.'[14]

Darwin did not develop this particular dimension of his studies further, however, and it was left for Haeckel to make explicit Darwin's implicit assumption of a developmental relationship between the evolution of the species and the development of the individual. This he attempted to do through the creation of what is known as the 'biogenetic law'. According to Gould,[15] this law was Haeckel's favourite argument. With it he coined the phrase 'ontogeny recapitulates phylogeny' by which he meant that the development of the embryo of every species repeats the evolutionary development of that species.

It might seem strange to invoke Haeckel given his well-documented ridicule of all things spiritual but it is with more than a hint of irony that we acknowledge the indebtedness of many contemporary Christian theologies of childhood to a man who could hold that 'Evolution and progress stand on the one side, marshaled under the bright banner of science; on the other side, marshaled under the black flag of hierarchy, stand spiritual servitude and falsehood, want of reason and barbarism, superstition and retrogression.'[16]

Although modern biology has proved his 'law' is false, Haeckel's ideas were profoundly influential on the emerging sciences of psychology and sociology and a refined version of his biogenetic law still has wide acceptance today. The refinement removed the biological determinative by claiming that ontogeny is *isomorphic* or *parallel* to phylogeny. Thus, according to Archard: 'The development of the child into an adult mirrors, without literally reproducing, the progress of humanity as a whole. The child is seen as the analogue of the "primitive" human or pre-human animal.'[17]

An immediate problem of this refinement is, of course, that it presupposes a common understanding of what an adult is – something that, as will be seen later, is as contestable in theology as it is in childhood psychology or human biology. If, however, we leave aside for the moment what state of maturity awaits the children of God and focus instead on the premise that Christ fully matured and become truly human then the language of this refined law invites a comparison with Irenaeus' presentation of recapitulation in Christ.

According to Osborne,[18] recapitulation for Irenaeus means incarnation: 'The Word, who was in the beginning and always present with mankind has, in the last days and at the appointed time, united himself to his workmanship', that is, to passible man. He recapitulated in himself the long line of human beings (that is, he united them in himself as head), 'so that in himself what was lost in Adam might be recovered'.[19]

The extent to which Irenaeus offers this theological counterpart to the biogenic law is easier to recognize in the following extract where he writes of Christ:

> He therefore passed through every age, becoming an infant for infants, thus sanctifying infants; a child for children, thus sanctifying those who are of this age, being at the same time made to them an example of piety, righteousness, and submission; a youth for youths, becoming an example to youths, and thus sanctifying them for the Lord. So likewise He was an old man for old men,[20] that He might be a perfect Master for all, not merely as respects the setting forth of the truth, but also as regards age, sanctifying at the same time the aged also, and becoming an example to them likewise. Then, at last, He came on to death itself, that He might be 'the firstborn from the dead, that in all things He might have the preeminence,' the Prince of life, existing before all, and going before all.[21]

Irenaeus was not, of course, the only theologian to propose this understanding of Christ as the firstborn child of God whose life is intended to act as mirror to the development of the children of God and hence humanity as a whole. It occurs first in the writings of St

Paul (Romans 8.29–30) and has been a locus for the doctrines of incarnation and salvation ever since. The problem is, however, that few of the theologies based on Christ's recapitulation have explored the underlying assumptions that are implicit in it. It is this that has, arguably, led to the paucity in all of the major traditions of fully coherent or systematic theologies of childhood. Developmental models of childhood, like those founded on the recapitulation of Christ, are based on three primary assumptions, which can be summarized in terms of 'teleology, necessity, and endogeneity'.[22]

As has already been acknowledged, the presupposition of the developmental model of childhood is that there is a known *telos* or end point – namely adulthood. Children are primarily understood as 'becoming' adults as distinct from 'being' children. Adulthood is the ideal end-state, worthy of celebration and commemoration – an achievement recognized as such by society as a whole as well as by the individual and the immediate family. Failure to attain adulthood is accordingly seen as an anomaly in the developmental process requiring some form of intervention or treatment to remove the 'problem' if at all possible.

The second assumption implicit in the developmental model is that of necessity. 'Development is the inevitable unfolding and bringing into being of a telos implicit within the child. Each stage must be gone through and is a necessary precondition of progress to the next.'[23] It is not possible to go from infancy to adulthood without first passing through youth. The fact that each stage in childhood is necessarily connected allows for a concept of continuous or ongoing development. There are no breaks in the process, although there may well be sharp and sudden changes as, for example, with the onset of puberty.

The third and final assumption is that of endogeneity. This requires the process of maturing to be self-propelled: the progress through childhood from the one stage to the next 'derives its motive force from structures, functions and processes which are rooted within the child's nature'.[24] The nature of the child is normally conceived of as biologically predetermined although this need not be the case. On this basis, a child can no more halt its own biological growth than it can stop its own heart beating by will power alone. Additional motivation, stimulation and even perhaps modification to the biological force can be provided by cultural or social factors. In times of war or famine, for example, children often mature quicker than in times of peace.

It is not difficult to recognize the parallels in the above with existent theologies of Christian maturing, in spite of the manifold differences in the understanding and application of the primary assumptions behind the developmental model. There may be no clear agreement as to what exactly the *telos* of the children of God is, but there is almost universal acceptance that an end point will be reached. Similarly, the concept of necessary progression is implicit in the coherence of the Christian doctrines of baptism, justification, sanctification etc., even though churches and theologians may argue with regard to their individual order and necessity. Lastly, endogeneity is implicit in the anthropologically oriented doctrines of original sin, purgatory, predestination and prevenient grace, to name but a few as well as in such christologically oriented doctrines as incarnation and *perochoresis*.

From this it would seem that Christianity has proffered countless doctrines that are concerned with the development of humanity and are derived from an understanding of Christ's life as the recapitulation of the intended evolution of the whole human race. Yet it has managed to do so without producing a single systematic or consistent and coherent conception of childhood for the children of God. Christian anthropology has, on the whole, skipped over this particular dimension of human existence. Doctrines that address particular aspects of childhood *telos*, necessity or endogeneity tend, on the whole, to abstract the context they were created to address. Even given the post-modern aversion for overarching meta-narratives, it is evident that this state of affairs has impoverished the Christian faith and helped to provide a rational basis for those wishing to argue that Christianity is an insubstantial childish dependency that modern humanity has outgrown. In the absence of an alternative, Christian childhood can seem to be an over-romanticized self-indulgent playground for those who will not face up to the harsh realities and pressing responsibilities of adult life.

A theological conception of childhood

Certain aspects of childhood, such as education and moral and spiritual formation were seriously reflected upon by many theologians prior to the nineteenth century, although they seldom presented their reflections in either a systematic or even deliberately focused treatise on childhood. Nonetheless, Marcia Bunge is undoubtedly correct in her claim that '[c]hildhood has not always been a marginal theme in Christian theology'.[25] The problem has been that where childhood has been engaged with theologically, it has tended to be for the sake of some other cause or doctrine. Childhood *qua* childhood has received little attention from a Church whose primary responsibility has been (metaphorically speaking) to turn the developmental model on its head and convert adults into children, that is, children of God. The influence of the Church in the development of children cannot be underestimated however. The Church's role in society as educators, pastors and even judges has had a profound impact on how the rights of children have been perceived historically[26] and on the sociological understanding of childhood.

The idea of childhood as a 'social construct' has been highly influential in the sociology of childhood but has also been seriously challenged by those outside of the discipline as being ambiguous and either false or highly exaggerated. The argument centres on the feasibility of contrasting the biological as a fixed, normative given, and the social as variable and artefactual. The fact that children are biologically undeveloped adults cannot be disputed, but childhood, it is claimed, is not a fact in and of itself, it is a cultural interpretation of physical immaturity.[27] The argument is similar to that found in theological discussions of childhood that attempt to contrast ontology as that which is fixed and normative with faith or spirituality as variable and artefactual.

However, Christian ontology, by which is meant the created nature of a child of God, has been no more fixed or immutable than human biology has proved itself to be. Human biology has changed over time. The average age of the onset of puberty, for example, has been steadily decreasing in response to social pressures in the western world. Similarly, Christian ontology has, over time, changed from perfect and sinless to fallen and sinful, largely, it could be said, as a result of external pressures.

As Archard points out 'there is a danger of relying on an unhelpful and distorting mutual exclusivity of nature and society'.[28] This is just as true of ontology and faith. Childhood is a period of immaturity that is understood in a particular way. Thus, the concept of childhood is unlike the concept of any other object. Ontological facts alone are insufficient to describe it unambiguously. Christian childhood is an ontological phenomenon *and* a spiritual and religious construction in much the same way that human childhood is both biologically determined and socially and culturally constructed.

It is impossible to define a theological concept of childhood without some reference to what it is not – namely adulthood. All being well, the expectation is that children will grow and mature with age into 'adults'. Every specific conception of childhood, however, predetermines how it compares or contrasts with adulthood. The converse is even more telling: 'it may well be our judgments as to what matters in being an adult that explain why we have the particular conception of childhood we do.[29] It has certainly been possible, for example, to recognize the adult in the child in the theologies of Augustine or Aquinas, both of whom adopted developmental models of childhood.

There have been many partial theological conceptions of Christian childhood, each with its own particular claims about how long childhood lasts, what attributes or qualities childhood possesses, and what the significance of childhood is in the overall scheme of God's work of creation and redemption. Some of these, such as those emerging out of the Eastern Orthodox churches, incorporate an explicit understanding of Christian adulthood; others, for example, those rooted in the teachings of the Lutheran Church, have borrowed more implicitly from a scriptural or social analogy to formulate their theological conception of Christian childhood.

In what follows, I will attempt to explore John Wesley's conception of Christian childhood as one which is Protestant but which also has a clearly recognizable debt to the Eastern Orthodox tradition in the hope that, by so doing, the best of both traditions might be brought to bear. In order fully to appreciate and appropriate this conception, it is helpful once again to follow the lead provided by Archard and explore three basic respects – *boundaries*, *dimensions*, and *divisions*[30] – in which existing conceptions of childhood tend to differ, in order that their underlying judgements and assumptions can be more easily identified and evaluated.

Boundaries

The boundaries of childhood are what determines when it begins and when it ends. For human childhood, the question when does childhood begin is essentially the same as the question when does life begin. The complexities of the current philosophical and biological debates concerning conception and the onset of life mirror in many ways the debates concerning when Christian childhood is said to begin: does it begin with creation, with baptism, with the first stirrings of faith, or with justification? Just as human life is recognized as beginning in a pre-embryonic state, so too, according to Wesley, does the Christian life. Wesley was careful to distinguish between the states and stages of salvation, which together describe the life of humanity in God. He referred to the three states of being as the Natural Man, the Servant and the Son. The 'Natural Man' corresponds most closely to the pre-embryonic state of a human. The Natural Man has potential but no ability, he has no spiritual senses that might make him aware of his state and do something about it. He has, as Wesley states 'no more power to perform the actions of a living Christian, than a dead body to perform the functions of a living man.'[31] The state of the Servant is that which corresponds most closely to the human embryo. The Servant has an awareness of itself but cannot act independently to bring itself to birth. It can respond to its creator and be nurtured by its creator but has no control over its own nature. It is only when the Servant is given the gift of grace by which it receives justifying faith that it is born as a child of God and Christian childhood begins.

> The moment a man comes to Christ (by faith) he is justified, and born again; that is, he is born again in the imperfect sense (for there are two (if not more) degrees of regeneration), and he has power over all the stirrings and motions of sin, but not a total freedom from them. Therefore he hath not yet, in the full and proper sense, a new and clean heart. But being exposed to various temptations, he may and will fall again from this condition, if he doth not attain to a more excellent gift.[32]

The belief that it was possible to fall from this state once it had been attained also led Wesley to refuse to consider baptism as the boundary for Christian childhood.

> Say not then in your heart, 'I was once baptized, therefore I am now a child of God.' Alas, that consequence will by no means hold. How many are the baptized gluttons and drunkards, the baptized liars and common swearers, the baptized railers and evil-speakers,

the baptized whoremongers, thieves, extortioners? What think you? Are these now the children of God? Verily, I say unto you, whosoever you are, unto whom any one of the preceding characters belongs, 'Ye are of your father the devil, and the works of your father ye do.'[33]

To be a child of God, and to participate in the life of the children of God, that is, to experience Christian childhood is determined solely by response to God. Childhood begins when the individual becomes aware of their need for salvation and chooses to respond to this preventing grace of God and. Note that according to Wesley, this does not necessarily coincide with either the assurance of forgiveness or the gift of the Spirit. Forgiveness cannot be demanded, justification cannot be forced, both are gifts of grace.

What then can be said of the boundary that marks the end of Christian childhood? There has been a tendency for theology to avoid dealing with this question directly. It is most often classified an eschatological mystery and left as an uncertain stage of human flourishing. Some, like Rahner, have argued that there is no final boundary to childhood, there is only perpetual childhood,[34] while others, such as Macarius and Wesley, have argued that childhood does end, either in *theosis* or in Christian Perfection (sometimes referred to as entire sanctification).

The discernable judgements that shaped the choice of boundaries seem to be those of human worth and human nature. Wesley, it might be said, had a more optimistic view of human potential than many of his time, perhaps borne of the transformations that he witnessed in the children who attended his school at Kingswood, or perhaps, as Cubie has suggested borne out of his own transformation at Aldersgate.[35] His optimism is nonetheless a very cautious optimism. Wesley had a real and abiding sense of the intractable nature of sin. At times Wesley seems to have been quite torn on this whole issue. As Randy Maddox has shown, Wesley altered the prerequisites for claiming the state of perfection several times during his life in an attempt to find a balance between perfection being achievable in this lifetime and yet still being that which required considerable progress (responsibility) in the faith.[36] Wesley's repeated insistence on the possibility of backsliding, or regression, hints at a real pessimism of faith, a lack of confidence in the ability of the newly converted to stand firm: the early history of Methodism with the necessary frequent expulsions of members may have provided more than sufficient grounds for this.

Dimensions

The paucity of systematic theological reflection on childhood has resulted in a plethora of almost incoherent variations concerning the dimensions of childhood, that is, those perspectives that highlight the differences between childhood and adulthood. The most commonly appealed to dimensions include the innocence, morality, responsibility, educational and cognitive capacities of a child of God. The incoherence can generally be attributed to poorly defined boundaries and an ambiguous definition of Christian 'adulthood'. Thus, children are held to be more vulnerable, or more open, more trusting, more receptive and more determinedly in the 'now'. But each of these begs the question, more than what? More than an adult is, more than a youth is, more than a child two years older than it is? Such broad generalizations and categorizations appear to say more about the wish list of the adult society that creates it than the child that is said to embody it. A child is biologically vulnerable and open to physical abuse, but children also know how to play on and exploit the vulnerabilities of others and often do so. Trust, immediacy, receptivity, openness and even innocence are all found in adults as well as children and fail really to differentiate between the two natures. The same is true of the perspectives that enable us to differentiate between children of God and 'adults' in the faith.

Wesley refined his understanding and presentation of the dimensions of Christian childhood throughout his life as he reflected on his own experience and knowledge of the Scriptures.[37] While he was also inclined at times to over-generalize and hence be inconsistent in his teaching on childhood,[38] his recognition of the distinct states and stages of Christian life did allow him to be more specific about the dimensions of childhood that distinguished it from adulthood. The lens through which Wesley viewed the positive and negative attributes of Christian childhood was grace. The grace of God is available in all states of being and in all stages of life – but it is not the same grace. Childhood alone was the time when God made available the confirming and sanctifying grace. Prior to this, God provides prevenient, convincing and justifying grace in order to initiate that response that leads to adoption as a child of God. Wesley's belief that even those who attained the state of Christian perfection would continue to grow in grace meant that the children of God were no more or less needful of grace than an adult was – the distinction is one of kind not of quantity or quality.

It is possible to read Wesley and assume that knowledge and assurance were also dimensions of his theology of childhood. Wesley certainly placed great store on the assurance of forgiveness and on the knowledge of salvation, but there is no evidence to suggest that he believed that mature Christians had 'more knowledge' of God or greater assurance of their salvation. Mature Christians had a greater awareness of God and, a greater knowledge of the Scriptures – but above all they were recognized as having a greater love of God. These dimensions of Christian maturity were believed to flow from growth in grace. The child of God had nothing specific to its nature that the adult in Christ would want to aspire to.

There are several judgements implicit in Wesley's choice of distinguishing dimensions. First, it reiterated the optimism mentioned earlier while at the same time hints at Wesley's own methodical disciplined approach to faith. Wesley's dimensions are neat, orderly and categorical as could have been predicted from his predilection for rules and the timetable that he created for the children at Kingswood. The insistence that the grace of God is constant but is not the same at each instant speaks of an understanding of God as being in relationship with each individual rather than simply administrating salvation.

Divisions

The third and final respect in which the theological conceptions of childhood might be said to differ is with regard to the divisions of childhood. While this can, and often is determined by the age of the child, Christian childhood is more frequently divided into less empirical or immediately quantifiable stages. The earlier quotation from Wesley is evidence that he believed in the reality of several intermediary stages or divisions in the state of Christian sonship, although he only wrote consistently about three of them. These were the Babe, the Youth and the Father, Wesley having taken the terms from the epistles of St John.[39] The three stages of sonship represent two stages of Christian childhood, and one of adulthood.

The Babe in Christ, in Wesley's theology has only a limited ability to control its natural tendencies and still has an uncertain faith. Babes in Christ are not yet confirmed in their faith, they are only really aware of their desire to receive faith. In the same way that a child is completely and utterly dependent on its mother for food, so the child of God is completely dependent upon God for forgiveness and faith. The Babe in Christ knows that it is helpless, dependent and unable to save itself, but it is unable to do anything to hasten the moment of its salvation. It can no more demand forgiveness for its sin, than a child can demand milk. There is hope and expectancy, but no immediate certainty. It is only when, by grace, that tender faith is strengthened through receiving the gift of the 'abiding witness of the Spirit' that the Babe becomes a Youth in Christ.

According to St John, Christian Youths are strong because the Word of God is in them and – more importantly – they have overcome the wicked one (1 John 2.13). Wesley took this to mean that they had received the forgiveness of God. Those who are young in Christ have the assurance of their faith, but not yet the full knowledge of it. As a result of this assurance Youths are able to leave aside the first obsessions of childhood namely the pressing questions of repentance and forgiveness, and work towards maturity in faith. Youths are thus able to grow in grace through the application of their faith and the acquisition of their knowledge of God. The motivation for this is the goal of perfection. Although Wesley's doctrine of perfection allowed for the possibility of sanctification as an instantaneous gift of grace, he considered it more normative for perfection to result from a sustained response to the means of grace over time.

The difference between being a Youth in Christ and an adult Christian or Father in Christ is that the Father has the freedom from all inward as well as outward sin, a difference that suggests an ontological as well as spiritual transformation of the nature of the child. Wesley substantiates this suggestion by the claim that the transition from Youth to Father in Christ is marked not only by a negative blessing – namely a deliverance *from* sin, but also by a positive blessing – by the planting by God of all good dispositions in their place.

Behind the partitioning of childhood into two stages is an implicit appreciation of the fickleness of humanity. Backsliding was a real issue for Wesley who believed in perfection and in the real for necessity not just the desirability of it.[40] The real debate that these divisions address is the ontological dimension of entire sanctification or perfection. Wesley was determined that perfection was achievable this side of death, contrary to the considered opinion of the time, and that an ontological change did occur. His optimism was, as always, tempered by his pessimism concerning human nature, he was all too aware that some of those who claimed to have achieved perfection clearly needed to continue to grow in grace!

Theosis or Christian perfection – towards a theology of Christian childhood

In the preceding sections I examined Wesley's developmental theology of childhood which was clearly based on a refinement of Haeckel's law but which also allowed the freedom of God to act anachronistically to transform the life of any one of God's children.

It has been often been claimed that the Protestant understanding of sanctification is equivalent to the Orthodox doctrine of *theosis*[41] (literally 'ingodded' or 'becoming god'). This doctrine has its origins in the first few centuries of Christianity and is supported by scriptural texts such as Psalm 82.6 and John 10.34. It can be found in the writings of many of the Church Fathers[42] and has been preserved and developed by the Eastern Orthodox Church. The deifying union, or restoration of the *imago dei*, is believed to result from a mysterious coinciding of a gift of divine energy and human freedom. *Theosis* as a union with God, 'is not the result of an organic or unconscious process: it is accomplished in persons by the cooperation of the Holy Spirit and our freedom'.[43]

The similarity between this understanding of the process of *theosis* and Wesley's doctrine of Christian perfection with its stress on the need for growth in grace and holiness throughout should not be surprising: it is known that Wesley had read and approved of the patristic doctrine of *theosis*.[44]

The fact remains however, that in the end, Wesley balked at the idea of ascribing any dimension of unity with God or of divinity to humans. He insisted, in accordance with Scripture that: 'They who are sanctified, yet may fall and perish (Heb. 10.29). Even fathers in Christ need that warning.'[45]

Charles Wesley thought differently. The influence of patristic *theosis* is very evident in these verses of his well-known nativity hymn:

He deigns in flesh to appear,
Widest extremes to join;
To bring our vileness near,
And make us all divine:
And we the life of God shall know,
For God is manifest below.

Made perfect first in love,
And sanctified by grace,
We shall from earth remove,
And see his glorious face:
His love shall then be fully showed,
And man shall all be lost in God.[46]

For Charles Wesley, perfection was nothing less than a full restoration of the divine likeness. John Wesley, however, thought that this was setting the boundary of perfection too high as may be seen in one of his letters to his brother:

> June 27, 1766. Concerning setting perfection too high. That perfection which I believe, I can boldly preach; because I think I see five hundred witnesses of it. Of that perfection which you preach, you think you do not see any witnesses at all . . . I verily believe there are none upon the earth; none dwelling in the body . . . Therefore I still think, to set perfection so high is effectively to renounce it.[47]

There remains therefore a fundamental difference between John Wesley's doctrine of Christian perfection and the Orthodox doctrine of *theosis* which was hinted at in the previous section. Wesley's optimism of grace is in the end let down by his pessimism concerning humanity. He sold his doctrine short. Wesley's interpretation of the Scriptures and his theology of responsible grace led him finally to proclaim what can only be described as an imperfect conception of Christian perfection and an all too ordinary conception of holiness. In spite of his, at times, contradictory statements, 'Father's in Christ' were never really expected or allowed to become fully one with Christ in the same way that Jesus and the Father are one except perhaps just before the *eschaton*.[48]

Wesley is not alone in this peculiarly western reticence. Karl Barth likewise had a coherent and positive theological conception of the childhood of the children of God, yet was prepared to condemn them to what Johnson calls an eternal advent.[49] Johnson writes that Barth's 'eschatological interpretation of the Holy Spirit and redemption is a unique combination of boldness and reticence. The boldness lies in his belief that human beings, incredible though it may seem, will one day enjoy the fellowship of life with God. But there is a lingering reticence as well. This reticence results in the fellowship or "presence" of God that Barth refers to, being displayed most reliably as "an honest and basic lack".'[50] Johnson concludes that for Barth, 'Life in the Spirit is "a permanent Advent", a perpetual waiting for a revelation that is yet to be consummated'.[51]

Were Wesley and Barth correct to refrain, at the last, from claiming too much for a child of God? Is childhood merely an imperfect metaphor that should never be taken to the extremes, or is it simply the case that those who believe are merely given the power to become 'children of God' and no more? Surely the idea of heaven as 'Never-Land' ridicules the generosity of grace and mocks the costliness of the redemption of humanity. Such a limitation on human potential is nothing more than an inverse projection, based on fear and worthy of the best criticisms of Feuerbach, Nietzsche, Freud, and all those who challenge and taunt Christians to 'grow up'.

Perhaps the story of Peter Pan provides us with a clue as to why Christian children are seldom told that their childhood is destined to end in the divinity that Christ has won for them according to Scripture:

> Thus he has given us, through these things, his precious and very great promises, so that through them you may escape from the corruption that is in the world because of lust, and may become participants of the divine nature.
>
> 2 Peter 1.4

The story of Peter Pan is subtitled – the boy who *would not* grow up (my italics). It is not that Peter could not grow up, nor even that Peter should not grow up, but that Peter would not grow up. It was a wilful, pointless refusal that denied Peter his real birthright – including, of course, any relationship with his mother. Far from being a wonderful tale of magic and innocence, Peter Pan is a frightening illustration of how the evasion of memory, time, sex and even death is not life affirming but life denying as everything of value is forgotten and rendered meaningless as just one more adventure.[52] Even love itself is lost. J. M. Barrie's play speaks powerfully to the Church's refusal to allow the children of God to grow up as it takes on the role of Peter in trying to persuade those who know no better to stay and play rather than go and grow.

Thus any theology of childhood must be prepared to take seriously the necessity of real maturity and the fact that, in the end, childhood is something that the children of God must be willing to leave behind. Once the kingdom of God has been received – once the gift of grace has been given – the child must be prepared to respond to it and grow. Recognizing the truth in Archard's claim that 'the way we see the difference between children and adults owes everything to what concerns us about being adults in an adult world',[53] we turn once again to the three primary assumptions of the developmental model on which most theologies of childhood are based and so begin our final stage in the formulation of a theological conception of childhood by considering how it all ends.

The assumption of *telos* is not more childhood but something almost inconceivable to the western mind, in spite of its scriptural mandate. The children of God mature to be so fully in-Christ that they become participants of the divine nature and so fulfil the words of the Psalmist: 'I have said you are gods; and all of you are children of the Most High' (Psalm 82.6). This is the *telos* decreed for the children of God. Humanity is called to 'know' God, to 'participate' in his life, to be 'saved', not simply through an extrinsic action of God's, or through the rational cognition of propositional truths, but by 'becoming God'.

Proponents of the doctrine of *theosis* have been less circumspect than most interpreters of the doctrine of sanctification have been in proclaiming what Christian perfection might actually mean as an end to Christian childhood and as a vision of human potential in Christ. They challenge those who attempt to present a developmental theology of childhood that takes seriously the idea that Christ recapitulates the whole human race, by insisting that if the incarnation, resurrection and ascension of Christ are more than a mere metaphor, so also must the intended deification of the human race be. Thus, for example, Athanasius writing about the incarnation, declares 'God became man so that man might become God'.[54] Similarly, Irenaeus proclaims: 'If the Word was made man, it is that men might become Gods.'[55]

That theosis is the natural conclusion to a doctrine of Christian perfection is more than suggested by Clement: 'being made perfect, we are made immortal, as the Scripture says "Ye are gods . . .".'[56]

The second assumption – that of necessity – provides a means of seeing how the two doctrines of perfection and theosis could be related. Both doctrines presume an order of salvation that cannot be bypassed by human endeavour.[57] Orthodox theologian and bishop, Maximos Aghiorgoussis, stated that, 'when Paul distinguished in Romans 8.28–30 among predestination, calling, justification, and glorification, these are all stages in one process, that of salvation'.[58] A possible fusion of the two doctrines could thus be as Charles suggests in the hymn mentioned earlier: The process begins with the pre-birth state of ignorance (predestination). This is followed by God's action in prevenient grace (calling), which leads to the individual's birth into Christ (justification). The newly born child of God then begins to grow in faith until it become a youth, at which point it is able to grow in grace and holiness until it receives the inner blessing of God and becomes not an adult, but an adolescent, a beneficiary who sees the maturing of Wesley's more achievable Perfection. At this stage the child of God possesses knowledge but not wisdom. The final stage sees the continuing growth in grace through the insights and knowledge obtained through this state of perfection until the child reaches full maturity adulthood and is able to receive the ultimate gift of theosis (glorification) and become perfected in Christ.

The third and final assumption of endogenity now presupposes the possibility of a theology of childhood that has both a clear objective and the necessary structure and motivation to achieve it, deriving solely from the nature of the child of God as it has been given to us in Christ. The distinction is important: It is the nature that we inherit in Christ that makes all this possible, not our human nature alone. Any theology of childhood that is predicated solely on what might be said of children born of human descent will fail to address the world's need for children born 'not of blood or of the will of the flesh or of the will of man, but of God' (John 1.13).

The nature of a child of God is inherited from Christ, it is both ontologically fixed *and* spiritually determined by the participation of the child in the process of their own becoming. The child utilizes and adapts their God-given nature to grow in grace and holiness by responding to the work of the Holy Spirit. Through the means of grace that God provides, the life of the individual is transformed until they are no longer conformed to the desires that they formerly had in their ignorance. As the one who called them is holy, they too accept their calling and strive to become holy in all their conduct (1 Peter 1.14–16). Thus, the goal of *theosis*, union with Christ, and the process of achieving are inseparable for Christ is the very source of the power and means which shapes and motivates the process.

The potential for a 'new' theology of childhood

So what? What difference could it possibly make to either human flourishing or to contemporary Christianity if a theology of childhood is constructed that effectively fuses Eastern Orthodoxy and the very best of Wesleyan perfection and that is neither afraid nor embarrassed to take seriously the interdependency of natural childhood and the childhood of a child of God?

To begin with, such a theology would warrant a change in the way that children are perceived and parenting is undertaken. It would demand that children cease to be viewed as either possessions or 'gifts' from God. Not only would this finally end the assumption that people have a 'right' to children, it would also in part resolve some of the anger and pain of those whose 'childlessness' has been treated as abnormal, wrong or a sign of God's displeasure. Put simply, those who have the potential in Christ to become 'gods' cannot belong to other people in any way other than as all belong to one other in Christ. Gods do not possess, but in practising *perichoresis* they own everything. Those who expect to be in Christ can expect also to have inherited that perichoretic nature and be able to utilize it in the care of their biological offspring. The closest analogy to the parenting role that arises out of such a theology is that of a loving regent. The role imposes an imperative to prepare the child well for the office it will one day hold, while at the same time, instilling a respect for and consideration of the final office that the child is expected to hold.

Attitudes to human nature would also change as the possibility that humanity is called to be so much more is accepted and the fullness of the life that is exemplified in Christ is explored. It will not be enough merely to divinize and emulate a few select attributes of Christ's nature as narrated in the Gospels, such as his humility or perceived pacifism. The Gospels also make it clear that Christ suffered pain, knew grief, exasperation and tiredness. These too are a part of what it must mean to be in Christ. At the very least, a theology that has as its goal full communion with Christ might help to end the current disabling practice of dividing human nature up into that which causes it pleasure and that which causes it pain, and ascribing the one to God and blaming the other on the devil. So much unnecessary pain and waste of human potential occurs through the fear of owning and recognizing the transforming power and constructive value of those things that lie outside of the comfort zone. Being allowed to cry out to God in grief rather than being required to 'deal with it', being transformed through pain and suffering rather than being made outcast because of it, being angry, frustrated, vexed and yet still feeling that it is acceptable to enter fully into the presence of God, to seek union with God through grace, is not just a form of liberation, it is a means of salvation.

But Christ's humanity is not all that humanity aspires to and can expect, by grace, to be united with. It is the union of his human nature with his divine nature that draws humanity forward out of its childhood. Could it be possible that one day humans could also replicate some of the healing and nature miracles of Christ by being so completely in union with God? Recognition that humans might have, through Christ, access to a greater power to change themselves and the world for the better could prompt a re-engagement with the subject of metaphysics. The very least that could be hoped for would be that the end of the heresy that names God as the one who limits and constricts, who keeps humanity infantile and stunted would undoubtedly provoke and invite changes in other currently accepted abusive power structures.

Within the life of the Church, the means of grace would be recovered as necessary, not just for the well-being of the congregation or even for the education of the faithful, but for the transformation of the children of God for the glory of God. This would necessitate significant changes in the practice of worship, the understanding of Scripture, the sharing in fellowship, the observance of the sacraments, the communion of prayer, the discipline of fasting and so much more. Discipline and discipleship would be forged into one pattern of living as the child of God determined to grow in grace and holiness according to the pattern of Christ.

Attitudes towards the education and discipline of children would also be affected. Education would be recognized as needing to do more than inform the mind or the hand: greater assimilation of facts and improved human dexterity will not release the potential for human evolution. Will this put an end to child violence or delinquency? Probably not, but the question should at least be put as to whether children who see no value in their lives because they are not academically or physically gifted might see themselves as different if they saw real appreciation being given to the status 'child of God'. On the whole, the expression 'child of God' carries no meaning or cudos with the younger generation: it is not 'cool' or 'wicked', just 'religious' and 'yeah yeah'. It is offered as a consolation prize rather than something to aspire to that is within the reach of every child. There is some hope. The trend towards lifelong learning suggests that there could come a time when the period called childhood is seen as the necessary time committed to identifying, developing and initiating those habits of learning, being and doing that will ensure that the adult is able to continue to mature and grow in grace until their full potential is realized.

But above all this, what it would achieve would be the freedom of the gospel to be heard anew by each generation as good news, as challenging potential to become something more than they ever dreamed possible.

> Beloved, we are God's children now; what we will be has not yet been revealed. What we do know is this: when he is revealed, we will be like him, for we will see him as he is.
>
> John 3.2

Notes

1 Philippe Ariès, *Centuries of Childhood*, New York, Vintage Books, 1962.

2 Consider in particular, David Archard, *Children: Rights and Childhood*, London and New York, Routledge, 2004 and Kathleen Marshall and Paul Parvis, *Honouring Children: The Human Rights of the Child in Christian Perspective*, Edinburgh, St Andrew Press, 2004.

3 The term 'Christian childhood' is used throughout this chapter to signify the childhood of a child of God as distinct from the childhood of a 'natural biological' human child.

4 Calvin, *Institutes*, IV, 15.10.

5 James Patrick Bulger (16 March 1990 – 12 February 1993) was a two-year-old toddler who was abducted and murdered by two ten-year-old boys, Jon Venables and Robert Thompson (both born in 1982), in Merseyside, in the United Kingdom.

6 J. A. Hunter, A. Figueredo, N. M. Malamuthand and J. V. Becker, 'Juvenile Sex Offenders: Toward the Development of a Typology', *Sexual Abuse: A Journal of Research and Treatment* (2003) Vol. 15, No. 1.

7 Eighteen-year-old Stephen Lawrence and, more recently ten-year-old Damilola Taylor, were killed in London. Those that were brought to trial were under the age of majority at the time of the killings.

8 Anti-Social Behaviour Orders – a legal means of restricting the movements of those considered to be behaving in an anti-social manner. Largely, although not solely, used to control unruly teenagers.

9 As many as 300,000 children under the age of 18 currently serve in government forces or armed rebel groups. Some are as young as eight years old. Statistics taken from: http://hrw.org/campaigns/crp/facts.htm :(Oct 2006).

10 It is worth noting that there are several non-canonical texts which contain several infancy and childhood stories of Jesus.

11 Jean-Jacques Rousseau, Preface, *Émile or On Education* (1762) as quoted by Archard, *Children: Rights and Childhood*, p. 17.

12 Archard, *Children: Rights and Childhood*, pp. 37–50.

13 The publication of two texts, Wilhem Preyer's *Die Seele des Kindes* (1882) and G. S. Hall's article 'Contents of Childs Minds' (1883) is conventionally deemed to mark the origin of child psychology proper. Archard, *Children: Rights and Childhood*, p. 40.

14 Charles Darwin, 'A Biographical Sketch of an Infant', *Mind* (London) 7 July (1877).

15 Stephen Jay Gould, *Ever since Darwin: Reflections in Natural History*, New York, Norton, 1977.

16 As quoted in Stephen Jay Gould, *Ever since Darwin*, p. 217.

17 Archard, *Children: Rights and Childhood*, p. 16.

18 Eric Osborne, *Irenaeus of Lyons*, Cambridge, Cambridge University Press, 2001.

19 Irenaeus, *Against Heresies* III, 18, 1.

20 It is clear from his writings (*Against the Heresies* II, 22: 5–6) that Irenaeus believed that Christ was nearly 50 years of age at the time of his death – old indeed for that time.

21 Irenaeus, *Against the Heresies* II, 22: 4.

22 Archard, *Children: Rights and Childhood*, p. 41.

23 Archard, *Children: Rights and Childhood*, p. 43.

24 Archard, *Children: Rights and Childhood*, p. 43.

25 Marcia J. Bunge, *The Child in Christian Thought*,Grand Rapids: W. B. Eerdmans, 2001, p. 9.

26 See, for example, Marshall and Parvis, *Honouring Children*.

27 See Archard, *Children: Rights and Childhood*, p. 25.

28 Archard, *Children: Rights and Childhood*, p. 31.

29 Archard, *Children: Rights and Childhood*, p. 31.

30 Archard, *Children: Rights and Childhood*, pp. 32–6.

31 John Wesley, *The Complete Works of John Wesley, Vol. 5, Biography and Sermons 1–39*, Oregon, Ages Software, 3rd edn 1996, p. 33.

32 John Wesley, 'The Principles of a Methodist', *The Bicentennials*

Editions of the Works of John Wesley, ed. Rupert E. Davies, Vol. 9, Nashville, Abingdon Press, 1989, p. 64.

33 John Wesley, *Works, Vol. 8*, p. 302.

34 Karl Rahner, 'Ideas for a theology of Childhood', *Theological Investigations*, Vol. 8, p. 363, *FurtherTheology of the Spiritual Life II*, p. 33–50, London, Darton, Longman & Todd, 1971.

35 David Livingstone Cubie, 'Placing Aldersgate in John Wesley's Order of Salvation', *Wesleyan Theological Journal*, Ohio, 1989, p. 24.

36 See chapter 7 in particular in R. L. Maddox, *Responsible Grace*, Nashville: Kingswood Books, 1994.

37 For a fuller treatment of this see Cubie, 'Placing Aldersgate'.

38 Most notably with regard to his teaching on infant baptism and its relationship to being born in the Spirit.

39 Wesley was quite clear on the distinction between the general states of human existence (natural man, the servant and the son) and the stages of Christian growth which occur within the state of the son.

40 The same threefold distinction once underpinned the structure of the Methodist societies with the Band being reserved for the more mature Christian, the class for the serious converted Christian and the Meeting open to all.

41 See Lucian Turcescu, 'Soteriological issues in the 1999 Lutheran-Catholic Joint Declaration on justification: an Orthodox perspective', *The Journal of Ecumenical Studies*, Philadelphia, 38.1, 2001.

42 Christensen claims that it is possible to identify two distinct interpretations of *theosis* in Patristic theology: '(1) The union model envisions humanity literally becoming divine (i.e. gods and goddesses, perfected sons and daughters in the family of God); (2) The communion model metaphorically imagines humanity becoming like God while remaining creature (i.e., perfected humanity may assume some qualities of divinity but never be divine in nature, always creature in relation to Creator).' Michael J. Christensen, 'Theosis and Sanctification: John Wesley's reformulation of a patristic doctrine', *Wesleyan Theological Journal* 31.2, 1996.

43 Vladimir Lossky, *The Mystical Theology of the Eastern Church* (Crestwood, NY, St Vladimir's Seminary Press, 1976, p.216) as quoted in Kelly S. McCormick, 'Theosis in Chrysostom and Wesleyan Eastern Paradigm on Faith and Love', *Wesleyan Theological Journal*, vol. 26, no. 1 (1991), pp. 38–103.

44 See, for example, Michael J. Christensen, 'Theosis and Sanctification: John Wesley's reformulation of a patristic doctrine', *Wesleyan Theological Journal* 31, 2,1996, and Randy L. Maddox, *Responsible Grace*, Nashville, Kingswood Books, 1994, p. 122.

45 John Wesley, *A Plain Account of Christian Perfection*, London, Epworth Press, 1952, p. 25.

46 Charles Wesley in *Hymns & Psalms*, no. 109.

47 John R. Tyson, *Charles Wesley – A Reader*, New York, Oxford University Press, 1989, p. 131.

48 Wesley taught that all those who were sincerely growing in grace would

somehow attain perfection before the *eschaton*. As Maddox points out, his most interesting idea was that those who needed to would somehow 'ripen' in paradise while waiting for the final *eschaton*. Maddox, *Responsible Grace*, p. 191.

49 William Stacy Johnson *The Mystery of God*, Louisville, Westminster John Knox Press, 1997, p. 131.

50 K. Barth, *Church Dogmatics: IV 3.1 The Doctrine of Reconciliation*, Edinburgh: T&T Clark, 2nd edn 1997, p. 322.

51 Johnson, *The mystery of God* , p. 131.

52 Archard, *Children: Rights and Childhood*, p. 48.

53 Archard, *Children: Rights and Childhood*, p. 36.

54 Athanasius, *On the Incarnation of the Word*, Book IV, 65.

55 Irenaeus, *Against Heresies Book V*, Pref.

56 Clement, *Stromateis*, chapter 6.

57 Both *theosis* and complete sanctification, however, can be given as an instantaneous gift of grace from God.

58 Maximos Aghiorgoussis, 'Orthodox Soteriology' in John Meyendorff and Robert Tobias (eds), *Salvation in Christ: A Lutheran-Orthodox Dialogue*, Minneapolis: Augsburg Fortress, 1992, pp. 48–9.